FRAGRANT HARBOR TASTE

THE NEW CHINESE COOKING OF HONG KONG

Ken Hom

Wine in the Cuisine of the Fragrant Harbor by Darrell Corti

A Fireside Book

Published by Simon & Schuster

New York   London   Toronto   Sydney   Tokyo   Singapore

Fireside
Simon & Schuster Building
Rockefeller Center
1230 Avenue of the Americas
New York, New York 10020

Copyright © 1989 by Taurom Incorporated
"Wine in the Cuisine of the Fragrant Harbor" Copyright © 1989
by Darrell Corti
First Fireside Edition 1992

FIRESIDE and colophon are registered
trademarks of Simon & Schuster Inc.

DESIGNED BY BARBARA MARKS
Manufactured in the United States of America

10 9 8 7 6 5 4 3 2 1
10 9 8 7 6 5 4 3 2 1 Pbk.
Library of Congress Cataloging in Publication Data

Hom, Ken.
    Fragrant Harbor taste: the new Chinese cooking of
Hong Kong/Ken Hom.
        p.   cm.
    Includes index.
    1. Cookery, Chinese.   2. Cookery—Hong Kong.   I. Title.
TX724.5.C5H665   1989
641.5951—dc20   89-35008
                                                                  CIP

ISBN 0-671-64469-6
ISBN 0-671-75444-0 Pbk.

Parts of this book appeared originally in slightly different form in
Bon Appétit, The New York Times Magazine, Gourmet Traveler [Aus-
tralia], *Cuisine* [New Zealand], *Taste Magazine* [London], *The
Times* [London], *The Peak Magazine* [Hong Kong], *Vogue* [Aus-
tralia], The London Times.

*For Susan Maurer,
whose vision helped me
open the window to
Hong Kong*

and

*for Willie Mark, my
Hong Kong teacher,
mentor, friend, and*
see fu *par excellence.*

DEDICATION

For almost a decade, I have conducted a series of extremely successful cooking classes in Hong Kong that a great many people helped to make possible. This book reflects much of what I learned and taught in Hong Kong, one of the most exciting food cities in the world. In offering it to you, I offer, too, my thanks to the people who assisted me in so many ways during all those years.

To begin, I thank Susan Maurer and Willie Mark. Susan was the first to encourage me to do classes in Hong Kong and then worked hard to make the idea a reality. Her unwavering faith and confidence was a source of inspiration for many years. When I arrived in Hong Kong, Willie literally took me by the hand and introduced me to *everyone* I needed to know. Over the years, he has generously shared his enormous fund of knowledge concerning the Hong Kong food scene with me. I owe them both a huge debt and this book is dedicated to them, with my affection and deep appreciation.

ACKNOWLEDGMENTS

There are many to whom I owe thanks: Frank Bouwmeester of Singapore Airlines; Patricia Costello, Peter Borer, and Lilian Chang of the Peninsula Group; my many friends, past and present, from the Peninsula Hotel: Peter Gautschi, Felix Bieger, Urs Aebi, Eric Waldburger, Eric Brand, Erich Scaheli, Lynn Grebstad, Sian Griffiths, Karen Penlington, and Priscilla Chen. I shall never forget the kind assistance of the Hong Kong Tourist Association, especially Buster Hollands, Charmaine Kong, Rory Chan, Melina Hung, Penelope Byrne, Stephen Wong, and John Pain. And I offer special thanks to Sophia Cheong and the rest of her staff of Pacific World.

To my family in Hong Kong, with a special thanks to my cousin, Kwan Wing Ching, who was always to be relied upon for any assistance.

I note with affection and respect the many chefs and restaurateurs who opened their hearts as well as their kitchens to me: Pierre Tang, Frank Y. Yuen, Chan Hong Kuen (Edwin), Leung King, the late George Tang, Cheung Man, Ian Chung, Au Yeung Shung, Sandra Lee, Amy P. C. Cheung, Gebbard K. Scherrer, and R. Hardmeir, among others.

I shall never forget the kindness of Ginnie and Bob McKay, Helen and Bob Giss, and Irma and Noel Power.

I recall with great warmth the friendship of Grace Fung and Kendall Oei, always there and always scouting new restaurants for me; Jimmy Woo, whose charm and knowledge of good food was always much appreciated; Siew and David Bell, who always make me feel so welcome, and Belle and Barney Rhodes for their gracious support.

I offer my special thanks and deep respect to Carole Lalli, my editor at Simon and Schuster, who first suggested and then sustained me through this book, and to my other talented friends there, Kerri Conan, Lisa Kitei, Julia Knickerbocker, Frank Metz, and Eve Metz.

Finally, my warm thanks to Darrell Corti, dear friend, who came with me to Hong Kong so many times and contributed the wine essay to this book. His enthusiasm constantly renewed my love for Hong Kong. And, as always, to Gerry Cavanaugh, Mimi Luebberman, Gordon Wing, Ted Lyman and Martha Casselman for their support and friendship.

CONTENTS

AUTHOR'S NOTE

The spellings of Chinese words and place names in this book follow both the pinyin system and the Cantonese system of converting Chinese characters to the Roman alphabet. The pinyin system has been officially adopted by the People's Republic of China since 1979 and it closely resembles actual Mandarin pronunciation. I have used this system especially when referring to certain regions within China, such as Sichuan, which I use instead of Szechuan. However, I have made an exception for the spellings of certain Cantonese names, such as Chiu Chow, which is the term you will find used in Hong Kong.

INTRODUCTION

~~~~~~

"A gradual mixing of ideas and foods, supported by increased transportation and communication, has given rise to modification, adaptation and variation of all regional foods. . . . The [Chinese] cookery of the moment is not one entity but an amalgam of the variety of cuisines that existed, united by geography and politics yet divided by climate, agriculture and tradition. Regional styles are no longer mutually exclusive. There are more similarities than there are differences between them."

— JACQUELINE M. NEWMAN[°]

"Hong Kong! A free port, an outpost of free trade, a capitalist back door to the People's Republic of China. . . . Once there was no Hong Kong. It is something that has had to be invented."

— ALESSANDRA CHIAPPERO

THE NEW CHINESE COOKING OF HONG KONG

The pot is boiling in Hong Kong, again and as ever. The fateful year approaches — 1997 — when British sovereignty over the territory of the "Fragrant Harbor" (Hong Kong's original Chinese place name) reverts to China. There is feverish speculation about what it all means, what it will entail, how it will affect Hong Kong, this dot on the mainland coast, this geographic place and state of mind that has been called by the writer Jan Morris "the last jewel of the Empire," a "stupendous epilogue" to imperial history. The People's Republic has pledged to allow things to go much as they have been. Changes will come, but for the vast majority of Hong Kong's people — those who will remain and carry on no matter what the future brings — the best and only option is to continue as they have now for decades: working, gambling, building. And as always, they will have the great fortune to enjoy the most varied and delectable cuisine to be found anywhere in the world.

It is the consensus among food critics the world over that Hong Kong offers some of the world's finest Chinese cuisine. I am in full agreement with this judgment. It is a venerable cuisine whose concepts, techniques, and recipes are deeply rooted in the rich and ancient traditions of the grand Chinese food culture. Most interesting to me, however, and a source of delight to diners in Hong Kong today, are the innovations that are presently being introduced into that cuisine.

These innovations — in techniques, foods, recipes, attitudes, and concepts — form the subject of this book. I have observed much of the new Hong Kong Cuisine over the past ten years:

[°] Dr. Jacqueline Newman "Regional and Other Differences of Chinese Cookery," *Oxford Symposium 1981: National and Regional Styles of Cookery, Proceedings,* (London, 1981) Page 40.

new approaches to staple foods; innovative techniques that have transformed standard recipes; new attitudes about the relationship between food and health, which in turn bring changes in eating habits; the emergence of young chefs, masters of the ancient cuisine but influenced by the cosmopolitan atmosphere of Hong Kong that embraces, for example, Japanese aesthetics, nouvelle and California cuisines. In the chapter headings and in each recipe in this book, I shall note how and to what degree we may perceive these new influences at work. But first, we need to know something about Hong Kong and its cuisine, what it was, what it is, and what it is becoming. Food is, after all, a form of social history.

As a frequent visitor and having led many culinary and cultural tours to Hong Kong, I know in delightful detail the glories of the food to be enjoyed there. There is probably no other place on earth where such a large part of the population is engaged in the preparation of good, fresh, nutritious meals from the simplest dish to the most imaginatively complex menus. They, along with the bulk of the permanent and visiting population, are constantly thinking and talking and dreaming about food, with an appreciation that goes far beyond considerations of mere sustenance.

. .

E. N. Anderson, Jr. and Marja L. Anderson write in their contribution to *Food in Chinese Culture:*

> There is continual concern with the quality of food [in South China]. Surely no culture on earth, not even the French, is so concerned with gastronomy as the Chinese. Everyone from the lowest beggar (looking for scraps) to the highest official knows where to find the best. There was, and at last report still is . . . a wonton shop in Yuen Long, in the New Territories of Hong Kong, that was famous throughout the western New Territories; everyone yearned to eat there. It was a perfectly ordinary, working-class neighborhood wonton and noodle place: yet people from all walks of life flocked to it. Western gourmets tend to require an elegant ambience as part of a meal. Chinese are concerned with the food.

On the exotic side of the culinary scene, there are dishes concocted of snake, shark's fin, bird's nest, and other unusual items. It is now forbidden to use dogs and cats for human consumption, though that does not mean that those who delight in these treats can't find them. These items are sometimes contrary to Western tastes and pocketbooks, but, extraordinary and expensive as they are, they are highly regarded among Hong Kong diners. Another current rage is what the Chinese call "wild taste," what we would loosely categorize as game. This includes such exotic animals as civet, a kind of wild cat, barking deer, giant water turtle, and other reptiles. I have been told that when eating bear paws, one should always have the left paw, since that is the one that the bear licks and is therefore the more tender of the two. Much of the wild game is imported from China. For the Chinese, eating this type of "wild game taste" warms the blood and keeps one in good health for the rough winter months. Incidentally, these animals are not hung, as in the West. Instead, they are killed just before cooking and then stewed with aromatic herbs and spices (probably to mask their strong taste). It always strikes me as fascinating that the Chinese, despite (or perhaps because of) their traditional shortage of food, have devoted so much attention to turning unusual items into sought-after, expensive gastronomic experiences. It is truly conspicuous consumption, and that, I suppose, is enough to explain it.

For most, Hong Kong's culinary reputation is based on other, more appealing characteristics. There are thousands of restaurants in Hong Kong. From the smallest street food stalls to the most luxurious elite hotel dining rooms, they share these elements: quality, care, and a serious/playful attitude toward the necessary recreation or restorative we call eating. Along with work, gambling, shopping, and sex, food in all of its aspects is central to Hong Kong life. It is a topic of conversation, a serious study, a source of anticipation in people's lives as they contemplate their next repast.

Hong Kong is open to the world. It is constantly exposed to cultural influences and styles. It is quite literally a crossroad of international trade, commodities, ideas, and influences. And thus, the *new* Hong Kong cuisine is demonstrating its receptivity to what is best in other regional Asian traditions, assimilating new foods, ingredients, and styles of cooking.

What this means in practice is that, while holding fast to traditional Chinese recipes, chefs are creating refined versions that reflect the influences of Hong Kong's cosmopolitan style. In some cases, the finished dishes are lighter; in others, they are changed just enough to make reference to the different and changing tastes of their international clienteles. In Hong Kong today, along with restaurants that feature Chinese menus (of all regional styles), there are Burmese, Indian, Japanese, Korean, Malaysian, Indonesian, Thai, and Vietnamese restaurants, plus French, Middle Eastern, Italian, German, Russian, Hungarian, and Mexican places, not to mention McDonald's. Indeed, Hong Kong boasts that it offers the "Best of the West" cuisine, at the same time as claiming to be "Asia's Spicy Melting Pot." Under such circumstances, culinary cross-culturalization is inevitable.

Fried Rice with Pineapple, for example, is an adaptation of the Thai approach and influence. Deep-Fried Milk, a popular dish of uncertain provenance, otherwise goes against the Chinese aversion to dairy products. Stir-Fried Lamb is a stylistic blend, combining Cantonese technique and flavorings with a popular north China meat. Stir-Fried Asparagus with Garlic indicates the readiness to try new foods: asparagus was but recently introduced to Chinese cuisine. Always imported, it is very popular despite its costliness. Even mayonnaise, quite un-Chinese, shows up in recipes at posh restaurants. Wines, once unheard of in Chinese cuisine, are now integrated into the cooking of dishes as well as into menus.

It must be understood there is no revolution at the eating table: the grand Chinese cuisine still dominates the Hong Kong culinary scene. But the quickening absorption of new ingredients and the novel application of old techniques are indeed reshaping the traditional cuisine. I have noticed, for example, that Hong Kong dim sum dishes are lighter (pastries are fried in oil instead of the traditional lard) and are prepared with such new spices and flavorings as shrimp paste and Chinese chives. The venerable clay pot is now used not only for braising but also to infuse flavors in a quick and intense blast of heat; I particularly enjoyed the simplicity and modern adaptation of the Crab Casserole in a Clay Pot (page 92).

As it is with so many other consumer products, Hong Kong is one of the richest and most varied food markets anywhere. The acceptance of new food products today must, I feel, be something like the assimilation into Chinese cooking of tomatoes and corn about a hundred years ago. These were alien foods that rapidly became naturalized and perfectly ordinary components of the ancient cuisine.

This process of discriminating assimilation is an outstanding characteristic of Chinese cuisine in general and of the Cantonese style in particular. Cantonese cooks will try anything so long as it is fresh, wholesome, and has natural flavor, which the Cantonese sauces always enhance, never overwhelm.

But such innovations presuppose a clientele ready and willing to try something different — and that resource Hong Kong has in the extreme. In the narrow confines of the place, with almost six million tightly packed-in people, who have disposable incomes, who enjoy good food, who conduct much of their business affairs in public, especially while eating, and whose crowded living arrangements in any event induce much dining out, restaurants flourish. Dining out is a pastime, a form of recreation; and the players-participants are sophisticated and knowledgeable. To compete, therefore, Hong Kong restaurateurs have to be alert.

Although I was born and raised in America, images of Hong Kong are part of my life. My mother was from the Canton area and had many relatives and friends there — the Colony is predominantly a south China, Cantonese city. As I grew up, family conversations often centered on what was happening in Hong Kong, who was going off for a visit, who was returning, what was new. How exciting and interesting it all seemed! I recall very clearly that over family dinners people would discuss quite seriously and at great length the wonderful food that was available in Hong Kong: the consensus was that there was no place like Hong Kong when it came to good food.

At the time, I took these conversations for granted, assuming that in all families food was a serious matter. Not until I moved into the American social mainstream did I realize that most people are not so obsessed by cuisine; it wasn't until I traveled to France and Italy that I discovered other cultures in which food and dining figured so prominently.

I can remember, as early as the age of five, my mother taking me to the Chinese cinema in Chicago to see a Cantonese double feature. One of the films might have been Cantonese opera, with elaborately costumed performers, on some historical or allegorical theme; the other almost always was a modern melodrama or touching morality play, a real tearjerker (for which there *is* an equivalent word in Cantonese — *fuching pin* — that translates as "tragic, sad movie"), whose setting invariably was Hong Kong. The locale for these modern movies was dictated by historical necessity: in the 1940s and '50s, Hong Kong was the only Chinese city accessible to independent moviemakers. And it made a splendid backdrop, with its magnificent crowded harbor, mountains and seashores, skyscrapers and teeming streets, neon lights, mansions and tenements, poverty and prosperity. I learned about New York the same way; but I knew Hong Kong better, perhaps, because it was home to so many in my family.

In the 1960s and '70s Hong Kong was much in the news, as a tourist stop and bargain-shopping center; as a place of rest and rehabilitation for the military; as a burgeoning manufacturing and commercial state; and, of course, as the source of some of the finest dining in the world. By the time I finally made it to Hong Kong in 1980, the images, sounds, smells, and atmosphere were all familiar. In what should have been a strange, exotic place, I never felt so comfortable in my life.

As for the food, it was even more delightful than I had been led to expect. On my first visit, I explored every aspect of Hong Kong's dynamic culinary scene under the guidance of Willie Mark, who is perhaps the most expert food critic in Hong Kong, and even my boyhood fantasies were surpassed.

Lately, there has been a subtle yet significant shift in techniques, ingredients, and concepts in Hong Kong cooking. And here I quote the Andersons again, from their contribution to *Food in Chinese Culture:*

> South Chinese are usually quick to experiment with new and different foods — they show some resistance, as does everyone confronted with a strange diet, but they adjust much faster and more easily than do people from most other cultures.

This adjustment, this controlled reception of new and different foods, enriches and makes even livelier the already great Hong Kong cuisine. There is a glorious continuity and unity to Chinese cuisine but there is also a willingness to adapt, to accept diversity. This book is an attempt to document the subtle changes now taking place within the great tradition in one of the world's most exciting cities — Hong Kong.

As to the techniques, the traditional ways have been improved and refined — an important contribution to the *new* cooking of Hong Kong. One of these is the practice of coating meats in a marinade or a light froth of egg white, a technique often referred to as velveting. Another is the use of batters with the addition of yeast or baking powder, which results in a thin, crisp veneer that is very light and not oily. Although food so prepared must be eaten immediately, the technique emphasizes the attention to detail required of the best cooking to preserve freshness and natural taste. The use of clay pots, not just for braising but for preserving and intensifying flavors with a quick, very hot heat, is another Hong Kong refinement. The use of high-quality peanut oil that is heated to a very hot point and often used just once to leave the food relatively greaseless is also a matter of practiced technique more than anything else.

No doubt these techniques have evolved from long use, experimentation, and a general high level of cooking skills that is pervasive throughout Hong Kong. Even in the most humble of local restaurants, you will see many of these sophisticated and highly evolved cooking techniques skillfully practiced. One essential is the intensive heat that restaurants and even homes apply. Hong Kong, with its modern affluence compared to fuel-short China, has an abundance of propane gas. And the chefs make good use of it in their cooking. Food is seared in oil, water, or broth at very high heat — Hong Kong cooks often talk about cooking literally in fire. This type of heat, of course, is difficult to duplicate in modern Western homes. But I have found that you can get fairly close to the new flavors of Hong Kong if you follow the techniques in the Glossary.

A NEW CITY FROM AN ANCIENT CIVILIZATION

"Hong Kong has become a social, political and economic laboratory where practical — though intentional — experiments in social evolution are continuously conducted in an atmosphere of high pressure created by the Colony's compactness, large population and intense vitality. Neither wholly Eastern nor entirely Western, it is sui generis — a phenomenon never seen previously and never likely to be duplicated."
— ROBERT ELEGANT

It is true — Hong Kong is sui generis, and perhaps more than any other city, an invention. From being a "barren island," as Lord Palmerston accurately described it in 1843, Hong Kong, but thirty square miles around, has become the "vast emporium of commerce and wealth" that its first governor, Sir Henry Pottinger, more presciently saw as its destiny: he predicted that trade, commerce, and manufacturing were to be Hong Kong's central purpose and concern. Even he, however, would be astonished could he see it today. Its 150 years of history (brief by any standards), and particularly the past forty years of growth and transformation, have produced the unique city and state of mind we know as Hong Kong.

Whatever Hong Kong is today, its origins held many aspects of its future. For the Crown Colony, blessed as it was by nature and human resources, came into existence as the result of greed, violence, and the lust after Imperial power and domination. The island passed into British hands in 1842 as a result of the first Opium War. Not to put too fine a point on it, this was a war fought to open China to the opium trade. Britain, with some connivance of other Western powers, forced China to cease her strenuous efforts to stop the nefarious trade which was enervating her people and undermining her economy. Then, as now, there were enormous profits to be made from the business and powerful interests sought to maintain their lucrative trade with the help of armed forces. (A contemporary parallel would be if Colombian drug dealers today forced the United States to open her ports to the cocaine trade.) By the Treaty of Nanjing (1842), which ended the war, the opium trade was continued and Hong Kong was ceded to Britain in perpetuity.

China never accepted the terms of this treaty — indeed, the British occupied Hong Kong before it was ratified — and continued her efforts to stop the drug trade, resulting in the second Opium War (1856). Again, the fragility of the Chinese state and superiority of British firepower forced further concessions from China. In the Convention of Beijing (1860), the Kowloon area, about three and a quarter square miles on the Chinese mainland opposite Hong Kong, was also ceded to Britain.

Finally, in 1898, another convention extorted from an increasingly weakened China the so-called New Territories, an area of 355 square miles adjacent to Kowloon, leased to Britain for ninety-nine years. Successive Chinese governments of whatever political persuasion referred to these agreements as the "unequal treaties," which constitute an infringement on China's sovereignty. It has always been only a matter of time, in China's view, before so unequal a settlement would be rectified.

However that may be, it was thus that the Crown Colony took its geographic shape: The main island of Hong Kong and numerous smaller outlying isles (235 all told); the Kowloon Peninsula; the New Territories — a total of 410 square miles. Before man's inventiveness took over, Hong Kong was an area of mountains, beaches, sparkling bays, a magnificent deep-water harbor, bright sunshine, gentle mists, with a climate balanced between warm and humid and cool and dry seasons. These combined to create a generally pleasing prospect and environment. Once the tropical fevers were overcome, through advances in sanitation and medicine, the only natural deficiency remaining was the seasonal threat of typhoons; these cannot be contained by progress or technology, but at least the modern buildings can withstand them. All in all, a propitious place, although quite misunderstood and undervalued back home in Britain where, in the 1850s, a book on China was published with a chapter, "Hong Kong: Its Position, Prospects, Character, and Utter Worthlessness from Every Point of View for England."

From 1846 to 1941, it may be said that Hong Kong's history was one of relative calm, of slow development interspersed with episodes of crisis and stress. In 1850, there were fifteen thousand people on the island — mainly south China or Cantonese Chinese, but with a dominant political and economic elite of foreign merchants, officials, military personnel, missionaries and their dependents. In 1900, Hong Kong, Kowloon, and the New Territories combined had a population of 250,000. The percentage of Westerners had shrunk, but it formed a thin but obvious veneer of Westernization over an essentially south China city.

The basis of Hong Kong's economy in the nineteenth and early twentieth century was the entrepôt trade, shipping and its supporting facilities, warehousing and the occupations ancillary to that trade. From its beginnings to the present day, Hong Kong has been a free trade zone, with minimum regulation. Until 1900 the opium trade provided almost one half of the Colony's revenues, but the growth of other trading and commercial opportunities (and a belated recognition of opium's baleful consequences) led to the gradual abolition of the drug trade. Sadly, although Hong Kong's opium dens were officially closed in 1910, the continuing illegal trade into and through Southeast Asia and Europe to Hong Kong is one of the area's most serious social problems.

~~~~~~

After World War I, Hong Kong's manufacturing sector began its expansion, facilitated by a reserve of willing and needy workers, while the shipping business, serving as a conduit for goods to and from the West and China, still provided the basis for its economy. By 1930, the population numbered 860,000 and by 1941 had reached 1,600,000, with members of my family among them. It was this enormous human capital that was later to provide much of the impetus for Hong Kong's economic and industrial surge in the post-World War II period.

Until the 1920s, there was remarkably little friction between the tiny British Crown Colony and its huge Chinese neighbor. The so-called Boxer Rebellion of 1900, an early nationalistic, anti-foreigner uprising, increased the flow of immigrants from the mainland into Hong Kong, as did all disruptions of life on the mainland. From 1920 to 1949, China experienced chronic internal disruptions, foreign invasion and occupation, and ultimately, all-out civil war, which Mao Zedong's Communist forces finally won.

Hong Kong's fortunes were directly implicated in all of these, with her lowest point the period of the Japanese occupation, from 1941 to 1945. Much of the population was forcibly evacuated to China proper, but as soon as the war ended, people streamed back. A different and vitally important component of this renewed immigration manifested itself after the 1949 triumph of the Communist forces: the mainland, it was readily apparent, was no longer any place for capitalism, nor for capitalists. Among the new immigrant refugees were affluent and experienced businessmen and entrepreneurs from such manufacturing centers as Canton and Shanghai, some of whom arrived with crates of machinery, even entire factories in tow. Hong Kong now had labor and capital, and, for the time being, enough land to build on.

The story of Hong Kong from 1946 to the present is one of feverish adaptations to changing economic imperatives. Resuming her career as an entrepôt proved impossible for Hong Kong because of the turmoil on the mainland and, later, the embargo placed on trade with China during and after the Korean War. Experienced Shanghai businessmen, desperate to reestablish themselves, used their contacts and know-how to start up manufacturing — for export. The transition was assisted, even impelled, by the Colony's administration which reestablished an almost complete laissez-faire business environment; whatever may have been happening at home in Labor-dominated Britain, the Colonial administrators were left alone.

It was after 1965, after the worst excesses of the Cultural Revolution, which so troubled the mainland, that Hong Kong attained its position as one of the great trading states of the world. As it did so, it retained its lure as a magnet to Chinese immigrants: from a population of 2.4 million in 1951, it grew to number 5.3 million in 1984.

That same year, an agreement was signed between Britain and the People's Republic of China to provide for the peaceful transfer of sovereignty to China. Hong Kong, Kowloon, the New Territories — "lock, stock, and skyscrapers" — will revert to Chinese control. Under its terms, China is committed to preserving Hong Kong's capitalistic approach to business for at least fifty years beyond 1997: "one country, two systems." The stock market will remain, along with Hong Kong's convertible currency and its free port. There are many indications that the Chinese leadership wishes to maintain and even improve upon the economic status quo in Hong

~~~~~~

Kong. China is investing great sums of money in Hong Kong enterprises; moreover, trade with the mainland has steadily increased, and today accounts for more than a quarter of Hong Kong's total export trade.

Apparently, after a brief (by China's chronology) interruption, the "barren island" is returning officially to the homeland, but it is now transformed into a feverishly productive trading state. History is replete with such ironies, but this promises to be a more happy than bitter turn of events. Hong Kong's experiences over the past 150 years indicate it will make the best of things.

SPLENDID HONG KONG

"Hong Kong, squeezed between giant antagonists crunching huge bones of contention, has achieved within its own narrow territories a coexistence which is baffling, infuriating, incomprehensible, and which works splendidly — on borrowed time in a borrowed place."

— HAN SUYIN

Hong Kong's social life, especially as it has evolved over the past three decades, is endlessly fascinating. Consider the place: almost six million people crowded onto about 410 square miles; not all of it habitable. Parts of Kowloon are probably the most densely populated human habitats in the world, with close to 400,000 inhabitants per square mile. To say the streets teem with people is to understate the situation. The island of Hong Kong is almost as densely populated. These many millions of people crowded together in what sometimes appears as ordered chaos constitute the human basis of Hong Kong, and they interact for the most part cooperatively and productively. Whatever may happen after 1997, the great majority of these people — fatalistic, realistic, preoccupied, and ambitious — carry on in the Hong Kong tradition: working hard, building, gambling, eating, enjoying, enduring the actualities, and exploiting the possibilities around them.

The government has a monopoly on perhaps the only commodity that Hong Kong entrepreneurs cannot produce or duplicate: it owns all of the land. Its policy is never to sell but to lease land for specific improvements, and to let it out parsimoniously and at the highest possible rate. The effect is to maximize its revenues and to enable it to keep taxes low. Another effect is seen in the uneven development of the area, with some areas disconcertingly overbuilt and others still untouched.

Pressure for land was vastly exacerbated by the immigration flood after 1949. The state had done nothing to ease the way of the immigrants once they had legally or illegally entered Hong Kong; however, after a disastrous fire destroyed the hovels and shacks of fifty thousand Kowloon residents on Christmas Day, 1953, major public housing projects were undertaken as a large and ongoing program. It is true that the buildings are, inevitably, high rises, rather bleak and alienating in appearance and social effect. Yet despite this, the public housing program has been a success insofar as it has provided inexpensive shelter for millions: more than forty percent of Hong Kong's population lives in public housing. One of the reasons, in fact, that Hong Kong can support so many thousands of restaurants, cafés, and food stalls is because low rents give even those with marginal incomes the ability to patronize these eating places. And of course, the restaurants at the same time provide hundreds of thousands of jobs.

The other major social program supported by the state is the primary and secondary public school system, free and compulsory for all children under the age of fifteen. The result is one of the best-educated, most literate populations among the developing nations.

Practically everything essential for Hong Kong's existence must be imported; every article it produces for export is manufactured from imported materials. It is a Chinese place and culture with a Western tincture that paradoxically dominates at least its immediately visible aspects: the skyscrapers, the banks, the commerce, the modern stylish clothing, the neon lights, the jet planes. A closer look reveals the Chinese continuities.

The two main cultures confront each other, assimilating certain aspects, rejecting others, maintaining an uneasy, fluid coexistence. Westerners who have seen the motion picture *Ah Ying,* set in Hong Kong, will understand more clearly the human side of this cultural mélange. The heroine of the story longs to escape from the physical and spiritual confinement of her tenement existence and from the drudgery of her family's traditional fishmonger trade. Her way out is through the theater, in which she masters not only the ancient Mandarin style but Western pop culture as well: Simon and Garfunkel's "Scarborough Fair" is as meaningful to her as are the Chinese classics. She remains a creature of two cultures, neither one of which is entirely fulfilling, yet she is determined to do the best she can with both worlds. That may well serve as the working motto of all who live in Hong Kong. And visitors who are aware of these cultural and social polarities are able to savor more fully the remarkable sights, sounds, and tastes of Hong Kong.

THE
RECIPES

APPETIZERS
AND
DIM SUM

~~~~~~~~~~~~~~~~~~~~~~~

CHIU CHOW CHIVE DUMPLINGS

PRESERVED VEGETABLE DUMPLINGS

STEAMED SHANGHAI DUMPLINGS

WHITE CREPE DUMPLINGS WITH CHICKEN

CRISP HALF-MOON DUMPLINGS

BRAISED JELLYFISH

PIGS' FEET COOKED IN WINE AND VINEGAR

TWO-FLAVOR CHICKEN WITH CORIANDER

DEEP-FRIED SQUAB ROLLS

BRAISED CHIU CHOW DUCK

PICKLED YOUNG GINGER

DEEP-FRIED CRABMEAT AND HAM ROLLS

FRIED WONTONS WITH SWEET-AND-SOUR SAUCE

SICHUAN DUMPLINGS IN SPICY SAUCE

Dim sum are light snacks designed "to touch the heart," as the literal translation of the Chinese written characters proclaims. That they touch the heart by way of the palate and stomach is deliciously appropriate. Dim sum has been a significant category of the Cantonese cuisine for one thousand years. Throughout Hong Kong today, there are restaurants that specialize in dim sum, offering a great variety of savory, spicy, and sweet dishes from early morning to late afternoon. Such specialty restaurants are like Western cafés, tearooms, and bistros. There is an informality about them that is conducive to relaxation. They are places of animated and often noisy conversation, where friends and colleagues meet to gossip and to transact business. Dim sum is usually served from steaming bamboo baskets set on carts that are pushed slowly past the diners' tables. Whenever you wish to select an offering you simply nod or point to it and it is served up. One typically samples at least two to four dishes. Tea is drunk throughout; indeed, this repast is sometimes referred to in Hong Kong as yum char, Cantonese for "drink tea meal." As with all Chinese cuisine, dim sum dishes allow for the introduction of new ingredients and techniques. The recipes here reflect Hong Kong's subtle innovations and variations on the traditional themes.

CHIU CHOW CHIVE DUMPLINGS

Chiu Chow cuisine is one of the subcuisines of Cantonese cooking that has been quite popular recently in Hong Kong. It is a peasant cuisine that emphasizes strong, earthy tastes. Like Cantonese cooking, it pays great attention to the textures of the ingredients in all dishes and its recipes insure that each ingredient retains its natural flavor. Nowhere are these traits more evident than in these wonderful dumplings which I had for the first time in a Chiu Chow restaurant in Hong Kong. The filling is brimming with the earthy flavor of Chinese chives which have a strong, slight garlic taste (it is from the garlic side of the onion family). Chinese chives have been used for centuries in east Asia in the same manner Westerners used true chives in their cooking.

The dumpling skins require wheat and tapioca starch. The tapioca starch is often used in southern Chinese dumplings to give it a crisp texture and translucent sheen; wheat starch is wheat flour with the gluten removed. The mixture of the two makes for a malleable skin in which a tasty filling can be wrapped.

FILLING
1 tablespoon peanut oil
½ pound fatty ground pork, preferably pork butt
2 tablespoons finely chopped whole scallions
1½ teaspoons salt
½ teaspoon freshly ground pepper
1 teaspoon sugar
2 teaspoons sesame oil
1 tablespoon Rich Chicken Stock (page 221)
2 teaspoons rice wine
2 teaspoons light soy sauce
½ cup finely chopped yellow chives, if available; substitute additional Chinese chives if not
1½ cups finely chopped Chinese chives

DOUGH
1 cup boiling water
1 cup wheat starch
½ cup tapioca starch
1 teaspoon salt
2 teaspoons sesame oil

3 tablespoons peanut oil, for pan-frying

Heat a wok or large skillet until it is hot. Add the peanut oil and when it is quite hot, quickly stir-fry the pork for about 3 minutes. Add the rest of the filling ingredients except the chives. Turn out all the contents of the wok into a bowl and allow to cool. When the filling has cooled, mix in the chives and set aside.

Add the boiling water to the wheat and tapioca starches in a gradual stream, mixing quickly. Add the salt and sesame oil. The dough will be slightly lumpy. Knead the dough on a floured board until it is smooth (about 3 to 5 minutes). Knead the dough for another 10 seconds, just to make sure it is smooth. With your hands, roll the dough into a log 1½ inches thick. Cut the dough into ½-inch chunks. Roll each chunk into a ball between your palms and then pat each ball into a 5-inch round pancake. Continue until all the pancakes have been formed. Lay the pancakes on a floured tray making sure that they do not overlap, and cover with a damp cloth to prevent them from forming a skin as you fill them.

Place two tablespoons of filling in the center of the pancake, gather up the sides and pinch the ends together at the top to seal. Flatten it slightly and continue to fill the rest of the pancakes.

Lightly oil a heat-proof platter, place platter on a rack in a tightly covered wok or pot, and gently steam the dumplings, seam side up, for 15 minutes. You may have to do this in 2 or 3 batches. Serve dumplings hot from steamer. If you then want to fry them, allow the dumplings to cool. They will look transparent when they have cooled.

Heat a large skillet until it is hot and add 1½ tablespoons of the peanut oil. Add the dumplings, turn the heat down, and brown on each side. Remove the cooked dumplings and present them with the seam side down. Continue to cook the remaining dumplings adding the rest of the oil. Serve immediately.

YIELD: MAKES 15 TO 20 DUMPLINGS

The dumplings are steamed first; they can either be eaten at this point or placed aside for future use. Then they are pan-fried to crisp them further. The result is a savory dumpling with much texture delighting tongue as well as palate.

Once you have made these dumplings you will see why they are so popular in Hong Kong. The chives can be found in Asian specialty markets and are well worth the search.

PRESERVED VEGETABLE DUMPLINGS

Preserved vegetables are a popular food in Hong Kong's colorful markets where they are displayed in stacks of different varieties. Traditionally they were served to stretch or supplement poor diets but today they are also often used as fillers or seasonings in ground meat dishes. Their earthy, distinct flavors add a new dimension to such foods. Here they are combined in a pork-based filling, then encased in wontons and gently steamed. The flavors of the vegetables and other seasonings permeate the filling. If you prefer, you may substitute other fresh or preserved vegetables, such as zucchini, Sichuan preserved vegetables, or cabbage (finely chopped) in place of the pork, for an equally tasteful vegetarian dumpling. Either way, they will serve deliciously as an appetizer or a dim sum snack.

FILLING

½ cup dried Chinese black mushrooms
1 pound fatty ground pork
¼ cup finely chopped Tianjin preserved cabbage
3 tablespoons finely chopped whole scallions
2 tablespoons finely chopped fresh coriander
1 tablespoon finely chopped peeled fresh ginger
2 teaspoons light soy sauce
1 teaspoon dark soy sauce
2 teaspoons sugar
1 tablespoon rice wine
2 teaspoons cornstarch
2 teaspoons sesame oil
½ teaspoon freshly ground white pepper

DOUGH
40 to 45 large thin wonton wrappers, 4 by 4 inches

Soak the mushrooms in a bowl of warm water for about 20 minutes or until they are soft and pliable. Squeeze out the excess water and cut off and discard the woody stems. Finely chop the caps.

Mix all the filling ingredients together in a medium-sized bowl.

Add a generous tablespoon of filling to the center of the wonton wrapper and fold over to form the shape of a triangle. Continue until you have used up all the dough and filling. Place the dumplings on top of a damp, cheesecloth-lined bamboo steamer.

Place the steamer over water in a wok or pot, cover tightly, and steam over high heat for 15 minutes. Serve immediately.

YIELD: MAKES 40 TO 45 DUMPLINGS

STEAMED SHANGHAI DUMPLINGS

FILLING
½ cup dried Chinese black mushrooms
1 pound fatty ground pork
3 tablespoons finely chopped whole scallions
1 tablespoon finely chopped fresh coriander
2 teaspoons light soy sauce
2 teaspoons sugar
1 tablespoon rice wine
2 teaspoons potato starch mixed with
    3 tablespoons water
1 teaspoon sesame oil
½ teaspoon freshly ground white pepper

DOUGH
30 store-bought thick pot-sticker skins or wonton
    wrappers

Soak the mushrooms in a bowl of warm water for about 20 minutes or until they are soft and pliable. Squeeze out the excess water and cut off and discard the woody stems. Finely chop the caps.

Mix all the filling ingredients together in a medium-sized bowl. Set aside.

Add a generous tablespoon of filling to the center of each skin and pinch to form the shape of a bun. Continue until you have used up all the dough and filling. Place the dumplings on top of a damp cheesecloth-lined bamboo steamer.

Steam over high heat in a tightly covered wok or pot for 15 minutes. Serve immediately.

YIELD: MAKES 30 DUMPLINGS

Shanghainese in Hong Kong boast that the place was a sleepy backwater until they arrived in 1949, after the People's Republic was established on the mainland. There is some truth to this claim inasmuch as the Shanghainese did indeed bring with them their great commercial and manufacturing skills. They also brought their venerable culinary traditions. Shanghai-style restaurants quickly established those traditions in Hong Kong. Today, you can see such restaurants all over, their distinctive display windows offering passersby a chance to see expert cooks preparing these famous dumplings and other specialties.

In the original recipe, the dough is a mixture of flour and water that must be allowed to rest after mixing. This is laborious and time-consuming. Searching for an acceptable shortcut, I tried using round pot-sticker skins. It results in an effect very close to the original and it takes one-fifth the time and effort. In addition, the Cantonese Hong Kong chefs have refined this recipe to make them lighter than the traditionally heavier and oilier Shanghai style.

WHITE CREPE DUMPLINGS WITH CHICKEN

The sophistication of Hong Kong's cooking is apparent in such dishes as this. I first tasted these dumplings at the sumptuous Man Wah restaurant of the Mandarin Hotel. The recipe derives from the peasant cuisine of Chiu Chow, a fishing area in southern China, and its appearance on the menu of the Man Wah is another illustration of how Hong Kong chefs creatively exploit the richness of Chinese cuisine. In this version, a light, airy white crepe, made with egg whites, envelopes a savory filling. The crepe-dumplings are tied with green onions, then gently steamed; often they are served with a topping of fresh crab roe. The result is a delightful contrast of tastes, textures, and aromas, a most unusual treat.

The recipe does require a bit of work but it will impress your guests. It makes a dramatic appetizer for an elegant dinner.

WHITE CREPES
3 egg whites
2 tablespoons cornstarch
3 tablespoons Rich Chicken Stock (page 221)

2 tablespoons peanut oil

FILLING
½ cup dried Chinese black mushrooms
1 whole chicken breast (12 ounces), boned, skinned, and finely chopped
1 egg white
1 teaspoon cornstarch
2 tablespoons peanut oil
¼ cup fresh water chestnuts, finely chopped
1 teaspoon salt
3 tablespoons finely chopped whole scallions
2 tablespoons finely chopped coriander
About 10 long green scallion tops, blanched

SAUCE
¼ cup Rich Chicken Stock
1 tablespoon rice wine
½ teaspoon salt
Freshly ground white pepper to taste
1 teaspoon sesame oil

Mix the crepe ingredients together in a small bowl. Heat a well-seasoned or nonstick small skillet and add a small amount of oil. (To fry all the batter, use no more than 2 tablespoons oil.) When it is hot, add about 1 tablespoon of the crepe mixture, swirling the batter around the bottom of the skillet to make a small, thin crepe about 5 inches in diameter. Cook for about 15 to 20 seconds or until set. Continue making the crepes until the mixture is used up. You should have about 10 crepes.

Soak the mushrooms in a bowl of warm water for about 20 minutes or until they are soft and pliable. Squeeze out the excess water and cut off and discard the woody stems. Finely chop the caps and set aside.

In a small bowl, mix the chicken, egg white, and cornstarch.

Heat a wok or large skillet and add peanut oil. When it is hot, add the chicken mixture, mushrooms, and water chestnuts. Stir-fry for 30 seconds. Then add the salt, scallions, and coriander. Continue to cook for 1 minute. Remove and set aside to cool.

Place about 1 tablespoon of filling into the center of each crepe, pull up the sides, and tie the filled crepe with a strand of blanched scallion green. Continue until you have used up all the crepes and filling to make the dumplings.

Place the dumplings on a heat-proof platter on a rack inside a tightly covered wok or pot and gently steam for about 5 minutes.

While the dumplings are steaming, combine the sauce ingredients in a small pan, bring to a boil, and then remove from the heat. When the dumplings are done, pour the sauce over and serve at once.

YIELD: MAKES 10 DUMPLINGS

CRISP HALF-MOON DUMPLINGS

It is always a pleasure for me to experience these treats again when I visit Hong Kong. In banquets, they are usually served just before the noodles and rice, dishes which traditionally signal the closing of the feast. The dumplings come with their own clear, rich chicken broth, usually sprinkled with chopped yellow chives. One dips them into the broth just before eating them; the contrast of the delicate broth and the crisp morsels adds to the delectability of this dish. According to the theory of the banquet, these dumplings are supposed to provide a little something just in case you are still a bit hungry. I myself have observed that everyone who has this treat set before them finds them irresistible.

Potato starch gives these dumplings a slightly heavier texture. This recipe makes a large quantity, perfect for a large crowd as finger food. Again, much of the work can be done ahead of time once the steaming is done — fry the dumplings only at the last minute before serving.

Serve alone, with dipping sauces of your choice, or with Clear Soup with Yellow Chives (page 48).

FILLING

2 tablespoons salt
1 pound medium shrimp, peeled and deveined
1 cup shelled fresh sweet peas (1 pound unshelled), blanched
1 pound ground pork
2 tablespoons light soy sauce
2 teaspoons salt
1 teaspoon sugar
1 tablespoon rice wine
3 tablespoons finely chopped scallions, white part only

DOUGH

2¾ cups wheat starch
1 cup potato starch
1 teaspoon salt
3 cups hot water

2 cups peanut oil, for deep-frying

Fill a large bowl with cold water, add 1 tablespoon of salt, and gently wash the shrimp in the salt water. Drain and repeat the process, using fresh salted water. Then rinse the shrimp under cold running water, drain, and blot dry with paper towels.

Coarsely chop the shrimp and mix them with the rest of the filling ingredients. Set the mixture aside.

In a large bowl, combine the starches and salt. Add the hot water gradually, stirring constantly with chopsticks or a fork until the water is fully incorporated. The dough should hold together in a ball. Remove the mixture from the bowl and knead it with your hands until it is smooth.

Form the dough into a long roll about 1 inch in diameter. Cut the roll into about 28 to 30 equal pieces. Shape each of the dough pieces into a small, round flat pancake about ⅛ inch in thickness. Put about two to three tablespoons of filling in the center of each pancake, then fold over into a half-moon shape. Pinch the edges together to seal well. Transfer the finished dumplings to an oiled tray until you are ready to cook them.

Lightly oil a heat-proof platter. Arrange the dumplings

so that they do not touch or they will stick together. Place platter on a rack in a tightly covered wok or pot and steam them gently for 10 minutes. You will have to do this in several batches. Allow the dumplings to cool thoroughly.

Heat the oil in a wok or deep pan. When it is hot, add the dumplings and deep-fry them. They will be crisp and puffed when done, about 5 minutes. Drain on paper towels before serving.

YIELD: MAKES 28 TO 30 DUMPLINGS

BRAISED JELLYFISH

½ pound prepared packaged shredded jellyfish

SESAME SAUCE
½ teaspoon salt
2 teaspoons sugar
1 teaspoon white rice vinegar
1 teaspoon light soy sauce
2 tablespoons sesame oil

GARNISH
2 tablespoons finely chopped coriander

Rinse the jellyfish well in cold running water and drain. Put it in a stainless steel bowl and cover with boiling water. Keep the jellyfish in the water for about 15 minutes, or until it is tender. Drain and continue to soak in at least six changes of cold water for 10 to 15 minutes each time. Drain the jellyfish thoroughly, blot dry with paper towels and set aside.

Mix the sesame sauce ingredients together in a small bowl. Toss the sauce thoroughly with the jellyfish and let sit for at least 30 minutes. Garnish with the coriander before serving.

YIELD: SERVES 4 TO 6

This popular jellyfish recipe is but one of the many diverse regional influences reflected in Hong Kong's cuisine. It is of northern Chinese provenance and, like that region's Peking Duck and many lamb and mutton dishes, it has earned a place in the Cantonese–Hong Kong repertory. The jellyfish is preserved in salt and comes in sheets or in shredded form, available in Chinese food stores. Properly prepared, it is a bit like al dente pasta, and as palatable. Its texture is particularly prized by the Chinese. Easy to make, it is an excellent and exotic appetizer, especially when paired with other appetizers such as Pigs' Feet Cooked in Wine and Vinegar (page 36) and main courses such as Cold Drunken Chicken (page 115).

PIGS' FEET COOKED IN WINE AND VINEGAR

Just as tasty as Grandma used to make, but presented in a better fashion, these pigs' feet have been refined by gentle long cooking, then boned, then chilled and sliced like a fine paté. Thus transformed, this old home dish has made a fashionable entry into Hong Kong's elegant teahouses. Our palates tell us it is indeed pigs' feet but with a smooth and appealing taste and texture that is most pleasing. When you make them, be sure your butcher provides you with hind legs, which are meatier and can best take the long braising time necessary.

Because this dish must be prepared ahead of time, it is ideal as an appetizer or as a light summer refreshment. I like to serve these pigs' feet with the Cold Drunken Chicken (page 115) and Braised Jellyfish (page 35) as a traditional dish to open a Chinese banquet.

2 pounds large, meaty pigs' feet, about 3 to 4 pieces
½ pound fresh ginger, peeled and cut into 8 pieces
10 unpeeled garlic cloves, crushed
10 whole scallions, cut into pieces

BRAISING LIQUID
4 cups Rich Chicken Stock (page 221)
2 cups rice wine
1 cup white rice vinegar
¼ cup sugar
2 tablespoons salt

Have your butcher trim the pig's feet and cut them into halves. Blanch the pig's feet for 20 minutes in a large pot of boiling water. Drain the contents of the pot, refill with water, and bring it to a boil. Return the pig's feet, ginger, garlic, and scallions and simmer for another 20 minutes. Drain the contents of the pot and rinse the pot well.

Add the braising ingredients to the pot, bring to a boil, and return the pig's feet. Cover and simmer for about 1 hour or until the meat is tender. Drain and discard ginger, garlic, and scallions. Allow the pig's feet to cool thoroughly. Refrigerate without the liquid.

Remove the meat from the bones, trying to keep pieces intact, and cut into thin slices. Serve with the Garlic-Vinegar Dipping Sauce (page 226).
YIELD: SERVES 6 TO 8

TWO-FLAVOR CHICKEN WITH CORIANDER

Two 3- to 3½-pound chickens

CLEAR STEEPING LIQUID
2½ quarts water
2 tablespoons salt
1 tablespoon whole unroasted Sichuan peppercorns
6 whole scallions, sliced
6 slices unpeeled fresh ginger

SOY STEEPING LIQUID
2 quarts water
½ cup light soy sauce
1 cup dark soy sauce
2 pieces cinnamon bark
4 tablespoons rock sugar
3 star anise

GARNISH
Fresh coriander

Blanch each chicken in a pot of boiling water for 5 minutes. Remove the chickens, drain, and allow them to cool thoroughly.

Fill one large pot with the clear steeping liquid, and fill another large pot with the soy steeping liquid. Bring the two steeping liquids to a boil, add one chicken to each, and simmer for about 20 minutes. Cover the pots, take off the heat, and allow the chickens to steep for about 1 hour or overnight. If the chickens are to steep longer than 3 hours, let them cool in the liquid, then refrigerate.

Remove the chickens from the steeping liquid, slice, and serve garnished with fresh coriander.

YIELD: SERVES 6 TO 8

Visitors in Hong Kong are always impressed by the sight of so many different varieties of barbecue meats, sausages, and other delicacies displayed in shop windows. Two very popular Cantonese classics are the white-cut and the soy sauce chicken dishes, which are usually served together, as in this recipe. The contrast between the pure, subtle taste of the white chicken and that of the bracing soy-steeped chicken is what accounts for its popularity. All the work for this recipe can be done ahead of time. It makes a dramatic opener for any meal, and it can serve as a light lunch entrée.

DEEP-FRIED SQUAB ROLLS

This is my version of a delicious pigeon roll I had at the Lung Wah pigeon restaurant, which specializes in pigeon cooked in many ways and forms. The restaurant is located in Shatin which is in the New Territories. It is a favorite of families and often they make excursions there on Sunday, their day off. The restaurant is partly open-air, a real blessing in Hong Kong's hot and humid spring and summer. While the adults play mah-jongg, children frolic about in the special children's area; then all gather for dinner, eating the whole pigeons or pigeon dishes for which the restaurant is famous.

In this preparation, the caul fat keeps the squab mixture moist; as it fries the fat becomes crisp and is quite tasty. Once wrapped, the squab rolls can stay in the refrigerator, covered with plastic wrap, until you are ready to cook them.

FILLING
½ to 2 pounds squab (about 2 squab)
1 tablespoon rice wine
2 tablespoons light soy sauce
1 teaspoon sesame oil
2 teaspoons sugar
2 teaspoons oyster sauce
1 teaspoon ground Sichuan peppercorns
Salt to taste
½ cup coarsely chopped fresh water chestnuts
    (about ½ pound whole)
½ cup coarsely chopped bamboo shoots
3 tablespoons finely chopped whole scallions
2 teaspoons finely chopped peeled fresh ginger

½ pound caul fat
2 cups peanut oil, for deep-frying
Cornstarch, for dusting

Peel the skin off the squab. Remove the meat from the bones and coarsely chop it with the liver, giblets, and hearts. Combine the chopped meat with the seasoning and the rest of the filling ingredients.

Cut the sheets of caul fat into twenty-four 3-by-5-inch squares. Place 2 to 3 tablespoons of squab mixture on the edge of each caul-fat square. Roll the edge over the mixture once, fold over the ends, and roll up tightly to resemble a breakfast sausage. Set the finished roll on a clean plate and continue the process until you have used up all the caul fat.

Heat the oil in a wok or deep pan until it is hot. Dust the rolls lightly with cornstarch and deep-fry them until they are crisp and brown, about 5 to 7 minutes. You will have to do this in several batches. Drain thoroughly on paper towels and serve hot or wrapped in lettuce leaves with hoisin sauce, if you wish.

YIELD: MAKES 24 ROLLS

BRAISED CHIU CHOW DUCK

3½- to 4-pound fresh duck, or fresh young goose

BRAISING LIQUID
2 pieces dried citrus peel
1½ cups dark soy sauce
½ cup rice wine
¼ cup light soy sauce
3 tablespoons brown sugar
4 whole scallions, cut into 2-inch long pieces
4 slices unpeeled fresh ginger
6 star anise
2 pieces cinnamon bark
1 quart water

Blanch the duck or goose in a large pot of boiling water for 5 minutes. Remove and allow to cool.

Soak the citrus peel in warm water and when it is soft, combine it with the rest of the braising liquid in a large pot and bring it to a simmer. Add the duck, cover, and braise for 1 hour or until the duck is cooked through. Turn the duck from time to time to make sure it cooks evenly.

Remove the duck and allow it to cool thoroughly. Bone the duck leaving the skin on the meat, and cut it into attractive slices. Serve it with Garlic-Vinegar Dipping Sauce (page 226) on the side as a dipping sauce.

YIELD: SERVES 4 TO 6

This is a most delectable cold dish. I always order it in the Chiu Chow restaurants in Hong Kong that are known for cooking goose. The smaller Chinese goose is as readily available as ducks in Hong Kong. The goose is simmered in a spicy braising sauce, cooled, and then hung in windows in a deli area inside the restaurants. When you order it, it is thinly sliced and variously served on top of cooked bean curd sheets, with fried blood pudding, or with braised soybeans. A dip of garlic and white rice vinegar always accompanies it, and perfectly complements the richness of the goose.

Here I use the more readily available duck instead of goose. But if you have access to a young goose, the procedure is the same. It is also quite tasty and easy to prepare. Since it is served at room temperature, it may be made well ahead of time. The cold, rich duck makes a delightful warm weather dish — you can see why it is perfect in Hong Kong's subtropical climate.

PICKLED YOUNG GINGER

Slightly sweet and just a tad sour, pickled young stem ginger is usually eaten raw or with preserved eggs (also known as Thousand-Year Eggs) as a snack or an appetizer. Sometimes it is stir-fried with meats, poultry, or vegetables, which it always enlivens. Because it is young, it is less fibrous and has a milder tang than mature gingerroot. But it has the authentic fresh and fragrant ginger appeal, and it can be sliced and eaten as a vegetable. At the food stalls of Hong Kong you will see it served with rice porridge or as an accompaniment with rice in a quick meal.

You can make this with ordinary fresh ginger but young ginger is preferable. Rubbing the ginger with salt draws out its excess moisture, giving it more texture. This easy-to-make dish can be made well in advance, and it will keep for as long as three months in the refrigerator. Try it by itself or serve it stir-fried, as in Stir-Fried Pickled Ginger with Bean Curd (page 172).

1 pound young stem ginger
2 tablespoons salt
2½ cups white rice vinegar
1 teaspoon salt
6 large cloves garlic, peeled and lightly crushed
2½ cups sugar

Wash the ginger well under cold running water. Trim and peel the ginger and cut into 3- to 4-inch chunks. Rub 1 tablespoon of salt onto the chunks and let them sit for 20 minutes. Rinse well in cold running water, and repeat the procedure with the remaining tablespoon of salt. Dry thoroughly with paper towels and set aside.

Bring the vinegar, salt, garlic, and sugar to a boil in a large enamel or stainless steel saucepan. Put the ginger into a heat-proof bowl. Pour the vinegar mixture over, making sure that the liquid completely covers the ginger. When cool, pack the ginger and the liquid into a glass jar and refrigerate.

The ginger will turn slightly pink in about a week and will be ready to use.

YIELD: MAKES 1 POUND

DEEP-FRIED CRABMEAT AND HAM ROLLS

FILLING
2 ounces (1 small package) bean thread noodles
½ ounce dried Chinese black mushrooms
½ pound fresh crabmeat
¼ pound fresh water chestnuts, finely chopped
3 tablespoons finely chopped Smithfield ham
3 tablespoons finely chopped whole scallions
2 tablespoons finely chopped fresh mint
1 tablespoon finely chopped peeled fresh ginger
1 tablespoon light soy sauce
¼ teaspoon freshly ground white pepper

1 package Banh Tran brand rice paper rounds
2 cups peanut oil, for deep-frying

Soak the bean thread noodles in a bowl of warm water for about 20 minutes. Drain well, cut into 5-inch lengths and set aside.

Soak the mushrooms in warm water for 20 minutes or until they are soft. Squeeze out the excess water and cut away the stems. Finely chop the caps and set aside.

Combine filling ingredients in a medium-sized bowl.

When you are ready to make the rolls, fill a large bowl with warm water. Dip one of the rice paper rounds in the water and let it soften for a few seconds. Remove and drain it on a linen towel.

Add about 1½ tablespoons of filling at the end of the rice paper round. Roll the edge over the mixture once, fold up both ends of the rice paper, and continue to roll to the end. The roll should be about 3 inches long, compact and tight, rather like a short, thick sausage. Set it on a clean plate and continue the process until you have used up all the filling.

The rolls can be made ahead of time, covered with plastic wrap, and refrigerated for up to 4 hours.

Heat the oil in a wok or deep skillet until it is moderately hot, and deep-fry the rolls a few pieces at a time for 3 to 4 minutes or until they are a light golden brown. They have a tendency to stick to one another at the beginning of the frying so do only a few at a time.

Drain on paper towels and serve at once.

YIELD: MAKES ABOUT 28 TO 30 ROLLS

The use of Southeast Asian rice paper rounds is a recent innovation of the creative Hong Kong chefs. Rice paper rounds are lighter and more delicate than the usual flour and water variety and are especially appropriate when used with such subtle and refined flavors as crab and ham. In Hong Kong, Chinese ham is used but our Smithfield variety is a fine substitute. The mint and ginger flavors enhance the taste of both the crab and the ham, making a delectable ensemble. This is an impressive appetizer to serve with drinks; or it may serve as a first course.

FRIED WONTONS WITH SWEET-AND-SOUR SAUCE

Fried wontons with sweet-and-sour sauce are almost a cliché in the West. Often associated with Westernized Chinese food, the dish has been vulgarized. So, I was surprised and delighted when I sampled the dish in Hong Kong. As prepared at the Yung Kee restaurant, the wontons and sauce revealed virtues I had not experienced before. My host and guide, Willie Mark, Hong Kong's leading food critic, explained that the wontons were double-fried, the second time just before serving. This assures that they will be hot and crisp. He also pointed out that the sauce must never overwhelm the wontons. It is a dipping sauce, he said, not a gravy. Moreover, the sauce must be balanced and the tendency to make it too sweet avoided. Properly done, then, this venerable recipe manifests all of the delicious qualities that earned it a place in the classical repertory. I find that if you serve the wontons right away, there is no need to double-fry them.

2 tablespoons salt
½ pound shrimp, shelled, deveined, and coarsely chopped

FILLING
½ pound fatty ground pork, shoulder or butt
2 teaspoons salt
Freshly ground black pepper to taste
1 teaspoon sesame oil

1 package thin square wonton wrappers
2 egg whites
2 cups peanut oil, for deep-frying

To clean the shrimp, please follow the directions on page 34.

Mix the shrimp and the filling ingredients together in a medium-sized bowl.

Place a tablespoon of filling in the center of a wonton square. Dab some egg white on the corners of the wonton skin and then gather the corners together and pinch them firmly to seal. Continue this process until all the filling is used.

Heat the peanut oil in a wok or a large deep pan. When it is hot but not smoking, deep-fry the wontons in several batches and drain on paper towels. They should be golden brown. Serve them while they are still hot and crisp with Sweet-and-Sour Sauce (page 222).

YIELD: MAKES 45 WONTONS

SICHUAN DUMPLINGS IN SPICY SAUCE

FILLING
½ cup dried Chinese black mushrooms
1 pound fatty ground pork, preferably pork butt
4 tablespoons finely chopped Chinese chives or
    whole scallions
1 egg white
1 tablespoon cornstarch
2 teaspoons salt
2 teaspoons sesame oil

20 to 25 large thin wonton wrappers, 4 by 4 inches

SAUCE
1 tablespoon peanut oil
2 teaspoons chili oil
1 tablespoon finely chopped garlic
2 tablespoons finely chopped whole scallions
2 teaspoons Sichuan peppercorns, roasted and ground
3 tablespoons sesame paste
2 tablespoons dark soy sauce
1 tablespoon sugar
2 teaspoons chili bean sauce
½ cup Rich Chicken Stock (page 221)

Sichuan cuisine is famously spicy — too spicy for the Cantonese–Hong Kong palate. However, Sichuan's robust recipes have other virtues in terms of taste, textures, colors, and aromas. In Hong Kong, therefore, Sichuan cuisine has been tamed, made milder and less oily, while its other aspects have been retained, as in this recipe. The dumplings are lighter, as a result of the addition of egg whites, and the sharp spices have been partially replaced by less aggressive but still savory seasonings. You will find that these dumplings are a sparkling opener for any meal. Or they can be a light lunch in themselves.

Soak the mushrooms in a bowl of warm water for about 20 minutes or until they are soft and pliable. Squeeze out the excess water and cut off and discard the woody stems. Finely chop the mushrooms and combine them with the meat and the rest of the filling ingredients. Mix well.

Place about 1 rounded teaspoon of filling inside each wonton wrapper. Gather the four sides of the wrapper up over the filling, allowing the wonton skin to fold in pleats naturally — it will resemble a little closed sack. Gently pinch the wrapper together just at the top of the filling to seal. Continue until you have used up all the stuffing.

Heat a wok or large skillet until it is hot and add the peanut and chili oils. Add the garlic and scallion and stir-fry for 20 seconds, then add the rest of the ingredients and simmer for 5 minutes. Remove to a separate bowl.

Bring a medium-sized pot of water to a boil and poach the dumplings for 3 minutes or until they float. Remove them quickly and drain thoroughly. Serve with the sauce.

YIELD: MAKES 20 TO 25 DUMPLINGS

SOUPS

~~~~~~~~~~~~~~~~~~

CLEAR SOUP WITH YELLOW CHIVES

SMOKED HAM AND ALMOND SOUP

SPINACH FISH SOUP

CRAB AND SHARK'S FIN SOUP

DOUBLE-STEAMED SHARK'S FIN SOUP

BIRD'S NEST SOUP WITH CHICKEN

VEGETABLE DUMPLING SOUP

DOUBLE-STEAMED MUSHROOM SOUP

TIANJIN CABBAGE WITH CHICKEN CONSOMMÉ

CABBAGE AND CHICKEN SOUP

HEARTY EGG-FLOWER AND BEEF SOUP

In the Chinese cuisine, soups are an integral part of the meal, consumed as a beverage throughout. However, the virtues of Chinese soups are such that they may serve as a course in a Western-style menu. With an international clientele to consider, Hong Kong chefs cater to different styles and tastes. So, as in Hong Kong itself, where the best of East and West can be found, these soups may be enjoyed as a beverage accompaniment to clear and refresh the palate, as a course, or served with bread and a salad as a complete meal.

CLEAR SOUP WITH YELLOW CHIVES

One finds this simple, clear chicken broth, slightly reduced to concentrate its flavor, in good restaurants throughout Hong Kong. It serves as a refreshing finish to a banquet when paired with Crisp Half-Moon Dumplings (page 34), or it can simply be consumed by itself with chopped yellow chives. It is very much like a European consommé. The Chinese yellow chives have been grown in the dark and have a rich, earthy, slightly garlicky taste; and of course, the lack of sunlight is responsible for their distinctive color. The chives add a subtle taste that enhances the delicious flavor of the clear broth.

8 cups Rich Chicken Stock (page 221)
Salt to taste
3 tablespoons finely chopped Chinese yellow or green chives

In a large pot, slowly reduce the chicken stock to about 6 cups. Salt to taste.

Put the chicken stock in a soup tureen or in individual serving bowls. Garnish with the chives and serve at once.
YIELD: SERVES 4 TO 6

SMOKED HAM AND ALMOND SOUP

3 cups blanched and skinned almonds
4 cups water
4 cups Ham and Chicken Stock (page 222) or
  Rich Chicken Stock (page 221)
2 teaspoons almond extract
2 teaspoons sugar
Salt to taste

GARNISH
2 tablespoons finely chopped Smithfield ham
3 tablespoons finely chopped whole scallions

In a medium-sized pot, simmer the almonds and water for 30 minutes. Let the mixture cool slightly, then finely purée in a blender and strain through a fine sieve lined with cheesecloth if necessary. The resulting liquid will be almond milk.

Heat the stock in a large pot and add the almond milk together with the almond extract and sugar. Add salt to taste if you are not using the ham and chicken stock. Simmer the mixture for 15 minutes and ladle it into a soup tureen. Garnish with the ham and scallions and serve at once.

YIELD: SERVES 6 TO 8

NOTE: The texture of the soup will be slightly gritty from the ground almonds, even after straining. You must use a blender to grind the almonds; *do not* use a food processor.

I have had this unusual soup several times in Hong Kong, but there it is made with chopped pigs' innards. I have concluded, on the basis of very little research, that smoked ham is preferred by Western palates. The almond flavor in this recipe is stronger that one would expect, as two types of almonds are used: sweet and bitter. Bitter almonds have a pungent taste that is due to the same enzyme reaction by which prussic acid is produced. Although they are inedible in the raw state, like peach pits, they are quite safe to use in cooking, because the toxin is highly volatile and evaporates when heated. Once heated, the bitter almonds retain the flavor of ratafia (indeed, ratafia essence and the liqueur by that name rely on the essential oils of both sweet and bitter almonds). One bitter almond can bring out the flavor of an entire dish using sweet almonds.

Bitter almonds are distilled and used to make almond extract, and so, because bitter almonds are more difficult to find here than in Hong Kong, I have substituted extract here.

This delicious, rich soup is a wonderful way to open any elegant meal.

SPINACH FISH SOUP

Another clear soup typical of the Hong Kong cuisine, this one is delightful to both the palate and the eye. The delicate flavor of the fresh fish, slowly steeped so that it remains tender and moist, is set off nicely against the more assertive spinach. Separate cooking of the two preserves their special qualities so that one experiences fish, spinach, and soup as three distinct and yet blended tastes.

This is a delicious soup and easy to make.

1½ pounds fillets of red snapper, rockfish, sea bass, or any firm white-fleshed fish
6 cups Rich Chicken Stock (page 221)
4 whole scallions
4 peeled fresh ginger slices, about ¼ inch thick
2 teaspoons salt
1 pound fresh spinach, washed and trimmed, to yield about 10 ounces
4 tablespoons rice wine
2 teaspoons sesame oil

GARNISH
2 tablespoons Smithfield ham, finely chopped

Cut the fish fillets into 3-inch pieces. Bring the stock to a boil in a large pot, and add the scallions, ginger, and salt. Reduce the heat to a simmer, add the fish pieces, and gently simmer for 2 minutes. Turn off the heat, cover tightly, and let sit for 20 minutes.

Blanch the washed and trimmed spinach for 30 seconds in a large pot of boiling salted water. Drain and set aside.

Add the spinach to the stock and fish fillets and return to a simmer. Add the rice wine and sesame oil, garnish with the ham, and serve at once.

YIELD: SERVES 4 TO 6

CRAB AND SHARK'S FIN SOUP

½ pound prepared shark's fin, frozen and thawed
4 cups Ham and Chicken Stock (page 222)
2 teaspoons salt
2 teaspoons finely chopped peeled fresh ginger
2 tablespoons finely chopped scallions, white part only
1 egg white
1 teaspoon sesame oil
½ cup fresh crabmeat

GARNISH
1 tablespoon finely chopped Smithfield ham

Blanch the shark's fin in a medium-sized pot of boiling water for 10 minutes. Drain and rinse under cold running water.

Bring the stock to a simmer, add the shark's fin, salt, ginger, and scallions. Simmer for 5 minutes. Combine the egg white and sesame oil in a small bowl and add this to the soup, stirring slowly with a chopstick or fork to form long egg strands. Add the crabmeat, allowing it to warm through. Turn the contents of the pot into a soup tureen, garnish with the chopped ham, and serve.

YIELD: SERVES 4 TO 6

NOTE: To get shark's fin to an edible state is an onerous and complex procedure that involves a week of effort. First, the fresh fin is removed from the shark and is thoroughly cleaned of sand. The skin and bone are then removed and the fin is dried. To prepare the dried fin, it must be soaked in cold water overnight. The fin is then boiled for several hours in a mixture of water, ginger, and scallions. This softens the fin and removes any fishy taste. The fin at this point can be frozen without loss of flavor or texture.

Among Hong Kong's most extravagant banquet fare is shark's fin, which is the dorsal "comb fin" or the two ventral fins of any of a variety of sharks from all over the world. A shark's fin dish is a sumptuous extravaganza, a highly acclaimed specialty said to have been first created over a thousand years ago. In Hong Kong, the preparation of shark's fin has become a culinary refinement that borders on snobbery. The wholesaling of shark's fin is a multimillion-dollar business. In Hong Kong you will notice many shops selling dried shark's fin, which is the best way to keep them until ready to use.

To make a soup, the prepared shark's fin is finally cooked with what is known as a supreme stock — a rich chicken and ham stock that gives flavor to the bland gelatinous shark's fin. Shark's fin is often combined with crabmeat in soup, as in this recipe, or it may be braised in a rich sauce, or garnished with chopped ham or crabmeat.

DOUBLE-STEAMED SHARK'S FIN SOUP

Two of my best friends in Hong Kong, Grace Fung and Kendall Oui, introduced me to this superb dish. I dined at their beautiful apartment home overlooking Hong Kong harbor and was treated to an unforgettable ten-course banquet prepared by a master chef-caterer. The meal rivaled the very best I have ever enjoyed anywhere and this soup was the most striking course of the evening. It was served with an impressive portion of Yunnan ham (from southwest China) that cooked for hours in the broth; the meat was literally falling away from the bone but still retained its hearty flavor. It was served side by side with the soup.

Frozen though it may be, shark's fin is still expensive and should be reserved for that extra-special occasion. Your guests will be delighted and impressed, and you will sample the genuine taste of Hong Kong.

½ pound prepared and frozen shark's fin, thawed
1 chicken, about 3 to 3½ pounds
¼-pound piece Smithfield ham
6 cups Rich Chicken Stock (page 221)
4 peeled fresh ginger slices, about ¼ inch thick
2 tablespoons rice wine
Salt and freshly ground white pepper to taste
2 teaspoons sesame oil

Blanch the shark's fin in a medium-sized pot of boiling water for 10 minutes. Drain and rinse under cold running water.

Cut the chicken into quarters and blanch together with the ham for 10 minutes in boiling water. Drain and set aside. Bring the chicken stock to a boil in a large pot. Add the shark's fin, chicken, ham, ginger, and rice wine. Pour the mixture into a 2 quart, heat-proof casserole.

Cover the casserole and set it inside a large steamer. Set the steamer on a rack in a tightly covered wok or pot and steam over slowly simmering water for 1 hour. Replenish as necessary with hot water.

Remove the chicken, ham, ginger, and any surface fat. Season to taste with salt and pepper and swirl in the sesame oil. Serve at once.

YIELD: SERVES 4 TO 6

BIRD'S NEST SOUP WITH CHICKEN

1 cup loosely packed, dried bird's nest
1 chicken, about 3 to 3½ pounds
6 cups Rich Chicken Stock (page 221)
2 teaspoons salt
1 teaspoon freshly ground white pepper

Soak the bird's nest overnight in warm water. Drain and rinse under cold running water. Blanch the bird's nest in boiling water for 5 minutes. Drain thoroughly and set aside.

Cut the chicken into quarters and blanch for 5 minutes in boiling water. Drain and set aside. Bring the chicken stock to a boil in a large pot. Add the chicken, salt, and pepper. Simmer for 20 minutes, skimming frequently. Allow the chicken to simmer for another hour. Drain thoroughly, removing any surface fat. Add the bird's nest and simmer for 25 minutes. Season to taste and serve at once.

YIELD: SERVES 4 TO 6

You must try it, just once. You will come back for more. As exotic and special as it sounds, bird's nest soup is very popular in Hong Kong and many parts of Asia. It is held to be good for one's complexion, to have medicinal virtues, and to slow down the aging process. Furthermore, it has a great taste —slightly gelatinous with the subtle flavor of whatever sauce or broth it has been cooked in. The nests are made, usually on rocky cliffs at the shoreline, by a species of bird in Thailand, Vietnam, Java, and the Philippines. Basically, they are an easily digestible complex of protein and other nutrients. In Hong Kong, there are shops devoted entirely to providing bird's nests. Needless to say, they are expensive because of the labor costs involved in gathering and preparing them.

Hong Kong restaurants use varying grades of bird's nest — there seems to be a semimystical process surrounding this judgment —and the bill varies, but it is always near the top of the price list! Elaborate banquets often begin with this soup, but the nests are used in stuffings as well.

VEGETABLE DUMPLING SOUP

Vegetarianism may be in vogue or having a resurgence in America, but it is an ancient tradition among many Hong Kong families of the Buddhist or Taoist faith. A popular Sunday outing for such families is to visit one of the many temples in the New Territories. There, both mundane and spiritual needs may be satisfied; on the temple grounds there is usually a restaurant serving vegetarian fare. The vegetables themselves come in a variety of preparations — fresh, preserved, and dried — and they are often served in remarkably effective mock forms of meat, poultry, and fish dishes. At the Ching Cheun Koon Taoist Temple, a vegetarian dim sum is sometimes served. One of my favorites is this soup with vegetable dumplings, so delicious, so full of textures and flavors, that it renders meat or any other such filling superfluous.

Experimenting at home, I discovered a blanching technique that allows you to prepare the dumplings ahead of time, finishing them at the last moment when the soup is ready.

STUFFING
½ cup dried Chinese black mushrooms
¼ cup tree fungus
½ cup Tianjin preserved cabbage,
    finely chopped
¼ cup bamboo shoots, finely chopped
¼ cup Sichuan preserved vegetable,
    finely chopped
2 teaspoons sugar
2 teaspoons cornstarch
2 teaspoons light soy sauce
1 teaspoon freshly ground white pepper
1 teaspoon sesame oil

25 round wonton wrappers
4 cups Rich Chicken Stock (page 221)

Soak the mushrooms and tree fungus in a bowl of warm water for about 20 minutes or until they are soft and pliable. Squeeze out the excess water and cut off and discard the woody stems from the mushrooms. Finely chop them.

Combine the rest of the stuffing ingredients in a medium-sized bowl. Mix well.

Place a spoonful of stuffing in the middle of a wrapper. Rub the edges with water and fold over to close. (They should be half-moon shaped.) Press to seal. Continue until you have used up all the stuffing. Blanch the dumplings for 2 minutes in a pot of boiling water. Remove them with a slotted spoon, drain, add the dumplings to the heated stock and serve at once. They may be blanched in advance, cooled, and covered with plastic wrap until they are ready to be used in the soup.

YIELD: SERVES 6 TO 8

DOUBLE-STEAMED MUSHROOM SOUP

1 cup dried Chinese black mushrooms
4 ounces fresh oyster mushrooms or fresh button
   mushrooms
1 chicken, about 3 pounds
4 cups Rich Chicken Stock (page 221)
3 peeled fresh ginger slices, about ¼ inch thick
4 scallions, white part only
Salt and freshly ground white pepper to taste

Soak the mushrooms in a bowl of warm water for about 20 minutes or until they are soft and pliable. Squeeze out the excess water and cut off and discard the woody stems. Wash and finely slice the fresh oyster mushrooms or fresh button mushrooms.

Cut the chicken into quarters and blanch the pieces for 10 minutes in a large pot of boiling water. Drain and set aside. Bring the chicken stock to a boil in a large pot. Add the chicken, ginger, scallion, salt, and pepper. Simmer gently for 10 minutes. Pour the mixture along with the mushrooms into a 2-quart, heat-proof casserole.

Cover the casserole and set it inside a large steamer. Steam vigorously on a rack in a tightly covered wok or pot for 1 hour. Replenish with hot water as necessary.

Remove the chicken, scallion, ginger, and any surface fat. Adjust the seasoning with salt and pepper to taste. Serve at once.

YIELD: SERVES 4 TO 6

Double-steamed soups are now typical in the new Hong Kong cuisine. The Cantonese traditionally preferred a clear soup that was also rich, an elusive combination. Hong Kong chefs hit upon the technique of double-steaming; it produces a clear but concentrated and therefore rich consommé. In this recipe we use mushrooms as the flavoring. The result is an earthy and substantial broth that makes an elegant opener for any meal.

TIANJIN CABBAGE WITH CHICKEN CONSOMMÉ

The Hong Kong specialty of clear soup or consommé is best exemplified by the chicken stock, which is always superb, full of intense chicken flavor and taste. To this only the best and most appropriate vegetable is added, in this case Tianjin cabbage, which has just the right flavor and texture to accompany the light, distinctive taste of the broth. This is an elegant soup for a special dinner; it is easy to make if you have already prepared your stock.

4 cups Rich Chicken Stock (page 221)
1 chicken, about 3 pounds
3 peeled fresh ginger slices, ¼ inch thick
4 scallions, white part only
½ teaspoon salt
¼ teaspoon freshly ground white pepper
½ pound lean pork

MARINADE
2 teaspoons dark soy sauce
1 teaspoon rice wine
½ teaspoon cornstarch

½ pound Napa cabbage
3 tablespoons finely chopped Tianjin preserved cabbage
1 tablespoon peanut oil
1 tablespoon sesame oil

Bring the stock to a simmer in a large pot. Cut the chicken into 10 pieces and blanch in a large pot of boiling water for 10 minutes. Add the blanched chicken pieces, ginger, scallions, salt, and pepper to the stock and simmer for 30 minutes, skimming any scum and fat that may rise to the surface. Continue to simmer for 1 hour longer; remove the chicken, ginger, and scallions and discard, and skim off as much fat as possible from the stock.

Meanwhile, place the pork in the freezer for about 20 minutes or until it is firm to the touch. Then cut it into slices and finely shred the meat. Add it to a large bowl with the marinade ingredients and refrigerate for 20 minutes.

Finely shred the Napa cabbage and set aside. In a pot of boiling water, blanch the fresh and preserved cabbage for 1 minute, drain well, and set aside.

Heat a wok or large skillet until it is hot and add the peanut oil. Stir-fry the pork for 30 seconds, remove with a slotted spoon, and set aside.

Season the stock to taste and ladle it into a soup tureen. Add the stir-fried meat and vegetables, swirl in sesame oil, and serve at once.

YIELD: SERVES 4 TO 6

CABBAGE AND CHICKEN SOUP

4 cups Rich Chicken Stock (page 221)
1 chicken, about 3 pounds
3 peeled fresh ginger slices, ¼ inch thick
4 scallions, white part only
½ pound bok choy
½ pound Napa cabbage
Salt and freshly ground white pepper to taste

Bring the stock to a simmer in a large pot. Cut the chicken into pieces, add them to the stock along with the ginger and scallions, and simmer for 30 minutes, skimming off any scum and fat that may rise to the surface. Continue to simmer for 1 hour longer; remove the chicken, ginger, and scallions and discard, and skim off as much fat as possible from the stock.

Cut the bok choy leaves from the stalks and cut the leaves into 2-inch pieces. Peel the stalks and cut them into thin diagonal slices. Wash well in several changes of water.

Finely shred the Napa cabbage and set aside. In a pot of salted boiling water, blanch the bok choy leaves and stalks and the cabbage for 30 seconds.

Season the stock with the salt and pepper to taste and ladle it into a soup tureen. Add the blanched vegetables and serve at once.

YIELD: SERVES 4 TO 6

Hong Kong chefs know how to insure that vegetables in soup retain their own flavors and textures, congenially accompanying the rich clear stock itself. This recipe demonstrates that knowledge. This dish is often served throughout a banquet as a means of refreshing the palate. I find it excellent as an aromatic opening course or by itself, as an ideal light soup and Chinese vegetable lunch.

HEARTY EGG-FLOWER AND BEEF SOUP

This is a common hearty home-style soup that is enjoyed throughout Hong Kong. It is easy to put together and has a satisfying taste. Beef is inexpensive in Hong Kong, as it is not a favored meat. Ground beef is used here as a filler to give substance to the soup, but even then, it is used in a small quantity. Once made, this soup can easily be reheated. It is perfect for a family meal.

4 cups Rich Chicken Stock (page 221)
1 tablespoon peanut oil
½ cup celery, chopped
½ pound ground beef
1 tablespoon light soy sauce
1 teaspoon salt
1 teaspoon sugar
3 teaspoons sesame oil
2 egg whites
Salt and freshly ground white pepper to taste

Bring the stock to a simmer in a medium-sized pot. While the stock is simmering, heat a wok, add the peanut oil, and stir-fry the celery and ground beef for 1 minute. Then add the soy sauce, salt, sugar, and 1 teaspoon of the sesame oil. Continue to stir-fry for 2 minutes or until the beef is cooked. Remove the mixture with a slotted spoon and add to the stock. Simmer the soup for 5 minutes.

In a small bowl, beat together the egg whites and the remaining sesame oil; pour into the soup in a slow steady stream, mixing gently all the while with a chopstick or a fork. Salt and pepper to taste and serve at once.

YIELD: SERVES 4 TO 6

FISH
AND
SHELLFISH

~~~~~~

SMOKY GARLIC FISH STEW

FISH CAKE PEASANT-STYLE

FISH CAKES WITH VEGETABLES

FRIED OYSTERS FROM LAU FAU SHAN

FISH ROLLS WITH STIR-FRIED VEGETABLES

TASTY STIR-FRIED SHRIMP

ROCKFISH IN WINE SAUCE

SHRIMP–BEAN CURD DUMPLINGS

SHRIMP-SCALLOP ROLLS

DOUBLE-COOKED FISH WITH GINGER SAUCE

FISH FRIED IN PARCHMENT PAPER

FRIED FISH WITH CHILI AND GARLIC

SALT AND PEPPER SPICY SHRIMP

CANTONESE SHRIMP WITH ASPARAGUS

CURRIED CRAB WITH PEPPERS AND SHALLOTS

STEAMED FISH WITH HAM AND VEGETABLES

VELVET SHRIMP WITH MANGO

SCALLOPS STUFFED WITH SHRIMP

STIR-FRIED SCALLOPS WITH FRESH CHILIES

STIR-FRIED SQUID IN TWO SAUCES

CHIU CHOW–STYLE STEAMED CRAB

MUSSELS IN BLACK BEAN SAUCE

SICHUAN GARDEN SHRIMP WITH HOT CHILI AND GARLIC

PAN-FRIED FISH WITH LEMON SAUCE

DICED LOBSTER IN LETTUCE CUPS

FRESH CORIANDER SHRIMP WRAPPED IN RICE PAPER

STEAMED LOBSTER WITH GARLIC AND SCALLIONS

SHANGHAI-STYLE SHRIMP WITH LEEKS

CRAB CASSEROLE IN A CLAY POT

STIR-FRIED SHRIMP WITH CHICKEN LIVER

SHRIMP WITH CASHEW NUTS

LAI CHING HEEN'S PEAR WITH SCALLOPS

SCALLOPS AND SHRIMP IN A CRISP TARO BASKET

A child of the sea, Hong Kong quite naturally draws much of her sustenance from the ocean. Fish and shellfish constitute an enormously important and popular aspect of the Hong Kong cuisine. This is a cultural matter as well: the Cantonese style, from which Hong Kong cuisine largely flows, also emphasizes seafood. In the Chinese tradition, hundreds of species of fish and shellfish have made their way into standard recipes, so it is no surprise that Hong Kong offers a rich and varied assortment of seafood dishes. The recipes here represent a sampling of the best of those dishes, with special regard for the Western preferences of Hong Kong's cosmopolitan clientele.

SMOKY GARLIC FISH STEW

I love to shop for my cooking classes in the food markets of Hong Kong. They are among the most colorful and varied I have seen anywhere in the world. A favorite seasoning of mine, which I have seen nowhere but in Hong Kong, is smoked garlic. I assume that it is a method or technique for preserving garlic. It gives food a wonderful, smoky flavor plus all the other tasty virtues that garlic imparts to any dish. Garlic, smoked or not, is used a great deal in the cooking of Hong Kong. It usually comes from the south of China, where the hot, humid climate makes the garlic even more pungent. As a flavoring agent it may therefore be used very economically — a little can make any dish very tasty. Garlic cooked long and slowly loses some of its pungent flavor and develops a sweet, delicate tang.

This stewed fish dish is made with whole fresh garlic cloves and shallots. (By all means, if you can buy smoked garlic, use it instead of the fresh.) Much of the preparation can be done in advance. The quick blast in the clay pot captures and seals in all the savoriness of this dish.

1 pound fillets of red snapper, rockfish, sea bass, or any firm white-fleshed fish

MARINADE
2 teaspoons light soy sauce
2 teaspoons rice wine
1 tablespoon ginger juice
1½ tablespoons cornstarch

½ cup peanut oil, for pan-frying
8 garlic cloves, peeled
½ pound whole shallots, peeled
2 tablespoons fermented black beans
2 tablespoons rice wine
4 garlic shoots or whole scallions, cut into pieces
2 tablespoons dark soy sauce
¼ cup water
2 teaspoons sugar

Cut the fish into large pieces. In a medium-sized bowl, combine the fish and marinade ingredients and let stand for 30 minutes.

Heat a wok or large skillet until it is hot and add the oil. Lightly fry the fish pieces for 2 to 3 minutes on each side until they are crisp and brown. Remove with a slotted spoon and drain on paper towels.

Drain most of the oil from the wok, leaving about 1 to 2 tablespoons. Reheat the wok and add the garlic, shallots, black beans, rice wine, and garlic shoots. Stir-fry for 2 minutes. Empty the contents of the wok into a clay pot or casserole. Add the fish pieces together with the soy sauce, water, and sugar. Cover and cook over high heat for 2 minutes. Serve immediately.

YIELD: SERVES 4 TO 6

FISH CAKE PEASANT-STYLE

FISH MIXTURE

1 pound fillets of red snapper, rockfish, sea bass, or any
   firm white-fleshed fish
1 egg white
1 tablespoon cornstarch
2 tablespoons coarsely chopped coriander
3 tablespoons finely chopped whole scallions
2 teaspoons finely chopped peeled fresh ginger
1½ teaspoons salt
3 tablespoons water

¼ cup peanut oil, for deep-frying

SAUCE

2 tablespoons fresh red chili pepper, finely shredded
1 tablespoon finely chopped garlic
2 teaspoons finely chopped peeled fresh ginger
1 tablespoon light soy sauce
4 tablespoons Rich Chicken Stock (page 221)
1 teaspoon cornstarch mixed with 1 teaspoon water

Remove any skin from the fish fillets and then cut them into small pieces. Combine all the ingredients of the fish mixture in a food processor and blend the mixture until it is a fine paste.

Heat a wok or large skillet; when it is hot, add the oil. Form the paste into a large flat cake about 1 inch thick and pan-fry it for 5 minutes or until it is golden brown and firm. Remove it with a slotted spoon or large metal spatula, and drain on paper towels. When the cake is cool, slice it into bite-size pieces.

Drain the wok, leaving 1 tablespoon of oil. Reheat the wok, add the chili, garlic, and ginger and stir-fry for 1 minute. Then add the soy sauce and chicken stock and continue to stir-fry for another 2 minutes. Add the cornstarch mixture and cook for another minute. Return the fish pieces to the sauce, mix gently, and heat through. Serve at once.

YIELD: SERVES 4 TO 6

This recipe illustrates Hong Kong's receptivity to innovation. This is a traditional peasant dish, identified with the poorer people of the countryside. However, because it is both nutritious and easy to prepare, as well as cheap, it is an ideal "convenience" food for the busy urban workers of Hong Kong, not all of whom are poor, by any means. Rather, food merchants and restaurateurs understand their market and are quick to supply any perceived demand. The mounds of puréed, fresh, raw fish are available in markets throughout the bustling city, ready to be shaped as desired, seasoned, and then steamed, poached, or pan-fried. This is south China peasant fare turned cosmopolitan.

In the Western kitchen, the dish is easily made from scratch with the aid of a food processor. It is a tasty alternative way to enjoy fresh fish.

FISH CAKES WITH VEGETABLES

Fresh fish from Hong Kong's markets are used in many ways. A popular method, as in this recipe, is to mince them into a paste. You may see piles of such paste at all fish markets. Food stalls and restaurants buy the paste to make fish balls for soups or for a hearty breakfast dish of rice porridge and fish balls. Or, the fish paste may be shaped, fried, sliced, and stir-fried with vegetables. This is a delicious and economical way to use fish which is often so expensive. Although this process involves a number of steps in the preparation, it is well worth the work. Once the fish cakes are fried and sliced (and this can be done way ahead of time), the rest is quite easy to put together.

The vegetables provide seasonal freshness, and the textures of the silk squash and cucumbers are especially appealing when paired with the fish cakes.

FISH MIXTURE
1 pound fillets of red snapper, rockfish, sea bass, or any whole, firm white-fleshed fish
1 egg white
2 teaspoons cornstarch
2 tablespoons finely chopped whole scallions
2 teaspoons ginger juice
1 teaspoon salt
2 tablespoons cold water

1 cup peanut oil, for deep-frying

VEGETABLE MIXTURE
8 cloud ears
1 tablespoon finely chopped garlic
5 peeled fresh ginger slices, ¼ inch thick
1 small onion, cut into wedges
½ pound silk squash or zucchini, roll-cut (page 267)
1 cucumber, roll-cut
3 tablespoons Rich Chicken Stock (page 221) or water

SAUCE
3 tablespoons oyster sauce
2 teaspoons light soy sauce
1 teaspoon sugar
1 tablespoon rice wine
¼ cup Rich Chicken Stock
1 teaspoon cornstarch with 1 teaspoon water

Remove any skin from the fish fillets and then cut them into small pieces. Combine all the ingredients of the fish mixture in a food processor and blend the mixture until it is a fine paste.

Heat a wok or large skillet until it is hot; add the peanut oil. Form the paste into ½-inch thick, 5-inch patties and deep-fry for 5 minutes or until they are golden brown. Remove them with a slotted spoon and drain on paper towels. When the cakes are cool, slice them into bite-size pieces.

In a medium-sized bowl, soak the cloud ears in warm water until they are soft and pliable, about 20 minutes. Rinse well in cold water, drain, and set aside until ready to use.

Drain the wok, leaving 1½ tablespoons of oil. Reheat the wok, add the garlic, ginger, and the onions and stir-fry for 1 minute. Then add the mushrooms and the rest of the vegetable mixture and continue to stir-fry for another 2 minutes. Pour in the sauce ingredients and continue to cook for another 2 minutes or until the vegetables are cooked. Return the fish pieces to the wok and mix gently to heat through. Serve at once.

YIELD: SERVES 4 TO 6

FRIED OYSTERS FROM LAU FAU SHAN

Lau Fau Shan is a remarkable fishing village in the New Territories outside of Hong Kong. It is located on the edge of Deep Bay, off the South China Sea, and the coast of China can be seen easily from its shores. One narrow street in the village, called Ching Alley, leads to a fish market near the pier where the fishing boats dock. This market is famous for oysters — specifically the Crassostrea gigas *type, which are elongated in shape and very large. These oysters are not eaten raw but cooked first, or sun-dried and used for oyster sauce. The shells are embedded in the clay walls that line the edge of the village and are otherwise scattered all around.*

The village features one of my favorite seafood restaurants. A small unpretentious place, like most of the crab and oyster restaurants on the west and east coasts of America, this restaurant offers the most delectable fried oysters. I love the crisp, delicate, light batter that surrounds them. I have learned that the secret to this batter is that it is made with yeast. It is allowed to ferment and rise, thus giving the oysters their crisp coating.

BATTER
½ cup flour
1½ tablespoons cornstarch
1 teaspoon dry yeast
2 teaspoons sesame oil
¾ cup water

1 pound large oysters, shucked
2 tablespoons salt
1 tablespoon cornstarch
Salt and pepper to taste
2 cups peanut oil, for deep-frying

In a medium-sized bowl, whisk the batter ingredients until smooth. Cover and let sit for 1 hour in a warm place.

In a large bowl, combine the oysters, salt, and cornstarch. Mix well, then rinse in cold water, and blot the oysters dry with paper towels. Season the oysters with salt and pepper.

Heat a wok or deep skillet until it is hot and add the oil. Dip the oysters into batter, making sure they are thoroughly coated, then deep-fry a few at a time for about 2 minutes or until they are golden brown. Drain them on paper towels and serve immediately.

YIELD: SERVES 4 TO 6

NOTE: You can serve them with Salt-and-Pepper Dip (page 227), or use any of the dipping sauces you like, or eat them just out of the hot oil, which is the way I prefer.

FISH ROLLS WITH STIR-FRIED VEGETABLES

FISH ROLLS
1 pound fillets of red snapper, rockfish, sea bass, or any
   firm white-fleshed fish
5 whole scallions, cut into 2-inch pieces
Cornstarch, for dusting

½ cup peanut oil, for pan-frying

VEGETABLE MIXTURE
2 teaspoons finely chopped peeled fresh ginger
1 teaspoon finely chopped garlic
2 tablespoons finely chopped whole scallions
1 pound large asparagus, roll-cut (page 267)
½ pound baby carrots, peeled and left whole

SAUCE
2 teaspoons light soy sauce
2 tablespoons oyster sauce
1 tablespoon rice wine
2 teaspoons sesame oil
1 teaspoon sugar
2 tablespoons Rich Chicken Stock (page 221) or water

Cut each fillet, crosswise into large pieces. Place a scallion on top of each fillet, roll up, and skewer tightly with a toothpick. Dust each roll lightly with cornstarch.

Heat a wok or large skillet until it is hot and add the peanut oil. Lightly pan-fry the fish rolls for about 3 to 4 minutes or until they are lightly browned all over. Remove and drain on paper towels.

Pour off most of the oil, leaving 2 tablespoons. Reheat the wok and add the ginger, garlic, and scallions and stir-fry for 30 seconds. Add the remaining vegetables and continue to stir-fry for 1 more minute. Then pour in the sauce ingredients, reduce the heat, and continue to cook for another 2 minutes or until the vegetables are tender. Return the fish rolls, heat through, and serve immediately.

YIELD: SERVES 4 TO 6

The term "fresh fish" is a redundancy in Hong Kong: if it isn't fresh it isn't fish. The most popular types of fish are from the grouper family. There are many different varieties, usually sold live at markets for very steep prices. The grouper family fish have meaty flesh and high-quality flavor that make them ideal for steaming, pan-frying, or braising.

The ingenious chefs of Hong Kong have even found a way to stuff these fish and mix them with vegetables. I have added my own touches of young carrots and the ever popular asparagus. And though the grouper from the South China Sea are impossible to get in this country, I have found that any fresh, firm white fish is an acceptable substitute.

TASTY STIR-FRIED SHRIMP

On any visit to Hong Kong, among the great dining treats are the shrimp dishes that are available there. Freshness is guaranteed, with shrimp still swimming about in tanks as you order. And anything that fresh deserves to be cooked in the most simple way possible, with a minimum amount of seasoning — just enough to enhance the virtues of the shrimp. Rarely have I found shrimp as enjoyable anywhere as I consistently do in Hong Kong.

This is, to my mind, one of the best, and certainly one of the quickest, ways to prepare them. A necessary preliminary step is to salt-wash them to firm the shrimp, which gives them a wonderful crunchy texture. Then it is necessary to coat them with a velvetlike egg-white and cornstarch mixture; this protects the delicate shrimp meat from the oil and prevents overcooking. Once those steps are done, this dish takes but minutes to cook. Always buy the freshest shrimp possible.

2 tablespoons salt
1 pound medium shrimp, peeled and deveined

COATING
1 egg white
2 teaspoons cornstarch
½ teaspoon salt

½ cup peanut oil, for velveting (page 271)
2 teaspoons finely chopped peeled fresh ginger
2 teaspoons finely chopped whole scallions
1 teaspoon rice wine
½ teaspoon white rice vinegar
½ teaspoon salt

To clean the shrimp, please follow the directions on page 34.

Combine the shrimp with the coating ingredients in a medium-sized bowl. Mix well and refrigerate for about 20 minutes.

Heat a wok or large skillet until it is hot; add the oil. When the oil is just warm, quickly add the shrimp, stir to separate, and turn off the heat. Allow the shrimp to sit in the warm oil for about 2 minutes. Drain in a colander set inside a stainless steel bowl, reserving the oil.

Reheat the wok, return 1 tablespoon of the drained oil and when it is hot, add the ginger and scallions and stir-fry for 30 seconds. Then add the rice wine, vinegar, salt, and the drained shrimp. Stir-fry for 1 minute, turn out onto a serving platter and serve immediately.

YIELD: SERVES 4 TO 6

ROCKFISH IN WINE SAUCE

½ cup dried Chinese black mushrooms
1 pound fillets of rockfish, red snapper, sea bass, or any
    firm white-fleshed fish

COATING
1 egg white
2 teaspoons cornstarch
½ teaspoon salt

½ cup peanut oil, for velveting (page 271)

SAUCE
1 teaspoon Chinese rose wine or vodka
1 tablespoon rice wine
2 teaspoons salt
1 tablespoon sugar
⅓ cup Rich Chicken Stock (page 221)
1 teaspoon cornstarch mixed with 1 teaspoon water

Soak the mushrooms in a bowl of warm water for about 20 minutes or until they are soft and pliable. Squeeze out the excess water and cut off and discard the woody stems. Finely chop the mushroom caps and set aside.

Cut the fish into 2-inch pieces. Combine the fish with the coating ingredients in a medium-sized bowl. Mix well and refrigerate for about 20 minutes.

Heat a wok or large skillet until it is hot; add the oil. When the oil is just warm, quickly add the fish, stir to separate, and turn off the heat. Allow the fish to sit in the warm oil for about 2 minutes. Drain in a colander set inside a stainless steel bowl.

Reheat the wok, add the sauce ingredients, and bring to a simmer; add the mushrooms and cook for about 2 minutes. Add the fish pieces and heat through. Serve at once.

YIELD: SERVES 4 TO 6

This is an elegant fish dish found on the menus of many of the best dining places in Hong Kong. Even though it calls for a rich wine sauce, it is surprisingly easy to make. The fish is coated with an egg-white mixture and then gently cooked (as always with fish) in oil; it is drained thoroughly, then mixed with the sauce. The mushrooms add a rich smoky flavor, a nice accompaniment to the subtle taste of the fish fillets. Because it is so delicious and so easy to make, this is an excellent recipe for a special dinner party.

Note, too, that just as Western wines are being introduced into Chinese menus, here you may experiment with other than Chinese liqueurs and rice wine. Compatibility and taste are all that matter.

SHRIMP–BEAN CURD DUMPLINGS

These fragile, delicate, delicious dumplings are a tribute to the creativity of Hong Kong chefs. They are the most beguiling dumplings I have ever enjoyed, reminiscent of French fish quenelles, and just as ethereal. They will add a gracious and impressive note to any dinner.

2 tablespoons salt
12 ounces large shrimp, enough to yield ½ pound after shelling, peeled and deveined

DUMPLINGS
½ pound bean curd
5 eggs
1 tablespoon finely chopped garlic
2 tablespoons finely chopped peeled fresh ginger
2 teaspoons salt
1 teaspoon freshly ground white pepper

2 cups peanut oil, for deep-frying

SAUCE
1 tablespoon finely chopped garlic
1 tablespoon finely chopped fresh ginger
1 tablespoon oyster sauce
2 tablespoons rice wine
1 tablespoon light soy sauce
2 teaspoons dark soy sauce
½ cup Rich Chicken Stock (page 221)
1 teaspoon cornstarch mixed with 1 teaspoon cold water

To clean the shrimp, please follow the directions on page 34.

Coarsely chop the shrimp in a food processor, about 5 seconds. Then combine the rest of the dumpling mixture and mix for 15 seconds. The dumpling mixture will be rather fluid.

Heat a wok or large deep skillet until it is hot and add the oil. When the oil is hot, with a large soup spoon, scoop a heaping portion of the dumpling mixture in and deep-fry until it is golden; you can make about five to six at a time. Drain well on paper towels. Continue until all the mixture is used up.

Drain off all but 1 tablespoon of oil. Reheat the wok; when it is hot, add the garlic and ginger and stir-fry for 30 seconds. Then add the rest of the sauce ingredients except the cornstarch mixture. Slowly stir in the cornstarch mixture and bring to a boil. Return the dumplings to the wok and cook for 10 seconds to reheat them. Serve at once.

YIELD: MAKES ABOUT 25 DUMPLINGS

SHRIMP-SCALLOP ROLLS

EGG CREPES
2 eggs, beaten
¼ teaspoon salt
2 teaspoons sesame oil

2 tablespoons peanut oil

BATTER
½ cup all-purpose unbleached white flour
1 tablespoon yeast
2 tablespoons cornstarch
½ cup warm water
2 teaspoons peanut oil

SHRIMP-SCALLOP MIXTURE
½ pound shrimp, peeled and deveined
½ pound scallops
1 teaspoon salt
2 teaspoons cornstarch

2 asparagus stalks, blanched
2 cups peanut oil, for deep-frying

In a small bowl, mix the crepe ingredients together. Heat a large skillet, preferably nonstick, until it is moderately hot and add 1 tablespoon of the peanut oil. Add half of the crepe mixture, tilting the pan to allow the batter to spread evenly over the surface, and cook for 1 minute or until the top has set. Turn the crepe over and cook for 10 seconds. Remove the finished crepe from the pan and make a second crepe. Set aside to cool.

Mix the batter ingredients together in a medium-sized bowl and let sit for 20 minutes.

In a food processor, combine the shrimp-scallop mixture until it is a fine paste. Spread this mixture on each of the crepes, add an asparagus stalk to each, and roll crepes up with the ends open. Dip the rolled-up crepes into the batter.

Heat a wok or large deep skillet until it is hot and add the oil for frying. When it is hot, deep-fry the shrimp-scallop rolls until they are golden brown. Remove them with a slotted spoon and drain on paper towels. When the shrimp-scallop rolls are cool enough to handle, slice them into bite-size pieces and serve with Salt-and-Pepper Dip (page 227).

YIELD: SERVES 4

In America, the term "hotel dining" does not often evoke happy thoughts of good food. In Hong Kong, however, many hotel restaurants are world-class. This is so not only because the hotels have the resources to prepare great menus, but also because they are necessarily in touch with the needs and wishes of a discerning international clientele. Knowing that the competition is tough, the hotels rely upon some of the finest chefs in Hong Kong who, although rooted in the Cantonese tradition, allow their imaginations free play. Such chefs create elegant dishes that at once reflect both the traditional and the innovative.

Here we have a seasoned shrimp-scallop blend, stuffed with asparagus, and rolled in a delicate egg crepe — Western, but also very Hong Kong.

Although this is a rather complicated recipe, typical of restaurant kitchens, much of the work can be done well in advance — only the frying must be done at the last minute. This is a beautiful presentation, however, and the perfect opener or appetizer for that special dinner party.

DOUBLE-COOKED FISH WITH GINGER SAUCE

This highly unusual process makes for an excellent dish. The fish is deep-fried first in very hot oil, then drained, steamed, and finished with a sauce. The deep-frying seals the flesh of the fish, capturing the moist juices, while the gentle steaming finishes the cooking. When properly fried, it is not oily or greasy at all.

Just before the end of cooking, hot oil is poured over the seasonings on the fish to release their flavors. Finally the sauce is added just before serving.

1½ to 2 pounds whole red snapper, rockfish, sea bass or any firm white-fleshed fish
1½ cups peanut oil, for deep-frying
2 tablespoons finely chopped peeled fresh ginger
4 tablespoons finely chopped whole scallions
½ teaspoon salt

SAUCE
2 tablespoons light soy sauce
1 teaspoon sugar
4 tablespoons Rich Chicken Stock (page 221)
1 teaspoon sesame oil

3 tablespoons peanut oil

GARNISH
2 tablespoons finely chopped fresh coriander

Rinse the fish under cold running water and blot it dry with paper towels. Then place the fish on a platter. Heat a wok or deep skillet until it is hot and add 1½ cups of oil. When the oil is slightly smoking, carefully slide the fish in and deep-fry for 2 minutes on each side. Remove with a spatula and drain on paper towels.

Put the fish on a heat-proof platter and sprinkle over the ginger, scallions, and salt. Set the platter on a rack in a tightly covered wok or pot and steam over slowly simmering water for 8 to 10 minutes, or until the flesh flakes easily.

While the fish is steaming, combine the sauce ingredients in a small pot and bring to a simmer. Remove and set aside.

About 1 minute before the fish is done, heat 3 tablespoons of oil in a small pot until it is smoking. Pour this oil over the steamed fish, then pour on the sauce, garnish, and serve immediately.

YIELD: SERVES 4 TO 6

FISH FRIED IN PARCHMENT PAPER

1 pound fillets of red snapper, rockfish, sea bass, or any
    firm white-fleshed fish

MARINADE
1½ tablespoons oyster sauce
2 tablespoons ginger juice
1 tablespoon finely chopped whole scallions
1 teaspoon rice wine
½ teaspoon sesame oil
1 teaspoon finely chopped fresh coriander

Parchment paper cut into 6-by-6-inch squares, about 25
2 cups peanut oil, for deep-frying
Oyster sauce, for dipping

Cut the fillets into about 25 small pieces. Combine them with the marinade ingredients in a medium-sized bowl, cover and refrigerate for 1 hour.

When you are ready to make the parchment packages, take a square of parchment and place it so that it is diamond-shaped with one point toward you. Make a small fold in the corner, about ⅛ inch. Place a piece of fish in the center of the parchment sheet and fold partially over to cover the fish piece. Now fold in one side of the parchment, then the other. Turn the entire package in half, leaving a small flap. Tuck the flap in to secure the package. It should look like a miniature envelope. Repeat the procedure until you have used up all the fish and parchment sheets.

Heat a wok or large skillet until it is hot and add the oil and deep-fry the packages, a few at a time for about 2 minutes. Drain them on paper towels and serve. Each guest unwraps his or her packages. There should be about 4 or 5 per person.

Oyster sauce can be served on the side for dipping.

YIELD: MAKES 25 PACKAGES

Oyster sauce and ginger juice are staples in Hong Kong cooking, especially with fish or seafood, which they complement and enhance well. Oyster sauce adds a rich and almost meaty flavor to food while ginger juice works as an acidic counterpoint, much like the use of lemon in Western fish cookery, but more subtle. Here these flavorings unite in a marinade and imbue fish fillets with even more flavor; wrapped in parchment paper and deep-fried, the fillets are protected from the oil. The fish steams gently inside the parchment. This is a quick way of cooking fish, taking but one or two minutes, which makes it ideal for parties. The individual portions also stay hot for quite a while. There is great ceremony and fun as each diner unwraps the package and smells the delightful aromas — a hint of the delicious taste to come.

FRIED FISH WITH CHILI AND GARLIC

I characterize this as a simple but sophisticated dish. That is, it is a Hong Kong favorite but aside from the seasonings, which may be varied, of course, it is a universally enjoyed meal, whether at a restaurant or at home. The technique here is also widely employed: pan-frying, which imparts a crisp crust to the fish, a texture nicely setting off that of the vegetables and rice that usually accompany the dish.

1 pound fillets of red snapper, rockfish, sea bass, or any
    firm white-fleshed fish
½ cup peanut oil, for pan-frying

1 tablespoon finely chopped garlic
1 tablespoon finely chopped peeled fresh ginger
1 tablespoon fresh red chili pepper, finely shredded

SAUCE
2 teaspoons light soy sauce
2 teaspoons dark soy sauce
1 teaspoon sugar
1 teaspoon black vinegar
2 teaspoons rice wine
½ teaspoon cornstarch mixed with ½ teaspoon water

GARNISH
2 tablespoons whole scallions, finely chopped

Cut the fish into bite-size pieces. Blot completely dry with paper towels. Heat a wok or large skillet until it is hot and add the oil. When the oil is hot, fry the fish pieces for 1 minute on each side. Remove and drain well. Remove all but 1½ tablespoons of oil in the wok.

Reheat the wok, add the garlic, ginger, and chili and stir-fry for 1 minute. Add all the sauce ingredients and bring to a boil, return the fish to the sauce, and continue to cook for another minute or until the fish is cooked through. Garnish with the scallions and serve at once.

YIELD: SERVES 4 TO 6

SALT AND PEPPER SPICY SHRIMP

2 tablespoons salt
1 pound large shrimp, unpeeled and deveined
2 teaspoons coarse or kosher salt
1 teaspoon roasted Sichuan peppercorns, ground
1 teaspoon sugar
2 tablespoons finely chopped garlic
2 teaspoons finely chopped peeled fresh ginger
2 tablespoons finely chopped whole scallions
2 fresh red chili peppers, coarsely chopped

2 cups peanut oil, for deep-frying

To clean the shrimp, please follow the directions on page 34. Remove the feathery legs and blot the shrimp dry with paper towels.

In a small bowl, combine the coarse salt, peppercorns, and sugar and set aside. In another small bowl, combine the garlic, ginger, scallions, and the chopped chilies. Heat a wok or deep skillet until it is hot and add the oil. When the oil is very hot and smoking, add the shrimp and deep-fry for about 1 minute or until they are pink. Remove them immediately with a slotted spoon and drain well. Pour off all but 1½ tablespoons of the oil and reheat the wok. Add the salt-peppercorns-sugar mixture and stir-fry for 10 seconds. Add the garlic-ginger-scallion-chilies mixture and stir-fry for 10 seconds. Return the shrimp to the wok and stir-fry over high heat for about 2 minutes until the spices have thoroughly coated the outer shell of the shrimp.

Transfer the shrimp to a serving platter and serve at once.

YIELD: SERVES 4 TO 6

The range of fresh, live shrimp that is available in Hong Kong is quite astonishing. Many restaurants serve the larger size shrimp in this, one of the tastiest shrimp dishes I have ever sampled. The shells are left on, as they keep the juices and flavors of the shrimp inside. When the shrimp are deep-fried whole, the shells become transparent, crisp, and edible — just like soft-shell crab. The oil, however, must be very hot. Enhanced with aromatic seasonings and chilies, this is a feast for lovers of shrimp. Once the oil is heated, the actual cooking moves quite quickly. As with many of the best dishes in this type of cooking, it is best done and eaten immediately — the only preliminary step required is the chopping. You will find these shrimp irresistible.

CANTONESE SHRIMP WITH ASPARAGUS

The origins of asparagus are unknown, but I do know that it is not a Chinese vegetable. Only recently introduced, it has nevertheless become a Hong Kong favorite. At first, asparagus was served in European restaurants in the great hotels of Hong Kong. From there it spread to other restaurants and then to the general population. Most of the asparagus in Hong Kong is from Australia, Europe, or California. Although it is expensive, it is still quite popular. The Chinese love its grassy green color and its distinctive flavor. The larger sizes are more desired, as the Chinese feel that they are meatier and stir-fry better. In Hong Kong, one often finds it paired with fresh shrimp, as in this recipe. Here, the shrimp are salted, then velveted, before being stir-fried.

2 tablespoons salt
1 pound medium shrimp, peeled and deveined

COATING
1 egg white
2 teaspoons cornstarch
2 teaspoons sesame oil
1 teaspoon salt

½ cup peanut oil, for velveting (page 271)
3 peeled fresh ginger slices, ¼ inch thick
½ pound asparagus, roll-cut (page 267)
½ teaspoon salt

SAUCE
3 tablespoons rice wine
1 teaspoon finely chopped garlic
3 tablespoons finely chopped whole scallions
½ cup Rich Chicken Stock (page 221)
1 teaspoon sugar
1 teaspoon cornstarch mixed with 1 teaspoon water
2 teaspoons sesame oil

To clean the shrimp, please follow directions on page 34.

Combine the shrimp with the coating ingredients. Mix well and refrigerate for about 20 minutes.

Heat a wok or large skillet until it is hot and add the oil. When the oil is just warm, quickly add the shrimp, stir to separate, and turn off the heat. Allow the shrimp to sit in the warm oil for about 2 minutes. Drain in a colander set inside a stainless steel bowl, reserving some of the oil.

Return 1½ tablespoons of the drained oil to the wok and reheat. As soon as it is hot, add the ginger slices to flavor the oil. Remove the ginger after 30 seconds and discard. Add the asparagus and salt and stir-fry for 1 minute. Then add the rice wine, garlic, and scallions and continue to stir-fry for another minute. Add the stock and sugar and continue to cook for 1 more minute. Thicken the sauce with the cornstarch mixture, return the shrimp to the wok, and give the mixture several good stirs. Add the sesame oil, stir one last time, and serve.

YIELD: SERVES 4

CURRIED CRAB WITH PEPPERS AND SHALLOTS

One 1½-pound fresh whole crab, preferably live
2 tablespoons peanut oil
2 teaspoons finely chopped peeled fresh ginger
2 green peppers, seeded, deveined, and cut into
    large chunks
1 cup whole shallots, peeled

CURRY SAUCE
⅓ cup Rich Chicken Stock (page 221)
2 tablespoons Madras curry paste or powder
½ teaspoon salt
2 teaspoons light soy sauce
1 teaspoon sugar

If you are using a live crab, rinse and scrub the crab or crabs under cold running water. Place the crab or crabs top shell down on a heat-proof platter on top of a rack in a tightly covered wok or pot. Gently steam for 10 minutes or until the shell has turned bright red. Cut the body of the crab into quarters and lightly crack the claws.

Heat a wok or large skillet until it is hot and add 1 tablespoon of oil. Stir-fry the crab for 2 minutes and remove.

Wipe the wok clean, add the other tablespoon of oil and reheat. Stir-fry the ginger, peppers, and shallots for 2 minutes. Add the curry sauce ingredients and bring to a boil.

Pour the entire contents of the wok into a clay pot or casserole and add the crab. Cover and cook over high heat for 5 minutes. Serve immediately.

YIELD: SERVES 4

Crabmeat is a highly prized seafood in Hong Kong (as everywhere) and crabs are always bought live in the markets to insure that the delicate but fragile flavor is intact. The green crab is popular in Hong Kong, and I have found that the California Dungeness crab is very similar in its meatiness and flavor. When green crabs are sold in Hong Kong markets, they are sorted by sex: the females with roe (or eggs) are the more expensive, the roe being much in demand for use in special dishes.

Here we have a typical method for preparing crabs in Hong Kong: with a touch of curry and quickly cooked in the high heat of the clay pot. The result is a dish redolent of crab and curry, exotic and aromatic.

STEAMED FISH WITH HAM AND VEGETABLES

In Hong Kong, diners expect fresh fish to be served. In restaurants, therefore, it is common to see large tanks filled with live fish and shellfish from which diners make their own selection. It may be some time before this custom is widely adopted in America. However, one Hong Kong practice should be followed: fresh fish should be steamed. This method preserves all of the best qualities of the food. Most commonly, the fish is steamed with soy sauce and then treated with scallions and hot oil. But Hong Kong chefs are increasingly using other, nontraditional seasonings: after all, with fresh fish, the secret is to flavor it without detracting from its own splendid but delicate taste. For that, a variety of seasonings is appropriate.

This recipe follows the more elaborate Hong Kong style, but one may feel free to experiment. I use Smithfield ham as a substitute for the traditional Chinese ham, along with mushrooms and fresh young ginger slices. It may then be topped with a light sauce and a garnish of Chinese broccoli.

8 dried Chinese black mushrooms
1½ to 2 pounds whole fish, red snapper, rockfish, sea
   bass, or any firm white-fleshed fish
1 tablespoon rice wine
2 teaspoons sesame oil
8 thin slices peeled fresh ginger
8 thin slices Smithfield ham

SAUCE
⅓ cup Rich Chicken Stock (page 221)
3 tablespoons rice wine
1 teaspoon salt
½ teaspoon freshly ground white pepper
½ teaspoon sesame oil
1 teaspoon cornstarch mixed with 1 teaspoon water

GARNISH
6 stalks Chinese broccoli

Soak the mushrooms in a bowl of warm water for about 20 minutes or until they are soft and pliable. Squeeze out the excess water and cut off and discard the woody stems.

Make four incisions on each side of the fish and rub the rice wine and sesame oil all over the fish. Insert a mushroom and a slice of ginger and ham into each incision.

Place the fish on a heat-proof platter and steam over slowly simmering water on a rack in a tightly covered wok or pot for 8 to 10 minutes, or until the flesh flakes easily.

Bring all the sauce ingredients except the cornstarch mixture to a boil in a small pan. Stir in the cornstarch mixture. Set the sauce aside and keep warm. Blanch the broccoli in a small pot of salted boiling water.

Remove the fish from the steamer and pour any liquid that has collected on the platter into the sauce. Place the fish on a serving platter and pour over the sauce. Arrange the broccoli around the sides of the fish and serve at once.
YIELD: SERVES 4 TO 6

NOTE: Again, as in Hong Kong itself, substitute after due consideration of your own taste and that of your guests; that is, use local broccoli and wines and seasonings whenever you decide they work. But fresh fish is the essence of the dish.

VELVET SHRIMP WITH MANGO

2 tablespoons salt
1½ pounds medium shrimp, peeled and deveined

COATING
2 egg whites
2 teaspoons cornstarch
½ teaspoon salt
1 teaspoon sesame oil
Freshly ground pepper to taste

1 cup peanut oil, for velveting (page 271)
1 tablespoon finely chopped peeled fresh ginger
2 teaspoons finely chopped garlic
1 tablespoon rice wine
1 teaspoon salt
2 mangoes, peeled and cut into ¾-inch cubes

GARNISH
1 tablespoon finely chopped fresh coriander

This might be called "nouvelle Hong Kong" or "Southeast Asia Meets Hong Kong." It is an exotic and unlikely combination. I have had this dish several times in Hong Kong and found it delicious every time. The rich sweetness and soft texture of the mango, which is very popular in Hong Kong (by way of Thailand and the Philippines), works extremely well with the fresh sea fragrance and delicate taste of the shrimp. The mango is cooked a short time, just enough to warm through and, as this recipe indicates, mixes well with other distinctively flavored foods.

To clean the shrimp, please follow the directions on page 34.

Combine the shrimp with the coating ingredients in a medium-sized bowl. Mix well and refrigerate for about 20 minutes.

Heat a wok or large skillet until it is hot and add the oil. When the oil is just warm, quickly add the shrimp, stir to separate, and turn off the heat. Allow the shrimp to sit in the warm oil for about 2 minutes. Drain in a colander set inside a stainless steel bowl, reserving some of the oil.

Return 1½ tablespoons of the drained oil to the wok and reheat. Add the ginger and garlic and stir-fry for 30 seconds. Then add the rice wine, salt, and mangoes. Stir-fry gently for 2 minutes or until the mangoes are heated through. Add the drained shrimp, stir gently to mix well, and serve.

YIELD: SERVES 4 TO 6

SCALLOPS STUFFED WITH SHRIMP

Here is another Hong Kong favorite that is also universally enjoyed. However, the chefs in Hong Kong, masters of illusion and refinement, do not actually stuff the scallops. Instead, they make a thick paste of the shrimp and then cleverly mound it on top of the scallops, giving them the appearance of being stuffed. It is quite a pleasing surprise to experience the shrimp first, having been led to expect the scallops. This is a harmonious blending of two delicious foods that works perfectly as a first course or as an appetizer.

1½ pounds large sea scallops

MARINADE
1 tablespoon ginger juice
1 tablespoon rice wine
1 teaspoon salt
1 teaspoon cornstarch
1 egg white
½ teaspoon freshly ground white pepper
1 teaspoon sesame oil

2 tablespoons salt
1 pound shrimp, peeled and deveined

SHRIMP STUFFING
1 egg white
½ teaspoon salt
2 tablespoons Smithfield ham fat, finely chopped
½ teaspoon sugar
½ teaspoon freshly ground white pepper
1 teaspoon sesame oil
2 teaspoons finely chopped fresh coriander

Cornstarch, for dusting
2 cups peanut oil, for deep-frying

If the scallops are very large, cut them in half horizontally. Combine the scallops and the marinade ingredients in a large bowl and let sit for 30 minutes.

To clean the shrimp, please follow the directions on page 34.

In a food processor, combine the shrimp stuffing ingredients and the shrimp and make a thick paste. Remove the scallops from the marinade and dust with cornstarch. Then mound 2 tablespoons of shrimp mixture on top of each scallop and dust again with cornstarch.

Heat a wok or large deep skillet and add the oil. When it is very hot, quickly deep-fry the "stuffed" scallops until they are golden brown and drain them quickly on paper towels. Serve with Salt-and-Pepper Dip (page 227) and bottled Worcestershire Sauce.

YIELD: SERVES 4

STIR-FRIED SCALLOPS WITH FRESH CHILIES

MARINADE
1 tablespoon rice wine
1 tablespoon light soy sauce
2 teaspoons cornstarch

1½ pounds fresh scallops
2 tablespoons peanut oil

2 tablespoons finely chopped fresh red chili peppers
1 tablespoon finely chopped peeled fresh ginger
3 whole scallions, cut into 1-inch pieces
½ teaspoon salt
1 teaspoon sugar
1 teaspoon chili bean sauce
1 teaspoon light soy sauce
¼ cup Rich Chicken Stock (page 221)
½ teaspoon cornstarch mixed with ½ teaspoon water

Combine the marinade ingredients. If the scallops are large, cut them in half. Add the scallops to the marinade and let sit for 1 hour. Drain the scallops and pat dry with paper towels.

Heat a wok or large skillet until it is hot and add 1 tablespoon of oil. Stir-fry the scallops for 2 minutes and remove from the wok.

Reheat the wok until it is hot and add the remaining oil. Stir in the chilies, ginger, and scallions and stir-fry for 30 seconds. Then add the rest of the ingredients except the cornstarch mixture. Return the scallops to the wok and stir-fry for about 2 to 3 minutes. Add the cornstarch mixture and cook for another 30 seconds. Serve at once.

YIELD: SERVES 4

When you visit Hong Kong, be sure to make a side trip to the New Territories and to the fishing village Lau Fau Shan. There, lining its one central street, you will see gigantic tanks filled with fish of all sizes and varieties swimming about, waiting to be purchased. There are trays of aerated seawater filled with jumping shrimp and other crustaceans, such as fan-shaped scallops. My favorite restaurant in the town, the Oi Man, cooks these scallops with fresh chilies and ginger in a quick and simple stir-fry. These seasonings work beautifully with the delicate flavor of the scallops. And the dish is as delectable and easy to make if shrimp are preferred. Remember, as in Hong Kong, experiment with and vary your styles and seasonings.

STIR-FRIED SQUID IN TWO SAUCES

Contrasting tastes and textures are characteristic of Cantonese–Hong Kong cuisine. Here, two different sauces are employed, spicy oyster sauce for richness and chili sauce for tang. Once the squid has been blanched, it is a quick dish to make. The result is a charming combination, delicious with noodles or rice.

2 pounds fresh squid

SPICY OYSTER SAUCE
1 tablespoon oyster sauce
2 teaspoons light soy sauce
2 teaspoons rice wine
1 tablespoon garlic, finely chopped
2 teaspoons peeled fresh ginger, finely chopped
2 tablespoons whole scallions, finely chopped
3 tablespoons Rich Chicken Stock (page 221) or water
    mixed with 1 teaspoon cornstarch

CHILI SAUCE
2 teaspoons dark soy sauce
1 teaspoon chili bean sauce
1 teaspoon bean sauce
1 tablespoon rice wine
1 tablespoon garlic, finely chopped
1 tablespoon peeled fresh ginger, finely chopped
1 tablespoon fresh red chili peppers, seeded and
    finely chopped
1 teaspoon sugar
3 tablespoons Rich Chicken Stock or water mixed with
    1 teaspoon cornstarch

2 tablespoons peanut oil

To clean the squid, separate the tentacles from the body, removing the entrails as you pull. Cut the tentacles just above the eyes and with your fingers remove the hard beak. Split the body lengthwise without cutting through. Remove the transparent quill and any remaining entrails. Peel the skin. Score the body in a cross-hatch pattern by cutting halfway through the flesh at a 45-degree angle.

Blanch the squid in a large pot of salted boiling water (1 teaspoon for each quart of water) for 5 seconds. Remove with a slotted spoon, rinse under cold running water, and set aside to drain in a colander. Mix the oyster sauce, light soy sauce, and rice wine together in a small bowl and set aside. In a separate small bowl, combine the dark soy sauce, chili bean sauce, bean sauce, and rice wine.

Heat a wok or large skillet until it is hot and add 1 tablespoon of oil. Add the garlic, ginger, and scallions of the spicy oyster sauce and stir-fry for 30 seconds. Add the oyster sauce, soy sauce, rice wine, and chicken stock with cornstarch. Reduce the heat and let the sauce simmer for 1 minute. Add half of the squid, stir-fry for 30 seconds to mix well, and reheat. Remove to a large platter.

Immediately rinse out the wok and reheat. Add the remaining oil and when it is hot, add the garlic, ginger, and chili peppers and stir-fry for 30 seconds. Then add the rest of the chili sauce ingredients, reduce the heat, and let the sauce simmer for 1 minute. Add the remaining squid, stir-fry for 30 seconds to mix well, and reheat. Place on the platter side by side with the squid in spicy oyster sauce and serve at once.

YIELD: SERVES 4 TO 6

CHIU CHOW—STYLE STEAMED CRAB

An unusual crab sold in Hong Kong markets is called by the locals "flower crab" or "mask crab" because of the distinct markings on the shell. It is very meaty with a delicate flavor. Many in Hong Kong believe that the best way to enjoy this crab is cooked in the Chiu Chow style; that is, to simply steam them upside down, so that all the juices and flavors of the crab are retained in the large shell, rather than lost to the steaming liquid. They are then cooled and served with a vinegar and ginger dipping sauce that helps to display the richness of the crab. At many of the Chiu Chow restaurants in Hong Kong, there are these lovely crabs, cooked and hanging beside the roast goose and other delicacies waiting to be savored. This recipe is simple to execute and makes a wonderful dish especially during warm weather.

2½ **pounds fresh whole crab, preferably live (either 1 to 2 medium-sized West Coast Dungeness *or* 6 to 8 east coast blue crabs)**

DIPPING SAUCE
4 tablespoons Chinese red vinegar
3 tablespoons finely chopped peeled fresh ginger

Rinse and scrub the crab or crabs under cold running water. Place the crab or crabs top shell down on a heat-proof platter on top of a rack in a tightly covered wok or pot. Gently steam for 10 minutes or until the shell has turned bright red. Remove and allow to cool.

Combine the vinegar and ginger in a small saucer. Lightly crack the cooled crab and serve with the dipping sauce.

YIELD: SERVES 4

MUSSELS IN BLACK BEAN SAUCE

1½ pounds fresh mussels
2 tablespoons peanut oil
1 tablespoon finely chopped garlic
2 teaspoons finely chopped peeled fresh ginger
2 tablespoons fermented black beans
1 tablespoon bean sauce
1 teaspoon chili bean sauce
1 tablespoon rice wine
1 tablespoon light soy sauce
2 tablespoons Rich Chicken Stock (page 221)
3 tablespoons finely chopped whole scallions

Scrub the mussels under cold running water and pull off the wirelike beards. Soak the mussels in a large bowl in several changes of cold water. Drain them thoroughly just before cooking.

Heat a wok or large skillet until it is hot and add the oil. Add the garlic, ginger, and fermented black beans and stir-fry for 30 seconds. Then add the bean sauce and chili bean sauce and stir-fry for another 10 seconds. Add the drained mussels and continue to stir-fry for 1 minute. Then add the rice wine, soy sauce, and stock and continue to cook over high heat until the shells are completely open. Discard any unopened mussels. Turn the contents into a large deep platter, garnish with the chopped scallions, and serve immediately.

YIELD: SERVES 4 TO 6

The Chinese in Hong Kong enjoy fresh mussels stir-fried with fermented black beans, as in this recipe. Or they are dried in the sun and chopped for use in stuffings. Fermented black beans are often used in Hong Kong cooking, unchopped and left whole — they thus have a more subtle flavor and taste and are less pungent than when they are chopped. This is a Hong Kong variation on a traditional recipe and is quite delicious. You may substitute clams if you like, but the cooking time will be slightly longer. Remove the mussels as soon as they open to prevent overcooking.

SICHUAN GARDEN SHRIMP WITH HOT CHILI AND GARLIC

A restaurant that has always been high on my list of favorites is Hong Kong's Sichuan Garden. There, the finest Sichuan cuisine is consistently offered. My students in Hong Kong always experience the delight of at least one banquet there and almost everyone's favorite dish is this one. Large fresh shrimp are coated with a light, airy batter and deep-fried. Then they are tossed with a colorless hot sauce thick with split red chilies and mounds of sliced garlic. The sauce is at once hot and sweet. To combine it with the crisp, lightly battered shrimp is to create a match made in a gourmand's heaven. The key to success here is to deep-fry the shrimp twice in hot oil, but very quickly to prevent overcooking. Skill, which you acquire through practice and experience, is the secret. Because the batter is so light and delicate, it will not hold if not served immediately. Once you have made this dish successfully, you will see why my students love it so much.

BATTER
4 tablespoons cornstarch
¼ cup flour
1 teaspoon baking powder
½ cup water
½ teaspoon salt
1 egg
1 egg white

2 tablespoons salt
1½ pounds medium shrimp, peeled and deveined
2 cups peanut oil, for deep-frying

SAUCE
1½ tablespoons peanut oil
5 dried chilies, halved
3 tablespoons finely sliced garlic
1 teaspoon salt
3 tablespoons sugar
1 teaspoon white rice vinegar
½ cup water
1 teaspoon cornstarch mixed with 1 teaspoon water

Mix the batter ingredients together in a medium-sized bowl; it should be thick and smooth. Allow the batter to sit, covered, for at least 30 minutes.

To clean shrimp, follow directions on page 34.

Combine the shrimp with the batter. Heat a wok or large deep skillet until it is hot and add the oil for frying. When the oil is barely smoking, deep-fry the shrimp for 2 minutes or until the batter is just firm. You should do this in several batches. Remove the shrimp with a slotted spoon and drain on paper towels.

Heat a small saucepan; when it is hot, add the oil, dried chilies and garlic, and stir for 30 seconds. Then add the rest of the sauce ingredients and simmer for 2 minutes. Keep warm.

Reheat the oil in the wok until it is very hot, but not smoking. Deep-fry the shrimp again until they are golden and crisp, about 1 minute. Remove and drain, place on a warm platter, drizzle with the sauce, and serve immediately.
YIELD: SERVES 4

PAN-FRIED FISH WITH LEMON SAUCE

1 pound fillets of red snapper, rockfish, sea bass, or any
   firm white-fleshed fish

MARINADE
2 teaspoons ginger juice
1 tablespoon rice wine
1 tablespoon light soy sauce
2 teaspoons cornstarch

3 tablespoons peanut oil

SAUCE
2 teaspoons peanut oil
3 garlic cloves, crushed
4 tablespoons Rich Chicken Stock (page 221)
2 tablespoons lemon juice
3 slices lemon, ¼ inch thick
1 teaspoon light soy sauce
½ teaspoon salt
1 tablespoon finely chopped whole scallions
1 teaspoon sugar
½ teaspoon cornstarch mixed with ½ teaspoon water

This simple-to-make fish recipe perfectly combines with a subtle lemon sauce. Unlike some versions made in the West, this Hong Kong version has just enough sauce to coat and never drown the fish pieces.

Cut the fish into large pieces. Combine with the marinade in a large bowl and set aside for 30 minutes.

Heat a wok or large skillet until it is hot and add the oil. When it is moderately hot, pan-fry the fish until lightly brown. Remove and drain on paper towels. Arrange the pieces of fish on a warm platter.

Reheat the wok and add 2 teaspoons of oil. When it is hot, add the garlic and stir-fry for 30 seconds. Then add the rest of the sauce ingredients and bring to a simmer. Pour this sauce over the fish and serve.

YIELD: SERVES 4 TO 6

DICED LOBSTER IN LETTUCE CUPS

As everywhere, lobster is a favorite in Hong Kong; but it is not the most plentiful shellfish in the South China Sea and has until recently been available at only the more expensive restaurants. The spiny Pacific lobster is, however, appearing in many more eating places and is popular. I first enjoyed this treat at a delightful banquet at the Rainbow Room at the Lee Gardens Hotel. This preparation is typical of the many recipes calling for chopped meats — usually pork or poultry — which are then stir-fried and wrapped in fresh crisp lettuce. Here, the chef has exploited the new availability of lobster; its flavor is enhanced by the crunch and taste of water chestnuts, celery hearts, and other vegetables. The vegetables are finely diced to show off the lobster. Admittedly, this is an expensive dish and one that requires some effort to prepare — but well worth it for a truly special occasion.

2 live lobsters, about 1 pound each
½ tablespoon peanut oil
2 tablespoons finely chopped fresh peeled ginger
1 tablespoon finely chopped garlic
3 tablespoons finely chopped whole scallions
½ cup finely diced fresh water chestnuts
½ cup finely diced celery hearts
½ cup finely diced red pepper
½ pound fresh peas or ½ cup frozen peas

SAUCE
2 teaspoons light soy sauce
3 tablespoons oyster sauce
1 tablespoon rice wine
2 teaspoons sesame oil

1 head Iceberg lettuce, separated into leaves
    to use as cups

Plunge the lobsters in large pot of boiling water for 3 minutes. Drain thoroughly and allow to cool. When cool, crack the shells, remove the meat with a fork, coarsely chop and set aside. If you are using fresh peas, blanch them in the same water for 2 minutes. Remove, drain thoroughly, and set aside.

Heat a wok or large skillet until it is hot and add the oil. When heated, add the ginger, garlic, scallions and stir-fry for 30 seconds. Add the water chestnuts, celery hearts, pepper, and blanched or frozen peas and stir-fry another 30 seconds. Then add the lobster meat and sauce ingredients and continue to cook the mixture for another 3 minutes, stirring constantly. Give the mixture a final toss and ladle onto a platter. Garnish with the lettuce cups and allow the diners to spoon some of the lobster mixture into a lettuce cup to eat with their hands. There is no need for any other sauces.

YIELD: SERVES 4 TO 6

FRESH CORIANDER SHRIMP WRAPPED IN RICE PAPER

2 tablespoons salt
1 pound medium shrimp, peeled and deveined

MARINADE
2 teaspoons light soy sauce
1 teaspoon dark soy sauce
1 teaspoon rice wine
1 teaspoon oyster sauce
½ teaspoon cornstarch

1 package Banh Tran rice paper rounds
Whole scallion segments, 3 inches long, cut in half,
    lengthwise
Fresh coriander leaves
2 cups peanut oil, for deep-frying

This Hong Kong innovation may be judged by its cover: Southeast Asian rice paper, the kind used in Vietnam, Thailand and the Philippines, delicate, light, translucent, yet very crisp and, to my taste, much superior to the classic Chinese wrappers made from wheat flour and water. The wrapper is adapted here for fresh briny shrimp and lusty coriander to create an outstanding appetizer or first course. It may be prepared well ahead of time and deep-fried at the last minute.

To clean the shrimp, follow the directions on page 34.

In a small bowl, combine the shrimp with the marinade ingredients and set aside for 1 hour at room temperature.

When you are ready to make the shrimp, fill a large bowl with warm water. Dip one of the rice paper rounds in the water and let it soften a few seconds. Remove and drain it on a linen towel.

Add one piece of shrimp, a scallion piece, and one coriander leaf to the edge of the rice paper. Roll the edge over the mixture once, fold up both ends of the rice paper, and continue to roll to the end. The roll should be about 3 inches long, compact, and tight, rather like a short, thick sausage. Set it on a clean plate and continue the process until you have used up all the shrimp. The shrimp can be rolled ahead of time, covered with plastic wrap and refrigerated for up to 4 hours.

Heat the peanut oil in a wok or deep skillet until it is moderately hot, and deep-fry the shrimp rolls a few pieces at a time for 3 to 5 minutes or until they are a light golden brown all over. They have a tendency to stick to one another at the beginning of the frying, so do only a few at a time.

Drain the shrimp rolls on paper towels and serve at once.

YIELD: MAKES 20 ROLLS

STEAMED LOBSTER WITH GARLIC AND SCALLIONS

Classic simplicity is the mark of this subtle and elegant steamed lobster dish, cosmopolitan Hong Kong cuisine at its best and in its purest form. The splendid taste of the lobster is expanded by the touch of garlic, scallion, and hot oil. Simple to make and noble in effect, this is a quick but impressive centerpiece to any meal.

1 live lobster, about 1¼ to 1½ pounds
4 garlic cloves, peeled and thinly sliced
4 tablespoons finely chopped whole scallions
1½ tablespoons peanut oil

Place the lobster upside down on a heat-proof platter and scatter the garlic slices around. Steam over slowly simmering water on a rack in a tightly covered wok or pot for 8 minutes. Remove the lobster and, when it is cool, cut it into serving portions. Arrange these on a serving platter and garnish with chopped scallions.

Heat the oil in a small pan until it is smoking, pour over the lobster, and serve at once.

YIELD: SERVES 2 TO 4

SHANGHAI-STYLE SHRIMP WITH LEEKS

2 tablespoons salt
1 pound medium shrimp, peeled and deveined
2½ tablespoons peanut oil
3 slices fresh peeled ginger
3 cloves peeled garlic, crushed
1 cup shredded leeks, white part only
1 teaspoon sugar
1 tablespoon rice wine
1 teaspoon salt
¼ cup Rich Chicken Stock (page 221)
1 teaspoon black vinegar
2 teaspoons sesame oil

To clean the shrimp, please follow the directions on page 34.

Heat a wok or large skillet until it is hot and add 1½ tablespoons of the oil. Add the ginger and garlic to flavor the oil and stir-fry for 30 seconds. Remove the ginger and garlic and discard. Add the shrimp and stir-fry for 1 minute. Remove them with a slotted spoon and drain on paper towels.

Wipe the wok clean and reheat over high heat. Add the remaining tablespoon of oil and then the leeks. Stir-fry for 2 minutes and add the rest of the ingredients. Return the shrimp to the wok and give the mixture several good stirs. Turn onto a platter and serve.

YIELD: SERVES 4 TO 6

Besides Cantonese offerings you find in the markets in Hong Kong, you will also discover many so-called Shanghai stalls, selling the famous Shanghai freshwater crabs, leeks, and other specialties. Many Shanghainese fled to Hong Kong after 1949. Their well-known business and manufacturing acumen helped fuel Hong Kong's economy, establishing Hong Kong's tailoring industry, among other enterprises. This dish is inspired by a recipe given to me at Kowloon's Mongkok Market by a recent emigré from Shanghai. Leeks are widely used in the northern and eastern part of China. They are flavorful but do not overwhelm the subtle taste of the shrimp.

CRAB CASSEROLE IN A CLAY POT

Here is an interesting, innovative technique employed by Hong Kong chefs. The clay pot traditionally is used for the long simmering and braising of foods; nowadays, however, it is as often used to infuse intense flavors over high heat in a short length of time, as in this recipe. The classic Cantonese dish is given a new twist; the fresh crab is stir-fried with aromatic seasonings and then quickly finished over high heat in the covered clay pot. The pungent black beans permeate the rich crabmeat, enhancing it and adding to its subtle flavors. This delicious casserole is quite easy to prepare and turns an ordinary dinner into a special occasion.

1½ pounds fresh whole crab, preferably live
2 tablespoons peanut oil
5 unpeeled garlic cloves, crushed
2 unpeeled fresh ginger slices, ¼ inch thick
3 whole scallions, cut into 2-inch pieces
3 tablespoons fermented black beans
2 fresh red chili peppers, seeded and shredded
3 tablespoons rice wine
2 tablespoons light soy sauce
½ cup Rich Chicken Stock (page 221)

If you are using a live crab, prepare it according to the technique on page 77. Cut the body into quarters and lightly crack the claws and legs.

Heat a wok or large skillet until it is hot and add the oil. Add the garlic, ginger, and scallions and stir-fry to flavor the oil. Then add the black beans, chilies, and crab. Stir-fry for 2 minutes and add the chicken stock. Turn the contents of the wok into a clay pot or casserole, cover, and cook over high heat for 5 more minutes or until the crab shell turns bright red. Serve immediately.

YIELD: SERVES 4

STIR-FRIED SHRIMP WITH CHICKEN LIVER

2 tablespoons salt
1 pound medium shrimp, peeled and deveined

COATING
1 egg white
1 teaspoon salt
2 teaspoons cornstarch

½ pound chicken livers
½ cup peanut oil, for velveting (page 271) and
    deep-frying
1 tablespoon finely chopped garlic
1 tablespoon finely chopped whole scallions
2 teaspoons finely chopped peeled fresh ginger

SAUCE
1 tablespoon oyster sauce
2 teaspoons bean sauce
3 tablespoons Rich Chicken Stock (page 221)
½ teaspoon cornstarch mixed with ½ teaspoon water

To clean the shrimp, follow the directions on page 34.
    Combine the shrimp with the coating ingredients in a medium-sized bowl. Mix well and refrigerate for about 20 minutes.

Rinse the chicken livers in cold running water, trim off the excess fat and veins. Blot dry with paper towels.

Heat a wok or large skillet until it is hot and add the oil. When the oil is just warm, quickly add the shrimp, stir to separate, and turn off the heat. Allow the shrimp to sit in the warm oil for about 2 minutes. Drain in a colander set inside a stainless steel bowl, reserving the oil.

Return the oil to the wok and reheat until very hot. Deep-fry the chicken livers for about 2 to 3 minutes or until they are crisp; remove with a slotted spoon, and drain on paper towels.

Drain all but 1½ tablespoons of oil from the wok, reheat, and when hot, add the garlic, scallions, and ginger and stir-fry for about 1 minute. Add the sauce ingredients and bring the mixture to a boil. Return the shrimp and livers to the wok and mix well with sauce. Serve at once.

YIELD: SERVES 4

Except for the spices and sauce, which may of course be varied to suit one's taste, this is a truly cosmopolitan dish: shrimp and chicken livers are universally appreciated. The notion of combining them is perhaps a novelty but as this recipe proves, it is an idea whose time was long overdue. Although each food has its own rich and distinct taste, the two blend congenially when appropriately seasoned and properly introduced to the right sauce. The blends and contrasts of the tastes and textures of this recipe make it a Hong Kong favorite.

It is a quick and easy meal, perfect for family dining, served with vegetables and rice.

SHRIMP WITH CASHEW NUTS

This easy-to-make shrimp dish is typical of tasty dishes you find in many restaurants in Hong Kong. The cashew nuts add an interesting textural counterpoint to the shrimp. This is fast food of great quality.

2 tablespoons salt
1 pound medium shrimp, peeled and deveined

COATING
1 egg white
1 teaspoon salt
2 teaspoons cornstarch

½ cup peanut oil, for velveting (page 271)
2 teaspoons finely chopped peeled fresh ginger
2 tablespoons finely chopped whole scallions
½ cup unsalted cashew nuts, roasted
½ teaspoon salt
1 tablespoon hoisin sauce
1 tablespoon rice wine
6 tablespoons Rich Chicken Stock (page 221)
½ teaspoon cornstarch mixed with ½ teaspoon water
1 teaspoon sesame oil

To clean the shrimp, please follow the directions on page 34.

Combine the shrimp with the coating ingredients in a medium-sized bowl. Mix well and refrigerate for about 20 minutes.

Heat a wok or large skillet until it is hot and add the peanut oil. When the oil is just warm, quickly add the shrimp, stir to separate, and turn off the heat. Allow the shrimp to sit in the warm oil for about 2 minutes. Drain in a colander set inside a stainless steel bowl, retaining some of the oil.

Wipe the wok clean, return 1½ tablespoons of the drained oil to the wok, and add the ginger and scallions, stir-frying for 30 seconds. Stir in the cashew nuts and salt and continue to stir-fry for another 30 seconds. Return the shrimp to the wok with the remaining ingredients and stir-fry for another 2 minutes. Turn out on a platter and serve at once.

YIELD: SERVES 4 TO 6

LAI CHING HEEN'S PEAR WITH SCALLOPS

2 tablespoons salt
½ pound medium shrimp, peeled and deveined

½ teaspoon salt
8 large sea scallops
¼-pound slice Smithfield ham
1 large Chinese pear apple or firm bosc pear
Fresh coriander leaves, rinsed and dried
2 cups peanut oil, for deep-frying
6 egg yolks, beaten and combined with 2 tablespoons of
    water
¼ cup or more cornstarch

DIPPING CONDIMENTS
¼ cup fresh lemon juice
Salt-and-Pepper Dip (page 227)

To clean the shrimp, please follow the directions on page 34. Put the shrimp in a food processor with the salt and mince until they form a firm but sticky paste. Set aside.

Cut the scallops in half horizontally. Finely slice the ham into 8 thin pieces about the size of the scallops. Peel and slice the pear into discs about the size of the scallops. Spoon about 1 tablespoon of shrimp mixture on each of the 8 scallop halves; top each with a pear slice, one slice of ham, and two fresh coriander leaves. Cover with the remaining eight pieces of scallop.

Heat a wok or large skillet until it is hot. Add the oil and continue to heat until it is very hot. With tongs or chopsticks, holding each scallop "sandwich" together, dip first into the egg-yolk mixture, then roll to cover all over with cornstarch. Drop immediately into the hot oil. Deep-fry the scallops, about four at a time, for about 3 minutes or until they are golden brown. Drain carefully on paper towels. Serve at once with the lemon juice and Salt-and-Pepper Dip.
YIELD: SERVES 4 TO 6

One of the most innovative restaurants offering the new Chinese cuisine of Hong Kong is Lai Ching Heen, in The Regent Hotel in Kowloon. Of the many dishes I have enjoyed there, this one epitomizes for me the virtues of carefully considered innovations that revise and enhance traditional and classical foods but retain their excellence.

Here the thoughtful chef has cleverly combined the crisp, slightly sweet, Chinese pear apple with scallops. The split scallops are stuffed with freshly made shrimp purée; they are topped with ham and fresh coriander and rest on a slice of pear apple. The combination is delicious, with all the tastes and textures coming together in a delightful and unexpected fashion. I have modified the recipe, for convenience, by placing the ham, coriander, and pear slice inside the scallop along with the shrimp purée, which does nothing to alter the basic taste.

SCALLOPS AND SHRIMP IN A CRISP TARO BASKET

Taro root needs some work to make it delectable and it is rarely a dish by itself. However, it can be used to sustain other, more flavorful foods, as in this recipe. Like the potato, taro root fries nicely and in this rather complicated recipe it may be prepared well in advance. The "basket" that results makes a splendid setting for the scallops and shrimp. Once the shellfish have been prepared, the actual stir-frying takes but a short time. This dish is well worth its cost in time and effort; your guests will experience an authentic Hong Kong banquet dish.

TARO BASKET
1 pound taro roots (potatoes may be substituted)
1 tablespoon cornstarch

3 cups peanut oil, for deep-frying
2 tablespoons salt
1 pound medium shrimp, peeled and deveined
½ pound scallops

COATING
1 egg white
½ teaspoon salt
2 teaspoons cornstarch

1 cup peanut oil, for velveting (page 271)
1 tablespoon finely chopped garlic
2 teaspoons finely chopped peeled fresh ginger
½ cup fresh water chestnuts, peeled and sliced
¼ cup canned bamboo shoots, sliced
6 scallions, diagonally sliced

SAUCE
2 teaspoons light soy sauce
¼ teaspoon salt
4 tablespoons Rich Chicken Stock (page 221)
1 teaspoon cornstarch mixed with 1 teaspoon water
1 teaspoon sesame oil

Peel and finely shred the taro roots or potatoes and soak in cold water for about 1 hour, changing the water twice. Drain and blot dry with a linen towel and sprinkle with cornstarch. This will help absorb any excess moisture.

Add the 3 cups peanut oil to a wok or large, deep pan and heat until almost smoking. Place the taro shreds between 5-inch and 7-inch stainless steel colanders or strainers and submerge into the hot oil, holding the top strainer down with a spatula to help keep the shape of the basket. Carefully ladle hot oil over any uncooked shreds. Continue to deep-fry until the basket is golden and crisp and thoroughly cooked. Drain on paper towels and then place on a serving platter. When the oil is cool, strain, and reserve for the velveting procedure.

Fill a large bowl with cold water, add 1 tablespoon of salt, and gently wash the shrimp in the salt water. Drain and repeat the process. Then rinse the shrimp under cold running water, drain, and blot dry with paper towels.

Combine the shrimp and scallops with the coating ingredients in a medium-sized bowl. Mix well and refrigerate for about 20 minutes. Heat a wok or large skillet until it is hot and add 2 cups of the reserved oil. When the oil is warm, quickly add the shrimp and scallops, stir to separate, and turn off the heat. Allow them to sit in the warm oil for about 2 minutes. Drain the shrimp and scallops in a colander set inside a stainless steel bowl. Strain the oil.

Return 1½ tablespoons of oil to the wok and reheat. Add the garlic and ginger and stir-fry for 10 seconds. Then add the rest of the vegetables and stir-fry for about 2 minutes. Return the shrimp and scallops to the mixture and give it a few good turns to mix well. Add the sauce ingredients and cook for another 2 minutes. Ladle the mixture into the taro basket and serve at once.

YIELD: SERVES 4 TO 6

POULTRY

~~~~~~

WINE-FLAVORED CHICKEN IN A CLAY POT

DICED CHICKEN AND SMOKED OYSTERS IN LETTUCE CUPS

CRISP SHRIMP-PASTE CHICKEN

STEEPED CHICKEN WITH SPICY SAUCE

SICHUAN-PEPPERCORN CHICKEN

SALT-BAKED SQUAB

SPICY ORANGE CHICKEN WITH BLACK BEANS

PEKING-STYLE ROAST SQUAB

SAVORY BLACK MUSHROOM AND CHICKEN CASSEROLE

BRAISED SOY SAUCE–FLAVORED SQUAB

TWO-COURSE PEKING DUCK, LEE GARDENS–STYLE

SICHUAN GARDEN'S SMOKED TEA DUCK

COLD DRUNKEN CHICKEN

GINGERY CHICKEN WINGS WITH PINEAPPLE

SHREDDED CHICKEN IN OYSTER SAUCE

RICE-PAPER CHICKEN ROLLS

VELVET CHICKEN WITH CRUNCHY WALNUTS

ROAST "PIPA" CHICKEN

FOUR-COLOR OMELET

THAI CURRIED CHICKEN AND POTATO STEW

DEEP-FRIED CHICKEN LIVERS WITH CASHEW NUTS

CHICKEN ROLLS

BRAISED SQUAB IN PORT WINE

MINCED DUCK WITH FRESH LETTUCE CUPS

BRAISED OYSTER-SAUCE SQUAB

PAN-FRIED CHICKEN WITH LEMON

DEEP-FRIED MILK WITH QUAIL EGGS

SICHUAN GARDEN'S SMOKED SQUAB

CHIUCHOW GARDEN'S CHICKEN WITH CRISP SPINACH

LAI CHING HEEN'S SPINACH AND CHICKEN ROLLS

After fish and shellfish, poultry provides most of the animal protein in the Hong Kong cuisine. Duck is a popular favorite but is relatively expensive. Chicken, pigeon (squab), and game birds (quail) comprise most of the poultry dishes in Hong Kong restaurants. The more robust flavors of duck and game birds allow for the use of stronger seasonings; chicken and squab, with their delicate flavors, call for more nuanced accompaniments. As these recipes indicate, Hong Kong chefs have taken advantage of the different characteristics of the various types of poultry available to them. They have created dishes of universal appeal.

WINE-FLAVORED CHICKEN IN A CLAY POT

I suspect the origins of this dish probably are in northern China. However, like many things in Hong Kong, new dishes are readily adapted, and origins and distinctions are blurred. Hong Kong chefs have no qualms about changing any dish to suit their own taste or their patrons' wishes. This cold chicken is extremely delicate and tasty and, as a bonus, much of it can be made ahead of time. The rose wine, found in Chinese supermarkets or groceries, adds a particularly attractive fragrance and is well worth the effort to obtain. It would make a great picnic dish. If you make it a day in advance, simply let it stay in the wine mixture in the refrigerator overnight and then cut it up when you are ready to enjoy it.

BRAISING LIQUID
3 tablespoons Chinese rose wine
½ cup rice wine
¼ cup light soy sauce
⅓ cup dark soy sauce
3 tablespoons sugar
2 pieces cinnamon bark
1 citrus peel, 2-inch piece
2 tablespoons dried ginger
3 star anise
1 tablespoon unroasted Sichuan peppercorns
2 teaspoons salt

3- to 3½-pound whole chicken

Place the braising mixture into a large clay pot or casserole, put it on the stove, bring to a boil, then turn the heat down, and let it simmer for 20 minutes. Add the chicken and continue to simmer for 20 minutes, rotating it once or twice during the cooking time. Turn the heat off and let the chicken rest in the liquid until it is thoroughly cooled. This will take 2 to 3 hours.

Remove the chicken from the pot, cut it into slices, and serve with some of the braising liquid.

YIELD: SERVES 4 TO 6

DICED CHICKEN AND SMOKED OYSTERS IN LETTUCE CUPS

3 tablespoons plus 1 teaspoon peanut oil
½-pound chicken breasts, boned and skinned,
    finely diced
¼ pound chicken livers, chopped

OYSTER MIXTURE
1 head iceberg lettuce, separated into leaves
    to use as cups
¼ cup cashew nuts, coarsely chopped
¼ cup smoked oysters, finely chopped; canned smoked
    oysters may be substituted
2 tablespoons finely chopped garlic
2 tablespoons finely chopped Smithfield ham
1½ tablespoons finely chopped peeled fresh ginger
3 tablespoons finely chopped fresh coriander
¼ cup finely chopped bamboo shoots
¼ cup finely chopped fresh water chestnuts
¼ cup finely chopped whole scallions

SAUCE
¼ cup Rich Chicken Stock (page 221)
5 tablespoons oyster sauce
2 teaspoons sugar
½ teaspoon salt
Freshly ground white pepper to taste

This recipe is typical of innovative dishes in Hong Kong that use new ingredients — in this case, iceberg lettuce — and combine them with traditional foods. Such a subtle variation transforms the dish into something new — something distinctive of Hong Kong, where to a real extent, East meets West and all points North and South. This recipe combines uncommonly good tastes and textures. The livers add richness and the dried oysters contribute their distinct smoky flavor. The lettuce offers a refreshing crunch and light note to the entire dish. You will see why it is so popular in Hong Kong.

Heat a wok or large skillet until it is hot. Add 2 teaspoons of the oil and when it is quite hot, quickly stir-fry the chicken breasts for about 1 minute. Remove with a slotted spoon, add 2 more teaspoons of oil, and stir-fry the livers for 20 seconds. Remove and add to chicken.

Trim the lettuce leaves into attractive cups, refrigerate.

Heat a wok or large skillet until it is hot. Add the remaining 2 tablespoons of oil and when it is quite hot, quickly stir-fry the oyster mixture for about 2 minutes. Then mix in the chicken and livers. Add the sauce ingredients and stir-fry for 1 more minute, stirring constantly. Turn the mixture onto a platter surrounded by the lettuce cups.

Ask guests to put a helping of the chicken mixture into a lettuce cup and eat it with their fingers like a taco.

YIELD: SERVES 4 TO 6

CRISP SHRIMP-PASTE CHICKEN

I first enjoyed this chicken dish at the Sun Tung Lok restaurant in Harbour City, and I was unprepared for the excellence of what I thought would be a simple fried-chicken dish. I immediately set out to duplicate the recipe in my own kitchen and have ever since incorporated it into the repertory of dishes I make frequently. The distinctive flavor comes from the shrimp paste, which gives an aromatic and exotic taste: it must be used with care, as it is quite strong. The secret to the extra crispness of the chicken is in the double-frying. Marinated and then fried the first time, the chicken is fried again just before serving, making it ideal to serve at a dinner party. This use of a seafood paste to flavor chicken is a typically southern Chinese touch: a Chiu Chow — southern Chinese seafood-oriented — inspiration.

The chicken is not boned; this helps the meat to remain flavorful and moist.

2½-pound chicken

SHRIMP-PASTE MARINADE
1 tablespoon shrimp paste
1 tablespoon ginger juice
2 teaspoons sugar
2 teaspoons sesame oil
1 teaspoon light soy sauce

2 cups peanut oil, for deep-frying
All-purpose unbleached flour, for dusting
3 tablespoons finely chopped whole scallions

Chop the chicken into bite-size pieces with a heavy knife or Chinese cleaver. In a medium-sized bowl, mix the shrimp-paste marinade ingredients, add the chicken, and let sit at room temperature for 30 minutes.

Heat a wok or large deep skillet until it is hot and add the oil. Lightly dust the chicken pieces with flour, shaking off any excess. When the oil is hot, deep-fry half the chicken for 5 minutes or until golden brown, then drain it on paper towels and set aside at room temperature for up to 1 hour. Then fry the rest of the chicken. Just before serving, remove any debris from the oil with a fine mesh ladle. Reheat the oil until it is very hot and refry the chicken for 1 minute or until golden brown and heated through. Drain on paper towels, sprinkle with chopped scallions, and serve at once.

YIELD: SERVES 4

STEEPED CHICKEN WITH SPICY SAUCE

3- to 3½-pound whole chicken
3 whole scallions, cut into 2-inch pieces
3 slices unpeeled fresh ginger
1 teaspoon salt

SAUCE
1 tablespoon peanut oil
2 teaspoons finely chopped garlic
2 tablespoons finely chopped whole scallions
2 teaspoons chili bean sauce
2 tablespoons Rich Chicken Stock (page 221)
1 teaspoon white rice vinegar
1 teaspoon sugar
Freshly ground white pepper to taste
½ teaspoon salt

GARNISH
3 tablespoons finely chopped whole scallions

This is a variation of the popular Chinese cold chicken salad, except it is made with a sauce that does not contain sesame paste. It is easy to make and is convenient to prepare in advance. It makes a wonderful appetizer.

Combine the chicken, scallions, ginger, salt, and enough water to cover in a large clay pot or casserole. Bring the water to a boil, then turn the heat down and let it simmer uncovered for 20 minutes, rotating it once or twice during the cooking time. Turn the heat off, cover, and let the chicken rest in the liquid until it is thoroughly cooled. This will take 2 to 3 hours.

Heat a wok or large skillet until it is hot. Add the oil and when it is hot, add the garlic, scallions, and chili bean sauce and stir-fry for 20 seconds. Add the rest of the sauce ingredients and simmer for 5 minutes. Set aside and allow the sauce to cool.

Skin the chicken and remove all the meat from the bones. Shred the meat with your hands and arrange on a serving platter. Pour the sauce over the meat and serve, garnished with chopped scallions.

YIELD: SERVES 4 TO 6

SICHUAN-PEPPERCORN CHICKEN

Chicken thighs are a common and well-liked food in Hong Kong. The dark meat can be paired with emphatic seasonings that go well with its stronger flavor. Here, the thighs are tossed in a Sichuan-peppercorn sauce after being marinated with some shrimp paste. The result is an uncommonly hearty and delectable chicken dish.

1½ pounds (about 6) chicken thighs

MARINADE
1 teaspoon dark soy sauce
1 teaspoon shrimp paste
1 teaspoon cornstarch
½ teaspoon sesame oil

2 tablespoons peanut oil

SAUCE
1 teaspoon Sichuan peppercorns, roasted and ground
2 teaspoons finely chopped whole scallions
1 teaspoon shrimp paste
2 teaspoons rice wine
1 teaspoon dark soy sauce
½ teaspoon sesame oil

Bone and skin the chicken thighs. Place the meat between pieces of plastic wrap and pound gently to tenderize. Cut the pounded meat into 1- by-3-inch-long pieces. In a medium-sized bowl, combine the meat with the marinade. Allow to marinate for 30 minutes.

Heat a wok or large skillet until it is hot. Add the oil and when it is quite hot, quickly stir-fry the chicken for about 3 minutes. Then add the sauce ingredients and continue to stir-fry for another 3 minutes or until the chicken is cooked. Serve at once.

YIELD: SERVES 4 TO 6

SALT-BAKED SQUAB

Two 14-ounce squab

MARINADE
1 tablespoon finely shredded peeled fresh ginger
2 whole scallions, coarsely shredded
2 tablespoons Chinese rose wine or rice wine
2 teaspoons five-spice powder

4 cups rock salt
2 pieces parchment paper, 8 by 12 inches
Two 12-inch-square sheets of aluminum foil

SAUCE
4 star anise
1 teaspoon ginger juice
1 tablespoon dark soy
2 teaspoons sesame oil

Along with Chiu Chow, Hakka cuisine is among the least-known branches of Chinese food. The Hakka women are seen throughout the New Territories wearing broad-brimmed, black-fringed hats as they tend the fields. They are historically nomadic and therefore many of their specialties include preserved vegetables. Especially well-known is their Salt-Baked Chicken, and this squab dish is a variation on that delicious peasant dish.

Dry the squab thoroughly inside and out with paper towels. Combine the marinade ingredients in a small bowl and rub this mixture all over the squab. Allow the squab to marinate for 1 hour at room temperature.

Preheat the oven to 400° F.

Pour the rock salt into a large heavy pot and smooth it so that it forms a level surface. Heat the pot over a medium flame for 5 minutes.

Combine sauce ingredients and pour an equal amount over the two birds. Wrap each squab in parchment paper and then completely seal each parchment package with foil. Place the packets on the hot rock salt, cover the pot, and bake for 25 minutes. Remove the pot from the oven and unwrap the foil just enough to expose the tops of the squab. Return the pot uncovered to the oven for another 15 minutes to brown. Transfer the squab to a platter and remove the foil. Let the squab sit for 15 minutes and then serve them still wrapped in the parchment paper.

YIELD: SERVES 2 TO 4

SPICY ORANGE CHICKEN WITH BLACK BEANS

Using the clay pot to complete the cooking of a quick stir-fried dish is a characteristic of Hong Kong cooking. Here, that innovative two-step process further enhances the flavors of traditional ingredients, and the resulting dish is an interesting and tasty variation on the traditional recipe.

1½-pound chicken, boned and skinned

MARINADE
2 teaspoons light soy sauce
1 teaspoon ginger juice
1 teaspoon rice wine
1 teaspoon cornstarch

3 tablespoons peanut oil

BLACK-BEAN MIXTURE
2 dried citrus peels, soaked and finely chopped
2 green peppers, cut into wedges
2 tablespoons orange zest, finely shredded
1 tablespoon fermented black beans
2 fresh red chili peppers, shredded
1 small onion, cut into wedges
2 teaspoons finely chopped garlic
1 teaspoon finely chopped fresh ginger

SAUCE
½ cup Rich Chicken Stock (page 221)
1 tablespoon rice wine
1 tablespoon light soy sauce
1 teaspoon salt

Cut the chicken into medium-sized pieces. Combine the marinade ingredients with the chicken. Let it stand for 30 minutes.

Heat a wok or large skillet until it is hot. Add half of the oil and quickly stir-fry the chicken for about 5 minutes or until it is brown. Remove the chicken with a slotted spoon and clean the wok.

Reheat the wok and when it is hot, add the remaining oil. Stir-fry the black-bean mixture for 1 minute, return the chicken to the wok, and continue to stir-fry for another 30 seconds to mix well. Remove the contents of the wok with a slotted spoon to a clay pot or casserole. Add the sauce ingredients, cover the pot, and braise over high heat for about 5 minutes. Serve at once.

YIELD: SERVES 2 TO 4

PEKING-STYLE ROAST SQUAB

2 squab (14 ounces or ¾ pound each)
1 teaspoon five-spice powder
1 teaspoon salt

BASTING LIQUID
2 teaspoons white vinegar
1 tablespoon malt sugar
2 tablespoons honey
2 cups water
2 tablespoons dark soy sauce
1 cup water

Hoisin sauce, for dipping

Season the inside of the squab with the five-spice powder and salt.

In a medium-sized pot, combine the basting liquid ingredients and bring to a boil. Turn off the heat and baste the squab several times with the hot liquid. Remove the birds from the liquid and allow them to dry on a rack, either in a cool, drafty place for 2 hours or in front of a fan for 1 hour. When properly dried, the skin will feel like parchment paper.

Preheat the oven to 450° F. Place the squab on a rack inside a roasting pan. Pour in 1 cup water. Roast the squab for 15 minutes. Reduce the heat to 375° F and continue to cook for 20 to 25 minutes. The skin should become crisp and a mahogany-brown color.

Remove the squab from the oven and cool for about 10 minutes before serving. Serve with hoisin sauce as a dipping sauce.

YIELD: SERVES 2 TO 4

Squab or young pigeons are a highly prized treat in Chinese cuisine and are often found on Hong Kong menus. It is said that more than 900,000 of these tasty birds are consumed there each year. Cantonese cooks have been ingenious in devising scores of innovative ways to cook them. So-called roast pigeon is really cooked for twenty minutes in a broth full of spices and seasonings. It is then drained, cooled, and dried. Just before serving, it is deep-fried so that the skin becomes parchment crisp with the meat remaining juicy and moist. Real roasting is uncommon and reserved mostly for pork or duck. In some restaurants in Hong Kong, however, I have sampled squab actually roasted in ovens like Peking Duck, which is especially easy for home cooks to do in the West. I like to serve it with just hoisin sauce and without the pancakes.

SAVORY BLACK MUSHROOM AND CHICKEN CASSEROLE

This hearty dish is served in restaurants, food stalls, and homes throughout Hong Kong. The recommended Chinese black mushrooms have been cultivated in the southern temperate parts of Asia for more than a thousand years. The Chinese never used them fresh, preferring them dried, because they keep longer and lose none of their flavor. They come in many grades but are always expensive and nevertheless widely used in Hong Kong cooking. They are highly esteemed for their distinct, robust flavor and succulent texture and for their ability to absorb the flavors of foods they are cooked with, without losing their own flavor. When mushrooms and poultry are combined, as in this recipe, the delicate flavor of the meat is subtly enhanced. The dish is very easy to make and goes perfectly with plain rice.

4 pounds (about 15 to 16) chicken thighs, skinned and boned

MARINADE
2 tablespoons rice wine
2 teaspoons salt
2 teaspoons sesame oil
½ teaspoon freshly ground black pepper
2 teaspoons cornstarch

1 cup dried Chinese black mushrooms
2 tablespoons peanut oil
3 unpeeled fresh ginger slices, ¼ inch thick
2 whole scallions, cut into 1-inch pieces

SAUCE
1 tablespoon light soy sauce
2 tablespoons oyster sauce
2 teaspoons sugar
¾ cup Rich Chicken Stock (page 221)
2 tablespoons rice wine
½ teaspoon cornstarch mixed with 1 teaspoon water
2 teaspoons sesame oil

Cut the chicken thighs into bite-size pieces and combine with the marinade ingredients. Marinate for 40 minutes.

Soak the mushrooms in a bowl of warm water for about 20 minutes or until they are soft and pliable. Squeeze out the excess water and cut off and discard the woody stems.

Heat a wok or large skillet until it is hot. Add the oil, ginger, and scallions and stir-fry for 30 seconds to flavor the oil, then discard. Add the chicken and stir-fry for about 5 minutes or until the chicken is lightly browned. Remove the chicken to a clay pot or casserole with a slotted spoon.

Add the sauce ingredients to the pot together with the mushrooms. Cover and braise over high heat for about 15 minutes. Serve at once.

YIELD: SERVES 6 TO 8

BRAISED SOY SAUCE–FLAVORED SQUAB

2 squab, about 14 ounces each
3 unpeeled fresh ginger slices
3 whole scallions, cut into 2-inch pieces

BRAISING LIQUID
¼ cup light soy sauce
½ cup dark soy sauce
3 tablespoons rock sugar
¼ cup rice wine
2 pieces cinnamon bark
4 star anise
1 tablespoon Sichuan peppercorns, unroasted
3 cups water

In a medium-sized pot of boiling water, combine the squab, ginger, and scallions. Boil for 5 minutes, drain, and set aside.

Bring the braising ingredients to a simmer, add the squab, and cook for 10 minutes. Cover, turn off the heat, and let the squab steep for 45 minutes. Remove and allow to cool slightly before cutting up and serving.

YIELD: SERVES 2 TO 4

Squab is fast becoming a standard item in Hong Kong restaurants, second only to chicken in the poultry category, and gaining in popularity. Farms in the New Territories (and, increasingly, deep in mainland China) ship them into Hong Kong every day. Chefs prepare them in many different ways: deep-fried, stir-fried, stuffed, and roasted. I enjoy them braised, as in this recipe. It is a technique that preserves all of the delicate taste and texture of the squab; it also allows one to introduce complementary and contrasting flavors by way of the braising liquid. And squab cooked this way can easily be reheated. I like to serve them at room temperature as a special picnic item or as an entrée for a simple but elegant summer luncheon.

TWO-COURSE PEKING DUCK, LEE GARDENS–STYLE

Although Peking Duck is a northern Chinese dish, it is not hard to see why it is also a Hong Kong favorite. The crisp skin is a delicious combination of tastes, color, and textures. It is made by air-drying the duck, which is then coated and roasted slowly in a special oven. At the Lee Gardens' Rainbow Room restaurant, it is brought out on a serving cart, hot from the oven, with the chef and two waiters in attendance. The skin is removed without any of the remaining underlying fat and then wrapped by the waiter in thin pancakes and served with finely shredded scallions. Because it is Hong Kong–style, the duck is served with hoisin sauce, a Cantonese touch, instead of the traditional sweet bean sauce of the North. Lee Gardens offers one of the best Peking Duck dinners in all of Hong Kong, which is saying a great deal.

In the second course, the rest of the duck meat is usually shredded and stir-fried with vegetables. One year, I challenged the chef at Lee Gardens to make something entirely different for the second course. He came up with this brilliant idea: duck rolls, in which the duck meat is shredded, mixed with seasonings

4 cups hot water
4- to 4½-pound fresh duck
1 teaspoon five-spice powder
1 teaspoon salt

BASTING LIQUID
2 tablespoons malt sugar
2 tablespoons honey
6 tablespoons dark soy sauce
1 tablespoon rice wine vinegar

1 cup water

SECOND COURSE INGREDIENTS
1½ cups finely chopped duck meat from thighs and legs
½ cup (about 5) fresh water chestnuts, peeled and sliced
3 tablespoons finely chopped whole scallions
¼ teaspoon salt
Pepper to taste
1 head iceberg lettuce
1 package rice paper rounds
2 cups peanut oil, for deep-frying
Cornstarch, for dusting
Hoisin sauce, for dipping

In a large pot, baste the duck several times with hot water. Place an "S" hook in the neck area to secure the duck and allow to dry either in a cool, drafty place for 5 hours or in front of a fan for 2 hours. When the duck is properly dried, the skin will feel like parchment paper. Season the inside of the duck with five-spice powder and salt.

In a large pot, combine the basting liquid ingredients and bring them to a boil. Turn off the heat and baste the duck several times with the hot liquid. Allow the duck to dry again; this time it should take about half the time or less.

Preheat the oven to 450° F. Place the duck on a rack inside a roasting pan and pour in 1 cup water. Roast the duck for 20 minutes. Reduce the heat to 350° F and continue to cook for 40 minutes. The skin should be crisp and a mahogany-brown color.

Remove the duck from the oven and allow it to cool for about 10 minutes before serving.

Skin the duck, slice the breast meat, and serve with Chinese pancakes (made according to the recipe on page 204), shredded scallions, cucumber sticks, and a bowl of hoisin sauce.

YIELD: SERVES 4 TO 6

For the second course, mix the finely chopped duck meat, water chestnuts, scallions, salt, and pepper to taste.

Separate the iceberg lettuce leaves into single cups. Keep refrigerated until ready to serve.

When you are ready to make the duck rolls, fill a large bowl with warm water. Dip a rice paper round in the water to soften for a few seconds. Remove and drain on a linen towel.

Place about 2 to 2½ tablespoons of the duck mixture on the edge of the rice paper. Roll the edge over the mixture once, fold up both ends of the rice paper, and continue to roll to the end. The roll should be compact and tight, rather like a short, thick sausage about 3 inches long. Set the roll on a clean plate and continue the process until you have used up all the mixture.

The duck rolls can be made ahead to this point, covered with plastic wrap and refrigerated for up to 4 hours.

Heat the oil in a wok or deep skillet until it is moderately hot, dust the duck rolls lightly with cornstarch, and deep-fry them a few at a time. They have a tendency to stick to one another at the beginning of frying, so do only a few at a time. Drain on paper towels.

To eat, place a duck roll inside a lettuce cup with a dab of hoisin sauce and wrap up.

YIELD: MAKES 20 DUCK ROLLS

and fresh water chestnuts for texture, then enclosed in delicate rice-paper wrappers and deep-fried. These are served rolled up in lettuce leaves with a bit of hoisin sauce. This works beautifully, capturing all the flavors of the various ingredients. The refreshing lettuce combined with the tasty duck rolls make a perfect second duck course.

This is a good example of the imaginative innovation that is going on all the time in Hong Kong. Chefs do not forsake their Chinese heritage but, like modern alchemists, change their traditional materials into something new and delightful. Food in Hong Kong is contemporary without compromising traditional approaches and techniques. It is hard to think that a Peking Duck dinner can be improved upon, but this second course shows it can be.

SICHUAN GARDEN'S SMOKED TEA DUCK

The Hong Kong cuisine may assimilate the best of all other cuisines, but it does not obliterate other great traditional styles. As a result, the Sichuan cuisine is very much alive throughout Hong Kong and most impressively in evidence in the Sichuan Garden Restaurant. The management recruited some of the best chefs from Sichuan province to train its staff. Inevitably, a touch of Cantonese–Hong Kong lightness and sensitivity came into play and, to my taste, brought even greater refinement to this classic dish. It is easy to see why it is so popular. The rich, smoky duck meat is uniquely delicious — vaguely reminiscent of excellent, aged smoked ham — while the skin is delightfully crackling-crisp. At the Sichuan Garden it is served with small, flat bread buns but I prefer Chinese pancakes (page 204).

The recipe does require a bit of labor but it is not nearly as involved as it would seem. The three cooking steps are quite straightforward, and although the process takes time, you will be rewarded and your guests will be impressed by a delicious and elegant centerpiece for your special dinner.

One 3½- to 4-pound duck

MARINADE
5 tablespoons salt
2 tablespoons Sichuan peppercorns, roasted and ground
2 tablespoons sesame oil
1 cup rice wine
2½ cups water

1 cup camphor wood chips or hickory chips
½ cup jasmine tea leaves
3 cups peanut oil, for deep-frying

Butterfly the duck by splitting it open along the backbone; remove the backbone. Flatten the duck with the palm of your hand. Make two small holes, one on either side of the breastbone, and tuck the legs through. This will help hold the shape of the duck when it is marinating and later when it is smoked.

Combine the marinade ingredients in a medium-sized bowl, mixing well to dissolve the salt. Place the duck in a shallow, noncorrosive pan and pour the marinade over. Cover with plastic wrap and refrigerate for 8 hours or over-night.

Blanch the duck in a large pot of boiling water for 2 minutes and dry it in front of a fan for at least 3 hours.

Soak the wood chips in water. Make a charcoal fire in a covered outdoor grill. When the coals are ash-white, using long tongs, push the hot coals to either side, leaving the center empty. Carefully place a pie tin filled with water in the empty space. Add the wood chips and tea leaves on the coals. Place the duck skin side down on the grill, cover, and let it smoke for about 35 minutes. Remove the duck from the grill onto a heat-proof platter. Heat water in a tightly covered wok or large steaming pot, set in a rack, and place the duck *and* platter on the rack. Gently steam the duck for 1½ hours. Cool thoroughly. The duck can be prepared ahead to this point.

Heat a wok or large, deep casserole until it is hot and add the oil. When oil is hot, deep-fry the duck until it is golden and crisp, about 8 to 10 minutes.
YIELD: SERVES 4 TO 6

COLD DRUNKEN CHICKEN

One 3- to 3½-pound chicken
2 teaspoons salt
3 unpeeled fresh ginger slices, ¼ inch thick
3 whole scallions, cut in half

WINE-BRAISING LIQUID
2 cups rice wine
3 tablespoons Chinese rose wine or vodka
2 teaspoons salt
¼ cup light soy sauce
5 cups Rich Chicken Stock (page 221)

Blanch the chicken in a large pot of boiling water for 3 minutes. Drain well. Rub the inside of the chicken with salt and stuff with the ginger slices and scallions.

Bring the braising liquid to a boil in a large pot. Add the chicken, reduce the heat, and simmer for 10 minutes; turn it over and simmer another 10 minutes. Cover, turn off the heat, and let the chicken sit in the liquid until it is thoroughly cool. Refrigerate the chicken overnight and then cut up and serve along with Braised Jellyfish (page 35).

YIELD: SERVES 4 TO 6

This is an example of the creativity of Hong Kong chefs. They have taken the blandly receptive meat of the chicken and transformed it into something of rich and exotic flavors. Classically, the dish was made with rice wine but in this recipe the chefs have innovatively infused the bird with the more assertive Chinese rose wine, but orange or other flavored liqueurs can be substituted as well. Like the Hong Kong chefs, experiment!

This dish can be made well ahead of time. It may be served at room temperature, as an appetizer, or warm to open a meal. Any way you choose, it is a winning recipe.

GINGERY CHICKEN WINGS WITH PINEAPPLE

The pineapple, originally native to South America, is now widely cultivated in Southeast Asia. The ones you find in Hong Kong are usually from Thailand or the Philippines. Although pineapple is sold as fruit to be eaten ripe or pickled in a mild brine as a snack, cooked pineapple is also widely used in Hong Kong recipes. This inexpensive home-style dish is typical of recipes in which pineapple is combined with meats. The tart, sweet taste of the fruit complements the rich, tasty chicken wings. This dish is easy to make and reheats well. Be careful not to overcook the pineapple.

1½ pounds chicken wings (about 10 wings)

MARINADE
1 tablespoon light soy sauce
1 tablespoon ginger juice
2 teaspoons rice wine
2 teaspoons cornstarch

3 tablespoons peanut oil
1 tablespoon finely chopped peeled fresh ginger
1 teaspoon sugar
2 cups fresh pineapple, cut up into 1-inch cubes
3 tablespoons Rich Chicken Stock (page 221)
2 tablespoons bean sauce
1 teaspoon salt

To bone the chicken wings, cut to the bone above the joint joining the wing to the wing drummette. Grab the joint with a paper towel and twist; the bone of the drummette should come out. Push the meat up, exposing most of the bone. With your finger, make a small pocket where the bone was lodged. Repeat the procedure for the joint between the wing and wing tip. Bone all the wings.

In a medium-sized bowl, combine the marinade with the prepared wings and let them marinate for 20 minutes.

Heat a wok or large skillet until it is hot and add the oil. Pan-fry the wings until they are nicely browned and set them aside.

Drain the wok, leaving 1 tablespoon of oil. Add the ginger and stir-fry for 30 seconds. Then add the remaining ingredients and stir to mix well. Add the browned chicken wings and continue to cook for about 7 minutes or until the wings are done.

YIELD: SERVES 4 TO 6

SHREDDED CHICKEN IN OYSTER SAUCE

¾-pound chicken breasts, boned (about 2–2½ breasts from a medium-sized chicken)

COATING
1 egg white
2 teaspoons cornstarch
1 teaspoon salt

½ cup peanut oil, for velveting (page 271)

SAUCE
1 tablespoon oyster sauce
2 tablespoons rice wine
4 tablespoons Rich Chicken Stock (page 221)
½ teaspoon cornstarch mixed with ½ teaspoon water
¼ teaspoon salt
1 teaspoon sesame oil

GARNISH
2 tablespoons finely chopped whole scallions

Place the chicken in the freezer for about 20 minutes or until it is firm to the touch. Cut it into slices and finely shred it. Add it to a bowl with the coating mixture and refrigerate for 20 minutes.

Heat a wok or large skillet until it is hot and add the oil. When the oil is moderately hot, add the chicken and stir quickly to separate. When the chicken turns white, remove immediately and drain in a colander.

Combine all the sauce ingredients in the wok and bring to a simmer. Return the chicken to the sauce and give the mixture a few turns to mix well. Garnish with scallions and serve at once.

YIELD: SERVES 2 TO 4

One of the tests of virtuosity in cooking as in other endeavors is to know when to leave the unimprovable as it is. In Hong Kong, many simple, home-style recipes have been untouched by the often radical innovations that characterize the new cuisine. This traditional Cantonese offering is one such classic. It is quick and easy to make. Serve it with rice and another vegetable dish and you have a tasty and nutritious meal.

RICE-PAPER CHICKEN ROLLS

I love these rice-paper chicken rolls because, unlike the traditional Cantonese spring rolls, these are lighter and more delicate. When fried, rice paper becomes translucent, almost transparent, and irresistibly crisp —and stays that way for a while. Combined with a tasty filling, it makes a delicious treat. Once the rolls are put together, they can be covered and refrigerated and deep-fried just before serving.

1 pound chicken breasts, skinned and boned

MARINADE
1 teaspoon finely chopped garlic
2 tablespoons finely chopped whole scallions
2 teaspoons oyster sauce
1 teaspoon light soy sauce
1 teaspoon rice wine or dry sherry
1 teaspoon sugar
½ teaspoon salt
½ teaspoon five-spice powder

One 8-ounce package Banh Tran rice paper rounds
¼ pound fresh water chestnuts, peeled and sliced
Fresh coriander leaves
2 cups peanut oil, for deep-frying

Cut the chicken into 3-inch by ½-inch strips. In a small bowl, combine the chicken with the marinade ingredients and marinate for 1 hour at room temperature.

When you are ready to make the Rice-Paper Chicken Rolls, fill a large bowl with warm water. Dip one of the rice paper rounds in the water and let it soften for a few seconds. Drain it on a linen towel.

Add a piece of marinated chicken, a slice of water chestnut, and one coriander leaf to the edge of the rice paper. Roll the edge over the mixture once, fold up both ends of the rice paper, and continue to roll to the end. The roll should be about 3 inches long, compact and tight, rather like a short, thick sausage. Set it on a clean plate and continue the process until you have used up all the chicken.

The Rice-Paper Chicken can be made ahead to this point, covered with plastic wrap, and refrigerated for up to 4 hours.

Heat the peanut oil in a wok or deep skillet until it is moderately hot, and deep-fry the chicken a few pieces at a time for 3 to 5 minutes or until they are a light golden brown. They have a tendency to stick to one another at the beginning of the frying so do only a few at a time.

Drain on paper towels and serve at once.
YIELD: MAKES 30 TO 35 CHICKEN ROLLS

VELVET CHICKEN WITH CRUNCHY WALNUTS

1 pound chicken breasts, boned and cut into
    ½-inch cubes

COATING
½ teaspoon salt
1 egg white
1 teaspoon sesame oil
2 teaspoons cornstarch

1 cup peanut oil, for velveting (page 268)
4 garlic cloves, peeled and finely sliced
2 teaspoons finely chopped peeled fresh ginger
6 garlic shoots or whole scallions, finely sliced
2 teaspoons salt
½ cup Rich Chicken Stock (page 221) mixed with
    1 teaspoon cornstarch
½ cup walnut halves

Combine the chicken with the coating ingredients in a medium-sized bowl and refrigerate for about 20 minutes.

Heat a wok or large skillet until it is hot and add the oil. When the oil is moderately warm, quickly add the chicken, stirring to prevent the pieces from sticking. Turn off the heat and allow the chicken to rest in the warm oil for about 5 minutes or until it looks completely white. Pour the contents of the wok into a colander set inside a large stainless steel bowl, reserving some of the oil.

Wipe the wok clean, return 1 tablespoon of the drained oil back to the wok and reheat. Add the garlic, ginger, garlic shoots, and salt, and stir-fry for 30 seconds. Add the chicken stock mixture and bring it to a boil. Return the drained chicken and mix well. Add the walnuts to heat through and serve at once.

YIELD: SERVES 2 TO 4

About walnuts, scholars tell us that the Chinese have been integrating their taste and texture into Chinese cuisine for two thousand years. It would be an understatement to say that they are a popular element in the Chinese cooking repertory. You may see mounds and mounds of them in Hong Kong food markets. As this recipe demonstrates, they add texture, rich body, and a unique flavor to other foods, especially bland foods like chicken. This is a quick and easy meal to prepare; serve it with plain rice and a vegetable, such as bok choy.

ROAST "PIPA" CHICKEN

The Chinese have a lute or mandolin called the pipa, *and there is in China a yellow loquat that, because of a similarity in shape to this musical instrument, is also called the* pipa. *The reference here is to a butterflied duck or chicken, opened to resemble the* pipa. *One can usually find this type of dish in a restaurant or deli in Hong Kong, where there are large commercial roasting ovens. It can be easily duplicated in homes in the West. You can even cook it on the barbecue.*

3- to 3½-pound whole chicken

COATING
4 tablespoons white rice vinegar
1 tablespoon red vinegar
2 teaspoons rice wine
2 teaspoons honey
3 tablespoons water

MARINADE
1½ tablespoons Chinese rose wine or rice wine
1 teaspoon red fermented bean curd
1 tablespoon black beans
½ teaspoon five-spice powder
1 tablespoon finely chopped garlic
2 teaspoons salt
2½ tablespoons sugar

Butterfly the chicken by splitting it open along the backbone and removing the backbone. Flatten it out with the palm of your hand, pushing against the top of the chicken. Make a small hole on each side of the breastbone near the tail, and tuck the legs through. This will hold the shape of the bird while roasting.

Bring a large pot of water to a boil and blanch the chicken for 5 minutes. Remove and allow to dry for 1 hour in a cool, drafty place or in front of a fan.

Bring the coating ingredients to a boil in a wok and coat the skin side of the chicken several times with this mixture. Allow the chicken to dry again. Meanwhile, combine in a blender the marinade mixture and rub this evenly on the inside of the chicken. Place the chicken skin side down on a rack to marinate for at least 4 hours in a cool, drafty place or overnight in a refrigerator, uncovered.

Preheat the oven to 450° F. Place the chicken, skin side up on a rack set inside a large roasting pan and bake for 5 minutes. Lower the oven temperature to 350° F and continue to cook for 30 to 40 minutes or until the chicken is brown and crisp.

Let the chicken cool for 10 minutes and then carve into serving pieces.
YIELD: SERVES 4 TO 6

FOUR-COLOR OMELET

1 preserved egg (Thousand-Year Egg)
1 salted duck egg
4 chicken eggs, beaten
2 tablespoons finely chopped whole scallions
1 tablespoon finely chopped fresh coriander
Freshly ground white pepper to taste
2 tablespoons peanut oil

Peel and cut the preserved egg into small dices and set aside. Crack the salted duck egg, cut the white into small dices, and combine with the beaten chicken eggs. Cut the yolk up into small dices and combine with the preserved egg.

Combine the beaten eggs with the scallions, coriander, and pepper.

Heat a wok or large skillet until it is hot and add the oil. Add the beaten eggs and stir-fry gently. When the eggs have barely set, add the preserved egg and salted egg yolk. Continue to cook for a few minutes until the eggs are warm through and cooked. Serve at once.

YIELD: SERVES 2 TO 4

Eggs are an esteemed food in Hong Kong as elsewhere. What is unique to Hong Kong is the availability of a vast variety of eggs: duck, quail, chicken, and pigeon and as many as twelve different types of each in any one market stall. Besides fresh eggs, there are sun-dried eggs; preserved eggs, including the Thousand-Year Eggs; duck eggs that have been preserved in a mixture of clay, fine ash, and salt, then rolled in straw; and salted duck eggs preserved in clay. And Hong Kong chefs do wonderful things with all of them. In a cooking school in Mongkok, a Kowloon neighborhood, I watched a master chef create this Four-Color Omelet. The various subtle colors blended together but were still discernible at the end, while the different tastes of duck and chicken eggs also came through. It is a truly unusual and delicious omelet. This is a recipe for an adventurous cook, but it will repay you with an impressive and beautiful meal.

The preserved and salted duck eggs can be found in Chinese stores or specialty shops.

THAI CURRIED CHICKEN AND POTATO STEW

Many of the cuisines of Asia can be sampled in Hong Kong. This recipe is inspired by those of Thailand and Indonesia. It combines an Indian staple, curry, with Indonesian coconut milk and chicken to make a perfect family dish. It can be made ahead of time and is easily reheatable. Over rice, it makes a simple meal full of exotic flavors and aromas.

2 pounds chicken thighs, skinned and boned (about 9 to 10 thighs)

MARINADE
1 tablespoon light soy sauce
1 tablespoon rice wine
2 teaspoons ginger juice
2 teaspoons cornstarch

1½ tablespoons peanut oil
2 teaspoons finely chopped garlic
1 teaspoon finely chopped peeled fresh ginger
2 tablespoons finely chopped whole scallions
3 tablespoons Madras curry paste or powder
2 teaspoons salt
1 tablespoon sugar
2 cups coconut milk
2 tablespoons light soy sauce
1 cup Rich Chicken Stock (page 221)
1½ pounds potatoes, peeled and cut into 1½-inch chunks

GARNISH
3 sprigs fresh coriander

Cut the chicken into bite-size pieces and combine with the marinade ingredients; let stand for 30 minutes.

Heat a wok or large skillet until it is hot. Add the oil and when it is quite hot, quickly stir-fry the chicken pieces for about 2 minutes, then add the garlic, ginger, and scallions and continue to stir-fry for 1 minute. Add the curry, salt, sugar, coconut milk, soy sauce, and chicken stock. Bring the mixture to a boil and pour the contents of the wok into a clay pot or casserole. Cover and braise over low heat for 15 minutes. Add the potatoes and continue to braise for another 15 minutes or until the potatoes are cooked. Skim off any surface fat. Garnish with coriander and serve at once.

YIELD: SERVES 4 TO 6

DEEP-FRIED CHICKEN LIVERS WITH CASHEW NUTS

1 pound chicken livers

MARINADE
1½ tablespoons light soy sauce
2 tablespoons Sichuan peppercorns, roasted and ground
1 tablespoon rice wine
2 teaspoons cornstarch

2 cups peanut oil, for deep-frying
2 teaspoons sesame oil
½ cup cashew nuts
2 tablespoons finely chopped whole scallions
1 tablespoon finely chopped peeled fresh ginger
2 teaspoons finely chopped garlic
2 tablespoons oyster sauce
¼ cup Rich Chicken Stock (page 221) mixed with
    ½ teaspoon cornstarch

Clean the chicken livers by removing the connecting veins and any bits of fat. Rinse in cold water and dry thoroughly with paper towels.

Combine the chicken livers and marinade in a small bowl and let sit for about 1 hour at room temperature.

Heat a wok or large deep skillet until it is hot and add the oil. When the oil is slightly smoking, deep-fry the chicken livers for 1 minute in two batches. Remove with a slotted spoon and set aside. Drain the wok and wipe clean, reserving 1 tablespoon of oil.

Reheat the wok and return oil along with the sesame oil. Add the cashew nuts, scallions, ginger, and garlic and stir-fry for 1 minute. Then add the oyster sauce and chicken stock blended with cornstarch; when the sauce is boiling, return the chicken livers and heat through. Serve at once.

YIELD: SERVES 4 TO 6

Chicken livers may be found wherever chickens can be had, that is, almost everywhere in the world. Though all chicken livers are equal, some are more equal than others: Hong Kong chicken livers are, it seems to me, richer, plumper, lighter, and smoother than others, reminiscent, really, of French duck and goose livers; Hong Kong chickens must be well fed. When in Hong Kong, I make a point of always showing off this lovely ingredient to my cooking classes. Chicken livers may be barbecued, stir-fried, or as in this recipe, deep-fried. This technique does not make them oily or too rich. Be assured that our local chicken livers make a delectable dish, especially with the addition of cashew nuts, which provide a nice contrast of texture and taste.

This is a simple and inexpensive dish that may serve as a first course or, with rice and a vegetable, as a meal in itself.

CHICKEN ROLLS

It is not difficult to see why this recipe is a Hong Kong favorite. The chicken livers are combined with ground pork and both are wrapped in caul fat. The pork flavor permeates everything and as the caul fat slowly dissolves, it adds a rich aromatic flavor and a crisp texture to the roll. It is a perfect appetizer, served with Salt-and-Pepper Dip (page 227). In Hong Kong it is innovatively served with Worcestershire sauce. This recipe can be halved easily.

½ **pound caul fat**
½ **pound chicken livers**
1 **pound ground fatty pork**

MARINADE
½ **tablespoon light soy sauce**
2 **teaspoons sugar**
2 **teaspoons rice wine**
1 **teaspoon freshly ground white pepper**
1 **teaspoon sesame oil**

3 **tablespoons finely chopped fresh coriander**
1 **tablespoon finely chopped peeled fresh ginger**
1 **teaspoon salt mixed with 2 teaspoons Sichuan
    peppercorns, roasted and ground**
Cornstarch, for dusting
2 **cups peanut oil, for deep-frying**

Soak the caul fat in a bowl of cold water for 5 minutes; this will allow it to unravel easily.

Trim the fat off the chicken livers. Blanch for 30 seconds in boiling water. Drain well, and when cool, cut them into slices. In a medium-sized bowl, mix the ground pork with all the marinade ingredients and let sit for 20 minutes. Combine the livers with the pork mixture and add the coriander, ginger, and peppercorns.

Cut the caul fat into twenty 5-inch squares. Lay out a square of caul fat and place several tablespoons of pork and liver mixture at one end. Roll the edge over the mixture once, fold up both ends of the caul, and continue to roll to the end. The roll should be about 3 inches long, compact and tight, rather like a short, thick sausage. Set it on a clean plate and continue the process until you have used up all the mixture. The recipe can be made ahead to this point. Wrap the chicken rolls well in plastic wrap and refrigerate until ready to cook.

Set up a steamer and gently steam the chicken rolls for about 5 minutes. Remove and allow the rolls to cool thoroughly. This may be done 2 hours ahead.

Just before serving, lightly coat the rolls with cornstarch. Heat the oil in a wok or deep skillet until it is very hot and deep-fry the chicken rolls until golden and crisp.

Drain the chicken rolls on paper towels and serve them at once with Salt-and-Pepper Dip (page 227) and bottled Worcestershire sauce.

YIELD: MAKES 30 TO 35 CHICKEN ROLLS

BRAISED SQUAB IN PORT WINE

Two ¾- to 1-pound squab
2 tablespoons peanut oil
2 peeled garlic cloves, crushed

BRAISING LIQUID
2 cups Rich Chicken Stock (page 221)
1 cup port wine
½ cup rice wine
1 teaspoon salt
2 tablespoons light soy sauce
2 tablespoons oyster sauce
2 teaspoons dark soy sauce
2 slices unpeeled fresh ginger
2 whole scallions, cut into 2-inch segments

Blanch the squab in a medium-sized pot of boiling water for 2 minutes. Drain and blot completely dry with paper towels.

Heat a wok or large skillet until it is hot and add the oil and garlic. Pan-fry the squab whole on each side for 2 to 3 minutes or until they are golden and crisp. Drain thoroughly on paper towels.

Combine all the braising ingredients in a clay pot or casserole and bring to a boil. Add the squab, cover, reduce the heat to low, and slowly braise for 1 hour or until the squab are tender. Skim off any excess fat and serve at once.

YIELD: SERVES 2 TO 4

Until recently, Western wines have been rather ignored by Asian chefs — there was nothing like coq au vin east of the Suez. In Hong Kong, however, chefs have begun playing with such new ingredients as port wine and they are producing memorable foods, as this recipe indicates. The braising technique allows the wine and the marinade flavors to be absorbed into the moist and tender squab meat. Less fatty than chicken, the squab can do with a bit of added richness — and this may be another reason for its growing popularity among health-conscious consumers. This meal reheats nicely and may be made well ahead of time. It smells and looks as good as it tastes.

MINCED DUCK WITH FRESH LETTUCE CUPS

This is a variation on the Lee Gardens' Rainbow Room innovative second-course Peking Duck. It is delicious and easy to make. The tender, richly flavored duck is balanced by the light crisp noodles and the refreshing coolness of the lettuce leaves.

2 cups peanut oil, for deep-frying
2 ounces (1 small package) bean thread noodles
1 small head iceberg lettuce

STIR-FRY MIXTURE
1 ounce dried Chinese black mushrooms
1 tablespoon peanut oil
2 tablespoons finely chopped garlic
2 teaspoons finely chopped fresh ginger
2 cups minced meat, from ½ roast duck (page 112)
¼ pound fresh water chestnuts, drained and finely chopped
¼ pound canned bamboo shoots, drained and finely chopped
1½ tablespoons oyster sauce
1 tablespoon light soy sauce
1 tablespoon dark soy sauce
1 tablespoon rice wine
2 teaspoons sugar
1 tablespoon whole scallions, finely chopped

Hoisin sauce

Heat a wok or deep-frying pan over high heat and add the peanut oil. Separate the bean thread noodles inside a paper bag to prevent them from flying all over your kitchen, and deep-fry them in the oil. They will puff up instantly. You may have to do this in several batches. Drain the noodles on paper towels and set them aside.

Separate whole leaves from the lettuce, trying not to break them. Trim them into manageable cups; you should get 9 to 10 cups. Refrigerate until ready to use.

Soak the mushrooms in warm water for 20 minutes or until they are soft and pliable. Squeeze out the excess water and cut away the stems. Finely chop the remaining mushroom caps and set aside.

Heat a wok or large skillet over high heat and add 1 tablespoon peanut oil. When the oil is moderately hot, add the garlic and ginger and stir-fry for 30 seconds. Then add the chopped duck meat and the rest of the stir-fry ingredients. Stir-fry over high heat for about 3 minutes. Turn off the heat.

Serve in the following manner: in each lettuce cup, add a generous portion of fried bean thread noodles, then add several tablespoons of the stir-fried duck mixture and a teaspoon or so of hoisin sauce. Fold the lettuce over and eat like a taco.

YIELD: SERVES 4

BRAISED OYSTER-SAUCE SQUAB

Two ¾- to 1-pound squab
1 cup dried Chinese black mushrooms
4 cups peanut oil, for deep-frying

BRAISING LIQUID
3½ cups Rich Chicken Stock (page 221)
2 teaspoons sugar
5 tablespoons oyster sauce
2 teaspoons dark soy sauce
2 slices unpeeled fresh ginger
2 whole scallions, cut into 1-inch segments

Blanch the squab in a medium-sized pot of boiling water for 2 minutes. Drain and allow to cool thoroughly.

Soak the mushrooms in a bowl of warm water for about 20 minutes or until they are soft and pliable. Squeeze out the excess water and cut off and discard the woody stems.

Heat a wok or large skillet until it is hot and add the oil. When oil is hot, deep-fry the squab for about 5 minutes or until they are golden and crisp. Drain thoroughly on paper towels.

Combine all the braising liquid ingredients in a clay pot or casserole and bring to a boil. Add the squab, cover, reduce the heat to low, and slowly braise for 1 hour or until the squab are tender. Skim off any excess fat and serve at once.

YIELD: SERVES 2 TO 4

There is something warm, comfortable, and "homey" about clay pots. And, of course, clay-pot food is invariably hearty, aromatic, and mouth-watering. Hong Kong chefs use this mundane cooking technique, adding a sophisticated touch or two, but preserving all the rustic charm of the process and the product, as in this recipe. The squab is first "double-cooked"— blanched to prepare the flesh and deep-fried to make the skin crisp and richly brown—and then braised slowly. The smoky, tangy, subtle flavors of sauce and mushrooms permeate the squab and fill the house with appetizing aromas. This hearty dish reheats very well and is perfect for a winter's evening.

PAN-FRIED CHICKEN WITH LEMON

This is my version, although slightly more lemony, of a delightful traditional dish I have enjoyed at the King Bun, one of the best Cantonese restaurants in Hong Kong. The master chef, Leung King, has subtly transformed this well-known dish into a delicious, lemon-flavored chicken. The batter is very light, and the sauce has a delicate lemon flavor, not too sweet or too thick. The lemon slices add a pleasing touch of color.

1 pound chicken breasts, skinned and boned (about 3 half breasts)

BATTER
3 tablespoons all-purpose unbleached white flour
½ teaspoon baking powder
2 teaspoons cornstarch
1 egg
½ teaspoon salt
2 tablespoons water

½ cup peanut oil, for pan-frying

LEMON SAUCE
2 tablespoons lemon juice
1 lemon, cut into thin slices
⅓ cup Rich Chicken Stock (page 221)
1 teaspoon rice wine
1 tablespoon sugar
1 teaspoon salt
Freshly ground white pepper to taste
1 teaspoon cornstarch mixed with 1 teaspoon water
2 teaspoons sesame oil

Pound the chicken breasts lightly between two pieces of plastic wrap.

Combine all the batter ingredients together in a medium-sized bowl and mix well. Add the pounded chicken and coat thoroughly.

Heat a wok or large skillet until it is hot and add the oil. Pan-fry the chicken pieces over moderate heat until they are brown and crisp, about 2 minutes on each side. Drain on paper towels.

Drain the wok and wipe clean. Add the lemon sauce ingredients and simmer for 2 minutes. Meanwhile, cut the chicken into bite-size pieces and arrange on a serving platter. Pour the sauce over the chicken and serve at once.

YIELD: SERVES 2 TO 4

DEEP-FRIED MILK WITH QUAIL EGGS

1½ cups milk
¾ cup evaporated milk
½ teaspoon salt
½ teaspoon freshly ground white pepper
5 tablespoons cornstarch
2 tablespoons finely chopped Smithfield ham
1 dozen fresh quail eggs

BATTER
6 tablespoons all-purpose unbleached white flour
6 tablespoons cornstarch
1 tablespoon baking powder
6 to 8 tablespoons water
2 teaspoons salt

1 cup peanut oil, for deep-frying

This is a recent innovation in the new Hong Kong cuisine and was a revelation to me when I first sampled it. The milk-based custard, not at all typically Chinese, is modified by the deep-frying technique. The result is a light, mild morsel, with a golden-brown-and-white crust and a creamy, tasty interior, a palpable contrast of textures when bitten into; and it pairs deliciously with the delicate quail eggs. The two together make an impressive first course or can be part of a light luncheon.

Combine the two milks, salt, pepper, cornstarch, and ham in a medium-sized saucepan and mix until smooth. Simmer over low heat for about 10 minutes or until the mixture has thickened. Oil a baking pan and pour in the cooked milk mixture and allow it to cool thoroughly. Cover with plastic wrap and refrigerate. This can be done the night before.

Add the quail eggs to a medium-sized pot of simmering water. Cook them for about 3 minutes. Gently remove, drain, and allow to cool.

In a medium-sized bowl, mix the batter ingredients and allow to sit at room temperature for 30 minutes. Cut the milk curd into diamond-shaped, 3-inch pieces. Gently crack and peel the quail eggs.

Heat a wok or deep skillet until it is hot and add the oil. When it is slightly smoking, dip some of the milk pieces into the batter with a slotted spoon, and deep-fry them for 3 minutes or until they are golden and crisp. Drain them on paper towels and repeat the process until you have fried all the milk pieces. Then dip the cooked quail eggs in the batter and deep-fry.

Arrange on a platter and serve at once.
YIELD: SERVES 4 TO 6

SICHUAN GARDEN'S SMOKED SQUAB

Second in popularity to the delicious, smoked-tea duck from the Sichuan Garden in Hong Kong is this tasty recipe made with squab. Less fatty than duck, squab require less cooking. Like the smoked duck, on page 114, it requires a triple-preparation cooking technique. However, most of the work can be done way ahead of time, with the last-minute frying to be done just before serving.

The smoked squab is an excellent main course for an elegant dinner party and well worth the effort.

Two ¾- to 1-pound squab

MARINADE
3 tablespoons salt
1 teaspoon Sichuan peppercorns, roasted and ground
2 teaspoons sesame oil
½ cup rice wine
1½ cups water

1 cup camphor wood chips or hickory chips
½ cup jasmine tea leaves
2 cups peanut oil, for deep-frying

Butterfly the squab by splitting them open along the backbone; remove the backbone. Flatten the squab with the palm of your hand. Make two small holes, one on either side of the breastbone, and tuck the legs through. This will help hold the shape of the squab when it is marinating and later when it is smoked.

Combine the marinade ingredients in a medium-sized bowl, mixing well to dissolve the salt. Place the squab in a shallow noncorrosive pan and pour the marinade over. Cover with plastic wrap and refrigerate for 8 hours or overnight.

Soak the wood chips in water for 20 minutes and drain. Make a charcoal fire in a covered outdoor grill. When the coals are ash-white, using long tongs, push the hot coals to either side, leaving the center empty. Carefully place a pie tin filled with water in the empty space. Scatter the wood chips and tea leaves on the coals. Place the grill back on and add the squab, cover and let them smoke for about 35 to 45 minutes. Remove them from the grill and allow to cool completely. The squab can be prepared ahead to this point.

When you are ready to serve the squab, heat a wok or large, deep skillet until it is hot and add the oil. When oil is hot, deep-fry the squab until they are golden brown and crisp. Serve at once.
YIELD: SERVES 2 TO 4

CHIUCHOW GARDEN'S CHICKEN WITH CRISP SPINACH

3 pounds chicken thighs
2 tablespoons dark soy sauce
1 teaspoon rice wine
1 teaspoon salt
1 teaspoon sugar
2 teaspoons cornstarch
½ pound fresh spinach
2 cups peanut oil, for deep-frying
1 teaspoon coarsely ground black peppercorns

Remove the skin from the thighs, and bone by cutting on one side with a sharp knife and scraping off the meat on the other. (Or have your butcher do it.) You should have about 1½ to 2 pounds of meat after boning. Cut the meat into bite-sized 1-inch pieces.

Combine the dark soy sauce, rice wine, salt, sugar and cornstarch and mix in the chicken pieces.

Remove the spinach leaves from their stalks; discard the stalks. Wash the leaves in several changes of cold water until thoroughly cleaned. Completely dry the spinach leaves in a salad spinner or on paper towels.

Heat the oil in a wok or deep skillet until it is very hot. Add a good handful of spinach leaves and deep-fry them until they become deep green and crisp — about 45 seconds. Remove with a slotted spoon and drain on paper towels. Continue to deep-fry the spinach leaves in batches until they are all fried. Pour off most of the oil, leaving about 2 tablespoons.

Reheat the wok until it is quite hot. Add the chicken mixture and stir-fry over high heat for about 5 minutes. Add the black pepper and continue to cook for 2 more minutes or until the chicken is completely cooked. Place the chicken on a platter, surrounded with the deep-fried spinach leaves and serve at once.

YIELD: SERVES 4 TO 6

This simple but very satisfying dish is a great favorite of mine. I first sampled it many years ago at the Chiuchow Garden restaurant in Kowloon. Savory stir-fried chicken is served with a mound of crisp deep-fried chili leaves. Robust chicken thighs are used here because they can take longer cooking than breast meat and they can also absorb more and richer flavors. The chicken is finally finished with a generous topping of freshly ground black peppercorns.

In this recipe, I have substituted spinach leaves for chili leaves, which I find work just as well. The crisp texture of the fried leaves, their rich, deep, jade-green color, and the appetizing chicken make an outstanding combination that is quick and easy to prepare and pleasing to the eye as well as the palate.

A word of caution — when deep-frying the spinach leaves, make sure to stand a good distance away, since the water from the spinach will initially make it sputter and pop.

LAI CHING HEEN'S SPINACH AND CHICKEN ROLLS

Rice paper used to wrap food to be steamed or deep-fried is a fairly recent innovation in Hong Kong cooking. Popular in Southeast Asian countries such as Vietnam and Thailand, rice paper entered Hong Kong with the influx of immigrants from these countries in the 1970s.

Chinese chefs in Hong Kong, always alert to new possibilities, quickly introduced dishes featuring these light and delicate wrappers. They hold their form nicely and, once fried, crackle like parchment paper. I especially like this version, which I first sampled at the Lai Ching Heen, one of the best Chinese restaurants in Hong Kong. They are a delightful appetizer.

2 tablespoons salt
½ pound medium shrimp, peeled and deveined
½ ounce dried Chinese black mushrooms
1 cup tightly packed fresh spinach leaves
2 tablespoons peanut oil
2 tablespoons finely chopped garlic
3 tablespoons finely chopped shallots
½ pound boneless chicken thigh meat, coarsely chopped
½ cup carrots, peeled and finely diced
2 teaspoons salt
2 tablespoons rice wine
1 package Banh Tran rice paper rounds
2 cups peanut oil, for deep-frying

To clean the shrimp, please follow the directions on page 34. Coarsely chop the shrimp and set aside.

Soak the mushrooms in warm water for 20 minutes or until they are soft. Squeeze out the excess water and cut away the stems. Finely chop the mushroom caps and set aside.

Remove the spinach leaves from their stalks; discard the stalks. Wash the leaves in several changes of cold water until thoroughly cleaned. Dry the spinach leaves thoroughly in a salad spinner or on paper towels.

Heat wok or large skillet and add the 2 tablespoons of oil. When the oil is moderately hot, add the garlic and shallots and stir-fry for 15 seconds. Add the chicken and stir quickly to separate; cook for 2 minutes, then add the shrimp, mushrooms, spinach, carrots, and salt and stir-fry for 1 minute. Add the rice wine and cook on high heat until most of the wine has evaporated. Remove all the filling ingredients from the wok and drain, retaining the liquid. Return the liquid back to the wok and reduce to 1 tablespoon over high heat. Add this to the filling mixture, mix well, and allow to cool thoroughly.

When you are ready to make the rolls, fill a large bowl with warm water. Dip one of the rice paper rounds in the water and let it soften for a few seconds. Drain on a linen towel.

Add about 1½ tablespoons of filling at the end of the rice paper round. Roll the edge over the mixture once, fold up both ends of the rice paper and continue to roll to the end. The roll should be about 3 inches long, compact, and tight, rather like a short, thick sausage. Set it on a clean plate and continue the process until you have used up all the filling. The rolls can be made ahead to this point, covered with plastic wrap, and refrigerated for up to 4 hours.

Heat the peanut oil in a wok or deep skillet until it is moderately hot, and deep-fry a few rolls at a time for 3 to 4 minutes or until they are light golden brown. They have a tendency to stick to each other at the beginning of the frying so do only a few at a time.

Drain the rolls on paper towels and serve at once.

YIELD: MAKES ABOUT 28 TO 30 ROLLS

MEAT

~~~~~~

SLOW-STEWED PORK IN A CLAY POT

SAVORY CUSTARD WITH PORK

STEAMED BEEF WITH ORANGE

DOUBLE-COOKED ORANGE SPARERIBS

BEEF AND GARLIC SHOOTS IN OYSTER SAUCE

SATAY-STYLE BEEF WITH CHINESE BROCCOLI

STIR-FRIED BEEF IN A NOODLE NEST

STIR-FRIED BEEF WITH PICKLED MUSTARD GREENS

STIR-FRIED LAMB WITH BAMBOO SHOOTS AND BLACK MUSHROOMS

STIR-FRIED MEATBALLS

BEEF WITH MUSHROOMS AND BABY CORN

SPICY PORK WITH FRESH MUSHROOMS AND CHINESE OLIVES

HAM AND MUSTARD GREEN CLAY-POT CASSEROLE

SPARERIBS WITH SALTED CHINESE PLUMS

FRIED PORK WITH SICHUAN PEPPERCORNS

STIR-FRIED BEEF WITH SICHUAN PRESERVED VEGETABLE

DRY-FRIED SICHUAN BEEF

SICHUAN SESAME BEEF

STIR-FRIED FROGS' LEGS IN BLACK BEAN SAUCE

CHINESE HONEY HAM

SHREDDED PORK WITH YELLOW CHIVES

SHREDDED CHILI BEEF

SIZZLING BEEF WITH SCALLIONS

STIR-FRIED PORK WITH WALNUTS

STIR-FRIED PORK WITH SALTED FISH

FRIED SPARERIBS WITH SPICED SALT

BRAISED BEEF SHANK

CURRIED BEEF STEW

As these recipes demonstrate, pork is the "red meat" of Chinese cuisine. For a number of ecologically sound reasons, pigs (along with chickens) are the main source of animal protein for most Chinese; only the northern Chinese have incorporated beef and lamb into their diets. In Hong Kong, however, with its easy access to world food supplies and with its cosmopolitan population, all types of meat dishes are readily available. While pork recipes predominate, there is a gradually increasing acceptance of other meats, especially beef, into the traditional canon.

In addition, the introduction of new flavorings such as orange juice, the use of Chinese rose wine and such ingredients as asparagus, and the frequent use of egg white to lighten the texture of meat have subtly but significantly altered classic recipes in the spirit of the new Chinese cuisine of Hong Kong.

SLOW-STEWED PORK IN A CLAY POT

One of the more unusual dishes to be enjoyed in Hong Kong is braised mutton, which I had for the first time at King Bun, a well-known, Cantonese-style restaurant in Hong Kong. The chef, Leung King, is acknowledged as one of the master chefs of the Colony. In fact, he is often referred to as the No. 1 chef —an honor not lightly bestowed. Cooking game is one of his many specialties, as is braised mutton, which probably has been introduced from northern China, either from Beijing or Outer Mongolia, where it is more common. The Cantonese, in general, are not fond of lamb, let alone mutton, though goat, which is leaner and less strong-tasting than mutton, is also prepared in Hong Kong. The dish I enjoyed at King Bun was served with highly seasoned dipping sauces, no doubt to hide any mutton taste remaining after the long braising.

Because mutton is difficult to find in America, I have substituted fresh pork belly, which is similar in that it is fatty. You may substitute beef brisket if you wish. In either case, long cooking turns an otherwise unpalatable piece of meat into a

15 large dried Chinese black mushrooms
3 whole dried citrus peels
2 sticks dried bean curd
3½ pounds fresh pork belly or beef brisket
2 tablespoons peanut oil
4 unpeeled fresh ginger slices, ½ inch thick
3 garlic cloves, peeled and crushed
¼ cup sliced bamboo shoots, ¼ inch thick
8 fresh or canned whole water chestnuts
4 tablespoons bean sauce
4 tablespoons oyster sauce
3 tablespoons sugar
2 lemon leaves or 2 slices lemon peel
3 tablespoons rice wine
2 tablespoons light soy sauce
3 tablespoons dark soy sauce
4 cups water

DIPPING CONDIMENTS
2 cubes fermented bean curd
4 finely shredded lemon leaves or 2 tablespoons
    lemon zest
4 fresh red chili peppers, seeded and finely shredded
1 tablespoon peanut oil

Soak the mushrooms in a bowl of warm water for about 20 minutes or until they are soft and pliable. Squeeze out the excess water and cut off and discard the woody stems.

Soak the citrus peels and the bean-curd sticks in a large bowl of hot water for about 20 minutes or until they are soft. Drain and set aside.

Cut the pork belly or beef brisket into bite-size chunks. Blanch for 20 minutes in a large pot of boiling water. Drain and set aside.

Heat a wok or large skillet and add the peanut oil, ginger, and garlic and stir-fry for 15 seconds. Then add the bamboo shoots, water chestnuts, mushrooms, citrus peel, and bean-curd sticks. Stir-fry for 30 seconds. Add the rest of the ingredients, bring to a boil, and turn off the heat.

In a large clay pot or heavy casserole, combine the blanched meat with the mixture from the wok. Bring this to a boil and simmer for 1½ hours or until the meat is very soft. Skim the surface from time to time to remove excess fat.

When you are ready to serve the stew, put the condiments together in a small serving dish. Heat the oil until it is smoking and pour it over the condiments.

YIELD: SERVES 4 TO 6

very palatable, even delicious, meal.

Guests can use the dipping sauces according to their taste. This hearty dish is definitely most suitable for winter. Here I have combined the condiments together into one simple condiment.

SAVORY CUSTARD WITH PORK

2 dried citrus peels
1 pound ground pork
4 eggs, beaten
1 tablespoon finely chopped fresh coriander
2 teaspoons finely chopped peeled fresh ginger
3 tablespoons finely chopped whole scallions
½ cup finely chopped onions
2 teaspoons finely chopped garlic
1 teaspoon salt
1 teaspoon sugar
2 teaspoons cornstarch
2 teaspoons sesame oil
1 teaspoon freshly ground black pepper

Soak the citrus peels in warm water for 20 minutes or until they are soft; drain and finely chop.

Combine the citrus peel, pork, and the rest of the ingredients and mix well. Turn into a clay pot or heat-proof casserole, cover, and set on a rack inside a steamer. Steam vigorously for 20 minutes.

Preheat the oven to 450° F. Remove the clay pot from the steamer and uncover. Bake in the oven for 15 to 20 minutes or until the top is lightly browned. Serve immediately.

YIELD: SERVES 4 TO 6

This home-style dish has been updated and employs the unusual technique of baking, which hardly exists in the traditional cuisine since Chinese kitchens do not contain ovens. Although steaming in a clay pot may seem strange to Western cooks, it does make sense; it gives a velvety smooth texture to the egg custard through gentle vapors rather than harsh heat and allows the delicate flavorings of the seasoning to permeate the pork without drying it out. The final baking — and this is the new twist in Hong Kong — gives the top a brown and crusty texture.

STEAMED BEEF WITH ORANGE

This might be termed the Chinese equivalent of meatloaf. Here, ground pork and beef are combined with dried citrus peel to form a hearty and zesty dish. Because it is steamed rather than baked, the meat retains the juiciness and the tang of the citrus. This is definitely an old-fashioned, home-style dish but it is now appearing on Hong Kong restaurant menus. It reminds me of the recent fad for basic "meat and potatoes" and "diner" food in America. Apparently, in Hong Kong as well as here, a generation has come of age that is too busy (or unwilling or unable) to cook for itself but, rather, seeks out food "like Mom used to make." Nostalgia takes many forms. This is a nutritious meal, easy to make, and it reheats nicely when gently steamed.

1 pound ground beef
½ pound ground fatty pork butt
3 dried citrus peels, soaked and finely chopped
2 egg whites
2 tablespoons finely chopped Smithfield ham
   (the fatty part)
½ teaspoon salt
2 teaspoons sesame oil
2 teaspoons sugar
2 teaspoons cornstarch
1 tablespoon water

GARNISH
3 tablespoons oyster sauce
3 tablespoons finely chopped whole scallions

Combine all the ingredients except the water together in a food processor. Mix for 30 seconds, then add the water and continue until the mixture is slightly sticky.

Oil a heat-proof platter and, with a spatula, spread the mixture on the platter; it should be about 1 inch thick. Set on a rack inside a large, tightly covered wok or pot. Cover and gently steam for 8 minutes or until the mixture is firm.

Cut the loaf into pieces, pour the oyster sauce over the top, and garnish with the scallions.
YIELD: SERVES 2 TO 4

DOUBLE-COOKED ORANGE SPARERIBS

1½ pounds pork spareribs

MARINADE
2 teaspoons salt
2 teaspoons light soy sauce
2 teaspoons sugar
1½ tablespoons cornstarch
1½ tablespoons ginger juice

2 cups peanut oil, for deep-frying

SAUCE
2 tablespoons finely chopped orange zest
2 teaspoons orange liqueur
½ cup orange juice
1 tablespoon cornstarch
2 teaspoons light soy sauce
2 teaspoons sesame oil

This innovative dish is an example of how chefs in Hong Kong are adapting their cuisine to suit more cosmopolitan tastes. It is an East-West dish, made by traditional methods and ingredients but combining them with other, new ingredients and flavors — in this case, quite far from traditional Chinese taste. The technique used here is double-frying, which is needed to tenderize the spareribs. The sauce, more familiar to Western chefs, makes a delightful combination because the tart yet sweet taste of the oranges perfectly complements the meat.

Have your butcher cut the spareribs into small, bite-size pieces.

Combine the marinade ingredients together in a medium-sized bowl. Add the spareribs and mix well with the marinade. Let them sit at room temperature for 1½ hours or overnight in the refrigerator. There is no need to drain the marinade.

Heat the oil in a wok or deep skillet. Deep-fry the spareribs in several batches for about 10 minutes. Remove them with a slotted spoon and drain thoroughly on paper towels. Reheat the oil until it is very hot. Deep-fry the spareribs a second time for about 5 minutes. They should look very brown and crisp. Drain them on paper towels.

Drain off the oil, leaving one tablespoon. Add all the sauce ingredients except the sesame oil, bring to a boil, and return the ribs to the wok. Stir well to coat the ribs with the sauce. Add the sesame oil and continue to cook for another 2 minutes. Serve at once.

YIELD: SERVES 4

BEEF AND GARLIC SHOOTS IN OYSTER SAUCE

This classic southern Chinese dish has been slightly updated in Hong Kong. In this version, the meat is coated and marinated in egg white to give it a fluffy, light texture. It is then stir-fried with young garlic shoots and slices of young ginger. The oyster sauce adds richness.

1 pound market steak, beef fillet, or New York steak

MARINADE
2 teaspoons light soy sauce
1 teaspoon rice wine
1 teaspoon sugar
1 egg white
2 teaspoons ginger juice
1 tablespoon cornstarch
2 teaspoons sesame oil

1 cup peanut oil

2 teaspoons finely chopped fresh garlic
6 garlic shoots or whole scallions, cut into 3-inch pieces
6 young ginger slices, ¼ inch thick
4 fresh or canned water chestnuts, peeled and sliced

SAUCE
½ cup Rich Chicken Stock (page 221)
1½ tablespoons oyster sauce
1 teaspoon light soy sauce
2 teaspoons rice wine
1 teaspoon cornstarch

Place the steak in the freezer for about 20 minutes or until it is firm to the touch. Then cut it, against the grain, into thin slices. Mix together the marinade ingredients, add the meat, and refrigerate for 20 minutes.

Heat a wok or large skillet until it is hot. Add the oil and when it is quite hot, quickly stir-fry the beef for about 3 minutes. Turn the contents of the wok into a colander set in a bowl to drain, reserving some of the oil.

Reheat the wok and return 1 tablespoon of the drained oil. Add the garlic, garlic shoots, and ginger and stir-fry for 1 minute. Add the water chestnuts and continue to stir-fry for another 30 seconds; add the sauce ingredients and bring the mixture to a boil. When the sauce has thickened, return the drained beef and mix well. Serve at once.

YIELD: SERVES 4

SATAY-STYLE BEEF WITH CHINESE BROCCOLI

¾ to 1 pound market steak, beef fillet, or New York
    steak

MARINADE
2 teaspoons dark soy sauce
1 teaspoon shrimp paste
2 teaspoons cornstarch
2 teaspoons rice wine

1 pound Chinese broccoli
1 cup peanut oil, for deep-frying

SAUCE
½ teaspoon shrimp paste
1 cup Rich Chicken Stock (page 221)
½ teaspoon satay sauce or 2 teaspoons chili bean sauce
1 teaspoon sugar
1 teaspoon dark soy sauce
2 teaspoons rice wine
½ teaspoon cornstarch mixed with ½ teaspoon water

Place the steak in the freezer for about 20 minutes or until
it is firm to the touch. Then cut it, against the grain, into
thin slices. Place the meat in a medium-sized bowl with all
the marinade ingredients and refrigerate for 20 minutes.

Separate the Chinese broccoli leaves and stalks, and cut
the leaves into 2-inch pieces. Now peel the stalks, and cut
them into thin diagonal slices. Wash well in several changes
of water. Blanch the broccoli for 2 minutes in a large pot of
salted boiling water. Drain well and arrange on a serving
platter; set aside in a warm spot.

Heat a wok or large skillet until it is hot; add the oil.
When the oil is very hot, add the meat and stir for 2 minutes.
Drain the contents of the wok into a colander set inside a
stainless steel bowl, reserving some of the oil. Return 1 tablespoon of the drained oil to the wok and reheat. Add the
shrimp paste and 3 tablespoons of the chicken stock and stir-
fry for 30 seconds; add the remaining stock and the rest of
the sauce ingredients and cook for another 30 seconds.
When the sauce has thickened, return the meat to the wok
and stir to mix well. Serve with the warm broccoli.

YIELD: SERVES 4 TO 6

*With the influx of Southeast
Asians in the mid-1970s into
Hong Kong, the effect on food
styles has been striking. You will
find many new restaurants in
Hong Kong serving food in the
style of Singapore, Indonesia,
and Thailand. Some of these
cuisines are even represented in
venerable Cantonese-Chinese
restaurants, the traditional
restaurants of Hong Kong. This
illustrates the flexibility of the
culinary traditions in Hong Kong
and the receptivity to new
techniques and influences. A
strong and venerable cuisine can
adapt to the new without feeling
threatened — this is what makes
food in Hong Kong new and
unique, as well as traditional.*

*This dish combines the flavors
of Southeast Asia by using satay
sauce and shrimp paste in a
combination of pungency and
spiciness that people in Hong
Kong love. Here the beef is paired
with Chinese broccoli, which, with
its slightly mustardy tang,
makes it a wonderful foil for the
other assertive flavors.*

*Satay sauce is very hot: use
it cautiously; and if you are
unable to find it, simply
substitute chili bean sauce.*

STIR-FRIED BEEF IN A NOODLE NEST

Such dishes as this are very popular in Hong Kong, and it is easy to understand why. The savory marinated beef is served in a crisp and very edible nest of noodles or taro root; together they make an eye- and palate-pleasing ensemble of great appeal that is not as difficult to make as you might think. The "nest," in any case, can be made hours in advance. After marinating, the beef is quickly stir-fried. With preserved mustard greens and chilis, and with the oyster sauce unifying the meat pieces, you have a mouth-watering and impressive centerpiece for any special dinner.

1 pound market steak, beef fillet, or New York steak

MARINADE
1 tablespoon light soy sauce
2 teaspoons rice wine
1 teaspoon dark soy sauce
1 tablespoon cornstarch
1 teaspoon sugar
1 teaspoon sesame oil

NOODLE NEST
1 small package (about 2 ounces) bean thread noodles
4 cups peanut oil, for deep-frying

2 tablespoons thinly sliced garlic
⅔ cup preserved mustard greens, thinly shredded
1 green pepper, seeded and finely shredded
2 small fresh red chili peppers, seeded and finely shredded

SAUCE
½ teaspoon salt
2 teaspoons sugar
3 tablespoons oyster sauce
2 tablespoons Rich Chicken Stock (page 221)

Place the steak in the freezer for about 20 minutes or until it is firm to the touch. Cut it into thin slices against the grain and then finely shred them by stacking the slices and cutting with a cleaver. Place the meat in a medium-sized bowl with all the marinade ingredients and refrigerate for 20 minutes.

Separate the bean thread noodles inside a paper bag to keep them from scattering. Heat the oil in a wok or large deep pan. Place the noodles between 5-inch and 7-inch stainless steel colanders or strainers and submerge into the hot oil, holding the top strainers down with a spatula to help keep the shape of the nest. The noodles should puff up immediately. Carefully ladle hot oil over any uncooked threads. Drain the nest on paper towels and then place on a serving platter. Strain and drain the oil from the wok to be reused another time, reserving 2 tablespoons for now.

Heat a wok or large skillet and return the 2 tablespoons oil. When it is hot, quickly stir-fry the beef for about 3 minutes. Remove the meat with a slotted spoon and set aside. Reheat the wok and add the garlic, preserved mustard greens, pepper, and chili and stir-fry for about 2 minutes. Add the sauce ingredients; when the mixture comes to a boil, return the meat and stir gently for 30 seconds to heat thoroughly. Place the stir-fried beef mixture in the noodle nest and serve at once.

YIELD: SERVES 4 TO 6

STIR-FRIED BEEF WITH PICKLED MUSTARD GREENS

Pickled mustard greens are a staple among southern Chinese. When properly made, they are like the half-pickled dill pickle, slightly sour but still crunchy, with some texture. Pickled mustard greens are often combined with pork or beef. The meat here is shredded rather than sliced and served on a bed of crisp-fried rice noodles. The noodles combine with the beef mixture to add to the textural quality of the dish. It should be eaten immediately, as the noodles have a tendency to get soggy.

¾ to 1 pound market steak, beef fillet, or New York steak
1 cup peanut oil, for deep-frying
4 ounces (¼ package) thin dried rice noodles

COATING
1 egg white
2 teaspoons cornstarch
2 teaspoons rice wine
1 tablespoon light soy sauce
1 teaspoon sesame oil
1 teaspoon sugar

1 cup preserved mustard greens, shredded
2 fresh red chili peppers, seeded and shredded
1 teaspoon finely chopped peeled fresh ginger
2 teaspoons finely chopped garlic

SAUCE
2 teaspoons oyster sauce
1 teaspoon light soy sauce
2 teaspoons dark soy sauce
1 teaspoon sesame oil
2 teaspoons sugar
3 tablespoons Rich Chicken Stock (page 221) mixed with ½ teaspoon cornstarch

Place the steak in the freezer for about 20 minutes or until it is firm to the touch.

Heat the cup of oil in a wok or deep pan until it is quite hot. Meanwhile, separate the dried rice noodles inside a paper bag to keep them from scattering. Deep-fry the noodles until they are crisp and puffed up — this will just take seconds. Remove the noodles immediately with a strainer or slotted spoon and drain on paper towels. Drain the wok, reserving 3 tablespoons oil.

Cut the meat, against the grain, into slices and then finely shred the slices into matchstick-size pieces. Place the meat in a large bowl with all the coating ingredients, mix well, and refrigerate for 20 minutes.

Heat a wok or large skillet until it is hot; add the reserved oil. Quickly stir-fry the meat for 1 minute until it is lightly browned. Remove immediately with a slotted spoon and add the pickled mustard greens, chilies, ginger, and garlic. Stir-fry for another minute. Then add all the sauce ingredients and bring the mixture to a simmer. Return the meat and stir to mix well.

Place the fried noodles on a plate, ladle the meat over the center, and serve at once.

YIELD: SERVES 4 TO 6

STIR-FRIED LAMB WITH BAMBOO SHOOTS AND BLACK MUSHROOMS

Although the Cantonese of Hong Kong are not particularly fond of lamb, you can find delicious lamb dishes in northern-style restaurants. Like many other recipes, the dish has been modified to the Hong Kong style. It is lighter, coated with an egg-white marinade, and served on a bed of crispy, airy noodles — a cloud of noodles. This is actually calculated to soften the impact of the strong-tasting lamb. In Hong Kong mutton or goat might be substituted as well.

The mushrooms add a lovely smoky touch, the peppers, color, and the bamboo shoots, texture. This is a quick and easy dish to put together and makes a very satisfying meal.

½ cup dried Chinese black mushrooms
1 pound boneless lean loin of lamb

MARINADE
1 egg white
2 teaspoons cornstarch
2 teaspoons light soy sauce
1 teaspoon sugar
1½ teaspoons rice wine
1 teaspoon sesame oil

1 small package (2 ounces) bean thread noodles
1 cup peanut oil, for deep-frying
2 fresh red chili peppers, seeded and shredded
½ cup bamboo shoots, shredded
1 tablespoon finely chopped fresh ginger
1 tablespoon finely chopped garlic

SAUCE
3 tablespoons oyster sauce
1 tablespoon light soy sauce
2 teaspoons sugar
2 teaspoons sesame oil
4 tablespoons Rich Chicken Stock (page 221)
1 teaspoon cornstarch mixed with 1 teaspoon water

1½ tablespoons finely chopped fresh coriander

Soak the mushrooms in a bowl of warm water for about 20 minutes or until they are soft and pliable. Squeeze out the excess water and cut off and discard the woody stems. Finely shred the caps and set aside.

Place the lamb in the freezer for about 20 minutes or until it is firm to the touch. Then cut it, against the grain, into slices. Place the meat in a large bowl with all the marinade ingredients and refrigerate for 20 minutes.

Separate the bean thread noodles inside a large paper bag to keep them from scattering. Heat a wok or large skillet until it is hot and add the oil. Deep-fry the noodles for 10 to 15 seconds until they have puffed up and are crisp but not brown. Remove with a slotted spoon, reserving the oil, and drain on paper towels. Place noodles on a serving platter.

Preheat the wok or large skillet until it is hot and return the oil. When the oil is very hot and smoking slightly, add the lamb and stir-fry for 2 minutes. Pour into a colander set inside a stainless steel bowl, reserving 1½ tablespoons oil.

Return the drained oil to the wok and reheat. Add the mushrooms, red peppers, bamboo shoots, ginger, and garlic and stir-fry for 2 minutes. Then add the sauce ingredients and continue to cook for 1 minute. Return the lamb to the wok, stir to mix well, add the coriander, and give the mixture a final stir. Ladle the meat and vegetables over the noodles and serve immediately.

YIELD: SERVES 4 TO 6

STIR-FRIED MEATBALLS

It may strike you as contradictory to discover comparatively fatty foods like these meatballs featured in the new Hong Kong cuisine. We are all so health-conscious today and beef is not exactly prescribed as a "health food." However, the Chinese diet is so very well-balanced and wholesome that even beef can be nicely integrated into it — in moderation, of course. Hong Kong chefs, striving to create tasty foods, are thus free to use beef such as this. My associate, Gordon Wing, and I tested various new Hong Kong recipes for this dish before we settled upon this one. The fatty meat has both taste and texture, and the egg white lightens it. Poaching the meatballs first keeps them moist and well-shaped; stir-frying gives them a firm, buoyant texture that opens up to the moist, soft core when you bite into them. The poaching can be done well ahead of time; the stir-frying should be done just before serving. This is an unusual dish, so delectable you will make it again and again.

MEATBALL MIXTURE
1 pound fatty ground beef, such as chuck
1 egg white
2 tablespoons finely chopped whole scallions
1 teaspoon salt
Freshly ground white pepper to taste
2 teaspoons cornstarch
1 teaspoon sesame oil

1 pound Chinese broccoli
1½ tablespoons peanut oil
2 teaspoons finely chopped garlic
2 teaspoons finely chopped fresh ginger
1 teaspoon shrimp paste
4 tablespoons Rich Chicken Stock (page 221)
1 tablespoon rice wine
2 teaspoons sugar

Combine the meatball mixture in a food processor and mix until it is a light paste. Wet your hands and form walnut-sized balls. Poach the meatballs in a pot of boiling water for 2 minutes. Remove them with a slotted spoon and drain on paper towels.

Separate the broccoli stalks and cut the leaves into 2-inch pieces. Now peel the stems, and cut them into thin diagonal slices. Wash well in several changes of water. Blanch the broccoli in a pot of salted boiling water for 3 minutes, drain, and set aside.

Heat a wok or large skillet until it is hot and add the oil. Add the garlic, ginger, and shrimp paste and stir-fry for 10 seconds. Then add the stock, rice wine, and sugar. Return the meatballs and broccoli to this mixture and continue to stir-fry for 3 minutes or until the meat and vegetables are heated through. Serve at once.

YIELD: SERVES 4 TO 6

BEEF WITH MUSHROOMS AND BABY CORN

1 pound market steak, beef fillet or New York steak

MARINADE
2 teaspoons light soy sauce
2 teaspoons rice wine
1 teaspoon cornstarch
1 teaspoon sesame oil

1 cup fresh husked or canned baby corn, drained
1 pound fresh oyster mushrooms or fresh button
    mushrooms
3 tablespoons peanut oil
2 garlic cloves, peeled and crushed

SAUCE
1 tablespoon oyster sauce
2 teaspoons rice wine
3 tablespoons Rich Chicken Stock (page 221)
1 teaspoon sesame oil

Place the steak in the freezer for about 20 minutes or until it is firm to the touch. Then cut it, against the grain, into slices. Place the meat in a large bowl with all the marinade ingredients and refrigerate for 20 minutes.

If you are using fresh baby corn, blanch it in boiling water for 2 minutes and drain in a colander. Rinse the canned baby corn well in cold running water, drain, and set aside. Wipe the mushrooms clean.

Heat a wok or large skillet until it is hot and add 2 tablespoons of the oil. Stir-fry the meat for 1 minute and drain. Wipe the wok clean, reheat, and add another tablespoon of oil. Add the garlic and stir-fry for 10 seconds. Then add the whole mushrooms and corn and continue to stir-fry for another 2 minutes. Add all the sauce ingredients except for the sesame oil and stir to mix well. Return the meat to the mixture, give it a few stirs, and stir in the sesame oil. Serve at once.

YIELD: SERVES 4 TO 6

With foods from all over the world available to them, Hong Kong chefs are inspired to use them creatively. They keep to their traditions but ingeniously adopt, adapt, and combine old and new ingredients, in this case Chinese straw mushrooms from China and baby corn from Southeast Asia. Fresh straw mushrooms are unavailable, unfortunately, outside of Asia but you may use local fresh mushrooms or fresh oyster mushrooms as substitutes. Fresh baby corn is becoming more widely available in America, working its way from Thai cuisine into the popular repertory.

This easy-to-make and nutritious dish can be stir-fried in minutes.

SPICY PORK WITH FRESH MUSHROOMS AND CHINESE OLIVES

One of the great treats available in the Hong Kong markets is fresh straw mushrooms; they were originally cultivated on rice straw and hence the name. They are like button mushrooms in the West but have a more subtle and delicate, earthy flavor. Because they are difficult to store and deteriorate rapidly, they are not exported. Although they are available in cans in the West, I prefer to use fresh straw mushrooms. Olives are believed to have been first planted in China during the sixth century A.D. but are not widely used in Chinese cuisine. Olive oil is viewed as incompatible with most Chinese cuisine as it intrudes its own distinctive flavor into dishes cooked in it and is never used for deep-frying. However, in Hong Kong one can find pickled olives in the markets, and, of course, with Chinese flavors. They are occasionally available in America in jars imported from China. You can substitute Greek black olives if you are unable to find the Chinese ones. The combination of the mushrooms, pork, and olives works very well in terms of color, taste, and texture.

1 pound ground pork

MARINADE
2 teaspoons light soy sauce
1 teaspoon cornstarch
1 teaspoon sugar
1 teaspoon rice wine

2 tablespoons peanut oil

½ pound fresh straw mushrooms
3 fresh red chili peppers, shredded
2 teaspoons finely chopped garlic
5 Chinese olives, pitted
2 tablespoons rice wine

Mix the pork with the marinade ingredients in a medium-sized bowl. Let pork marinate for 30 minutes.

If the mushrooms are small, leave them whole; if large, cut them in halves or quarters and set aside.

Heat a wok or large skillet until it is hot and add 1 tablespoon of oil. Add the pork, stir-fry for 2 minutes, drain, and set aside.

Wipe the wok clean and reheat. Add the remaining tablespoon of oil and when it is hot, add the chilies and garlic. Stir-fry for 10 seconds and then add the mushrooms. Continue to cook for 2 minutes and then add the olives and rice wine. Stir-fry for another minute and return the pork to the wok. Continue to cook for another minute and serve at once.
YIELD: SERVES 4 TO 6

HAM AND MUSTARD GREEN CLAY-POT CASSEROLE

1 cup dried Chinese black mushrooms
½ pound preserved mustard green stems
½ pound Peking (Napa) cabbage
2 tablespoons peanut oil
3 slices fresh ginger
¼ cup Smithfield ham slices, 3 inch by ⅛ inch
1 cup Rich Chicken Stock (page 221)

SAUCE
1 tablespoon oyster sauce
2 teaspoons light soy sauce
1 tablespoon rice wine
1 teaspoon dark soy sauce
2 teaspoons sugar
1 teaspoon sesame oil

Soak the mushrooms in a bowl of warm water for about 20 minutes or until they are soft and pliable. Squeeze out the excess water and cut off and discard the woody stems.

Cut the mustard greens and cabbage into 2-inch strips.

Heat a wok or large skillet until it is hot and add the oil. Add the ginger slices and stir-fry for 30 seconds. Then add the greens and cabbage and stir-fry for 2 minutes. Remove and place the vegetables in a small clay pot or casserole. Add the mushrooms and then a layer of ham slices. Add the chicken stock and bring the mixture to a boil. Cover and simmer gently for 30 minutes; then add the sauce ingredients and simmer for an additional 2 minutes. Serve at once.

YIELD: SERVES 4

This is another nostalgic recipe making a comeback in Hong Kong. Most of its residents were once peasants or are of peasant stock, and this dish is redolent of the family hearth with its traditional clay pot simmering away, wafting its promise of hearty, nutritious meals. It is really quite good, and one can see why, beyond nostalgia, it is a popular item. The few slices of ham judiciously introduced are enough to flavor and add some substance to this mainly vegetarian casserole. Serve it with plain rice and you have a most satisfying hot meal for a cold winter's eve.

SPARERIBS WITH SALTED CHINESE PLUMS

A treat I used to get as a child, instead of candy, was salted or pickled plums, so I was fascinated to see in Hong Kong entire stores filled with dozens of varieties of salted plums for eating and cooking. Innovative methods to use these plums to flavor foods have been created there, as in this spareribs dish. The plums should be removed before serving, because even after cooking, they have a strong flavor. I love them, but they are an acquired taste.

1 pound pork spareribs
1 tablespoon peanut oil
3 garlic cloves, crushed
3 large slices fresh ginger
4 whole scallions, cut into 1-inch pieces
4 salted plums
1½ cups Rich Chicken Stock (page 221)

Cut the spareribs into small 2-inch pieces or have your butcher do it for you. Blanch the spareribs in boiling water for 5 minutes. Drain and set aside.

Heat a wok or large skillet and add the oil. Quickly stir-fry the garlic, ginger, and scallions for 30 seconds. Then add the spareribs and continue to stir-fry for 2 minutes, or until the spareribs are lightly brown. Remove the contents of the wok with a slotted spoon to a clay pot or casserole. Add the salted plums and chicken stock and bring the mixture to a boil. Cover and slowly simmer for 1 hour or until the spareribs are tender.

Skim the surface fat and remove the salted plums. If the sauce seems too thin, bring the mixture to a boil and reduce it until it is slightly thickened. Serve at once. This dish can be prepared ahead of time and reheated.

YIELD: SERVES 4

FRIED PORK WITH SICHUAN PEPPERCORNS

1 pound pork fillet or lean pork chops

COATING
1 egg white
1 tablespoon cornstarch
2 teaspoons light soy sauce
2 teaspoons rice wine

3 tablespoons peanut oil

GARNISH
Salt-and-Pepper Dip (page 227)

Place the pork in the freezer for about 20 minutes or until it is firm to the touch. Cut it into slices, 3 inch by ¼ inch, place in a medium-sized bowl with all the coating ingredients, and refrigerate for 20 minutes.

Heat a wok or large skillet until it is hot and add the oil. Quickly stir-fry the pork for about 2 to 3 minutes or until it is lightly browned. Immediately remove the pork to a dish and serve with the dipping sauce.

YIELD: SERVES 4 TO 6

When first-time visitors to Hong Kong eat Chinese food, they are struck by the number of condiments and sauces placed before every diner. This is done so that the diner can determine what or how much more flavoring is needed for a particular bite of food. It is a sophisticated and highly refined style of eating, I think. It works especially well when you have a dish such as this one, where pork is treated in a simple and straightforward manner, perfect for adjustment by the eater, rather than by the kitchen.

This is a simple and delicious way to enjoy pork.

STIR-FRIED BEEF WITH SICHUAN PRESERVED VEGETABLE

The venerable Cantonese cooks of Hong Kong have long since recognized and accepted the genius of the Sichuan regional (western China) cooking style. Here we have a recipe that uses Sichuan preserved vegetables to enhance the flavor and texture of other foods. These Sichuan delights are cured in ground chili pepper and salt. They are intensely strong in taste but they mellow with cooking, and they have a crunchiness that is retained throughout. They add a piquant touch to meat dishes such as this. Serve with plain rice or noodles, whose regal blandness is a nice accompaniment to the fiery flavors of Sichuan.

1 pound market steak, beef fillet, or New York steak

MARINADE
2 teaspoons light soy sauce
1 teaspoon rice wine
1 teaspoon sugar
2 teaspoons cornstarch
1 teaspoon sesame oil

2½ tablespoons peanut oil
2 tablespoons finely sliced garlic
6 tablespoons Sichuan preserved vegetable, rinsed and finely chopped
2 tablespoons Rich Chicken Stock (page 221)
1 tablespoon rice wine
2 teaspoons sugar

Place the steak in the freezer for about 20 minutes or until it is firm to the touch. Then cut it, against the grain, into ¼-inch slices. Place the sliced meat in a large bowl with all the marinade ingredients, mix well, and refrigerate for 20 minutes.

Heat a wok or large skillet until it is hot and add 1½ tablespoons of the oil. Add the garlic and stir-fry for 20 seconds, then add the beef and stir-fry an additional 30 seconds; remove the mixture from the wok with a slotted spoon. Add the remaining tablespoon of oil, and when it is hot, add the preserved vegetables and stir-fry for 1 minute. Add the rest of the ingredients and continue to stir-fry for 30 seconds. Return the meat and garlic to the wok and give the mixture a good stir. Serve at once.

YIELD: SERVES 4 TO 6

DRY-FRIED SICHUAN BEEF

¾ to 1 pound market steak, beef fillet, or New York
  steak
1 cup plus two tablespoons peanut oil, for stir-frying
2 teaspoons chili bean sauce
1 tablespoon hoisin sauce

2 teaspoons finely chopped garlic
3 tablespoons finely chopped whole scallions
2 teaspoons sesame oil
1 teaspoon salt
2 teaspoons sugar
2 teaspoons finely chopped fresh ginger
1 teaspoon Sichuan peppercorns, roasted and ground

Place the steak in the freezer for about 20 minutes or until it is firm to the touch. Then cut it, against the grain, into slices. Finely shred the slices into matchstick-sized strips.

Heat a wok or large skillet until it is hot and add the oil; add the meat and stir-fry for 1 minute. Drain the meat in a colander. Add the 2 tablespoons of peanut oil to the wok and return the meat. Quickly stir in the chili bean and hoisin sauce and continue to stir-fry for another minute. Mix in the garlic, scallions, sesame oil, and salt and stir-fry for 2 more minutes. Finally, add the remaining ingredients, stir-frying all the while. By this time, the meat should be quite dry and browned. Remove the meat with a slotted spoon and serve at once.

YIELD: SERVES 4 TO 6

Sichuan food in Hong Kong has been slightly tamed under the influence of the Cantonese tradition. It is nevertheless still relatively fiery and full of the contrasting flavors that are its hallmark. In this recipe, beef is cooked until most of the moisture escapes, leaving it with what might be considered only the essence of beef and with a dry texture. This makes the beef ideal for combining with different flavors. The result is an unusually delicious new way to eat beef.

I have found this dish to be equally tasty served at room temperature.

SICHUAN SESAME BEEF

Again, Sichuan essences are adapted into Hong Kong's new cuisine. Modified, mellowed, and molded to the Hong Kong taste, we have here a rich but not overly spicy dish. The marinade is the key medium or vehicle in this recipe, while the sesame seeds contribute a toasty crunchiness along with their distinct flavor. With rice and vegetables, this is a delicious and easy-to-make meal.

¾ to 1 pound market steak, beef fillet, or New York steak

MARINADE
1 tablespoon light soy sauce
2 teaspoons dark soy sauce
1½ teaspoons rice wine
1 teaspoon sugar
2 teaspoons sesame oil

1 cup peanut oil
1 tablespoon white sesame seeds, roasted

GARNISH
2 tablespoons finely chopped whole scallions

Place the steak in the freezer for about 20 minutes or until it is firm to the touch. Then cut it, against the grain, into slices. Add it to a large bowl with all the marinade ingredients and refrigerate for 20 minutes.

Heat a wok or large skillet until it is hot; add the oil. When the oil is hot and slightly smoking, add the meat and stir-fry for about 2 minutes. Drain the contents of the wok into a colander set inside a stainless steel bowl, reserving 1 tablespoon oil.

Return the drained oil to the wok and reheat. Add the sesame seeds and stir-fry for 10 seconds. Return the meat to the wok and continue to stir-fry for another minute. Turn onto a serving platter, garnish with scallions, and serve.

YIELD: SERVES 4 TO 6

STIR-FRIED FROGS' LEGS IN BLACK BEAN SAUCE

1½ pounds frogs' legs

MARINADE
1 tablespoon light soy sauce
2 teaspoons rice wine
2 teaspoons cornstarch

2 tablespoons peanut oil
2 green peppers, seeded and cut into squares, 2 inch by 2
   inch

BLACK BEAN SAUCE
2 tablespoons finely chopped black beans
1 tablespoon finely chopped whole scallions
2 teaspoons finely chopped garlic
1 teaspoon finely chopped peeled fresh ginger
1 teaspoon sugar
2 teaspoons light soy sauce
2 teaspoons rice wine
3 tablespoons Rich Chicken Stock (page 221)

Cut the frogs' legs at the joint into segments and combine them with the marinade ingredients in a medium-sized bowl. Place in the refrigerator for about 20 minutes.

Heat a wok or large skillet and add the oil. When it is hot, stir-fry the frogs' legs for 5 minutes, and then with a slotted spoon remove them to a clay pot. Add the green peppers to the wok and stir-fry them for 1 minute. Add the black bean sauce ingredients and continue to stir-fry another minute. Return the frogs' legs to the mixture and give several good stirs. Ladle the mixture into a clay pot or heat-proof casserole, cover, and cook over high heat for about 5 minutes or until the frogs' legs are tender. Serve at once.
YIELD: SERVES 4 TO 6

Frogs' legs are a true delicacy everywhere. I much enjoy demonstrating their preparation to my cooking classes in Hong Kong. The freshness of the legs is guaranteed and the "chicken of the fields," as they are known in the Cantonese dialect, are transformed into a succulent dish of subtle flavor and pleasing texture. The sauce here is classic Cantonese: pungent black beans with garlic and ginger, but the delicate taste of the frogs' legs is not overwhelmed. Frogs' legs may be obtained fresh in many Chinese markets in large urban areas. However, the frozen legs found at fish stores or ordered from your local butcher work just as well. In any case, they will be cleaned and ready to cook whether fresh or frozen. The majority of frogs' legs used in the United States come from either Florida or Louisiana. Plain rice is the appropriate accompaniment.

CHINESE HONEY HAM

Chinese ham from Yunnan was frequently referred to during my childhood in Chicago. My mother used to buy Smithfield ham as a substitute but always admonished me that it was never as good as Yunnan ham. I finally sampled the exquisite taste of the Chinese ham when my Hong Kong mentor, Willie Mark, introduced me to its rich salty flavor; it was perfectly cooked and endowed with the heavy but not cloying sweetness reminiscent of honey. In fact, the sweetness came from cooked-down rock sugar. It was a revelation to me, and I immediately set out to learn how it was cooked. The Yunnan ham required a complex series of soaking, poaching, and steaming — about five hours worth in all. As few would choose to spend Saturday evenings on such a chore — besides, Yunnan hams are not available outside of China — I thus concocted an easier but still reasonably similar version. This recipe works quite well. You must use Smithfield ham — it is closest in taste and texture to Yunnan style. The dish makes a splendid first course in any banquet or formal dinner and the ingredients may be doubled or tripled for larger amounts.

1-pound piece Smithfield ham
4 tablespoons rock sugar or sugar
½ cup hot water
1 tablespoon Grand Marnier Liqueur

Blanch the ham in a medium-sized pot of boiling water for 5 minutes. Drain and place the ham in a heat-proof bowl, adding just enough hot water to cover the top.

Set the bowl over slowly simmering water on a rack in a tightly covered wok or pot and steam the ham for 1 hour. Remove the ham and slice, discarding the liquid. Return the sliced ham to the bowl, add the sugar and hot water, and steam for another 45 minutes. Drain the ham liquid into a small saucepan over low heat and add the Grand Marnier. Give the sauce several stirs and pour over the ham. Serve at once.

YIELD: SERVES 4 TO 6

SHREDDED PORK WITH YELLOW CHIVES

1 pound lean tenderloin pork or boneless pork chops

MARINADE
1 egg white
1 tablespoon cornstarch
1 tablespoon light soy sauce
1 tablespoon rice wine
1 teaspoon sesame oil

½ cup dried Chinese black mushrooms
1 cup peanut oil
½ pound Chinese yellow or green chives, cut into
    3-inch pieces
2 teaspoons finely chopped fresh ginger
1 tablespoon finely chopped garlic
1 teaspoon salt
2 teaspoons rice wine

Place the pork in the freezer for about 20 minutes or until it is firm to the touch. Then cut it into slices and then into shreds. Place the meat in a large bowl with the marinade ingredients and refrigerate for 20 minutes.

Soak the mushrooms in a bowl of warm water for about 20 minutes or until they are soft and pliable. Squeeze out the excess water and cut off and discard the woody stems. Finely shred the caps.

Heat a wok or large skillet until it is hot and add the oil. When the oil is hot, add the pork and stir-fry for 20 seconds. Remove the meat and drain off all but 2 tablespoons of oil. Reheat the wok and add the mushrooms, chives, ginger, garlic, and salt and stir-fry for 2 minutes. Return the pork to the wok and continue to stir-fry for another minute. Finally add the rice wine and give the mixture several stirs. Turn onto a platter and serve at once.

YIELD: SERVES 4 TO 6

Some things don't change. Here we have a traditional dish that resists modification. The "yellow chives" are simply Chinese green chives grown in the dark. They have a mildly pungent, earthy flavor reminiscent of onions and garlic that goes particularly well with pork. Because they add a pleasantly distinct taste to simple foods, they are much prized by chefs. Paired with mushrooms, as in this recipe, they help to create an unusual treat. If the yellow chives are unavailable, you may substitute fresh leeks. Be sure to trim the green leaves and wash the leeks well before cutting.

SHREDDED CHILI BEEF

Until recently, traditional Cantonese of Hong Kong cooking rarely made use of chili peppers. Today, however, they are an integral ingredient in many restaurant and family meals. As usual, Hong Kong chefs were alert to their patrons' wishes and tastes, and they took over what is essentially a Sichuan style and made it their own. The particular chilies used by Hong Kong chefs impart a rather mild bite and a bright red color to the dish, qualities that help make it a very popular meal. What's more, it's easy to make.

1 pound market steak, beef fillet, or New York steak

MARINADE
1½ tablespoons rice wine
1 tablespoon light soy sauce
1 egg white
2 teaspoons sugar
2 teaspoons cornstarch
2 teaspoons dark soy sauce

1 cup peanut oil
5 fresh red chili peppers, seeded and finely shredded
1 green pepper, seeded and finely shredded
1 teaspoon salt
1 tablespoon finely chopped garlic
1 tablespoon finely chopped peeled fresh ginger
2 tablespoons rice wine

Place the steak in the freezer for about 20 minutes or until it is firm to the touch. Then cut it, against the grain, into slices, and then into shreds. Place the meat in a large bowl with all the marinade ingredients, mix well, and refrigerate for 20 minutes.

Heat a wok or large skillet until it is hot and add the oil. When the oil is quite hot, add the beef and stir for 30 seconds. Remove and drain all but 2 tablespoons of oil. Reheat the wok and add the chilies, green pepper, and salt and stir-fry for 1 minute. Remove with a slotted spoon, add the rest of the ingredients, and continue to stir-fry another minute. Return the beef, chilies, and pepper to the wok and continue to stir-fry for another 2 minutes. Serve immediately.

YIELD: SERVES 4 TO 6

SIZZLING BEEF WITH SCALLIONS

¾ to 1 pound market steak, beef fillet, or New York
   steak

MARINADE
2 teaspoons sesame oil
2 teaspoons ginger juice
1 tablespoon rice wine
2 teaspoons light soy sauce
½ teaspoon salt
2 teaspoons cornstarch
1 egg white

½ cup peanut oil
10 whole scallions, cut into 1-inch pieces
2 fresh red chili peppers, seeded and shredded
1 teaspoon bean sauce
2 teaspoons chili bean sauce
1 teaspoon finely chopped garlic
3 tablespoons Rich Chicken Stock (page 221)
2 tablespoons oyster sauce

Place the steak in the freezer for about 20 minutes or until it is firm to the touch. Then cut it, against the grain, into slices. Place the meat in a large bowl with the marinade ingredients and refrigerate for 20 minutes.

Heat a wok or large skillet until it is very hot and add the oil. When the oil is smoking slightly, add the meat and stir quickly to separate. After 1 minute, drain the meat into a colander set inside a stainless steel bowl, reserving 2 tablespoons oil.

Meanwhile, heat a cast-iron frying pan on a separate burner until it is very hot.

Return the drained oil to the wok and reheat. Add the scallions, chilies, bean sauce, chili bean sauce, and garlic and stir-fry for 30 seconds. Pour in the chicken stock and oyster sauce and simmer for 30 seconds longer; return the meat to the wok. At the table, pour the entire contents of the wok into the sizzling hot frying pan. Stir once or twice and serve immediately.

YIELD: SERVES 4 TO 6

Fashion in food, as with clothes, is very much part of the Hong Kong scene. The fad I find most amusing and quite popular is what are called "sizzling platters." Dishes are partially cooked and presented at the table on a cast-iron plate that has been heated to very hot; the diners then shield their clothes and faces by placing their napkins in front of them, and the waiter pours the food on the platter. Because it is so hot, of course, it makes a wonderful and very appetizing sizzling noise. There is, however, a culinary purpose here because the food now continues to develop its aromas and flavors and completes its cooking. The result is a sense of the pure freshness of just-cooked food.

There is no need to run out and buy a special platter—I found the good old American cast-iron skillet works just fine. Make sure it rests on a heat-proof trivet. This method is a lot of fun and creates delicious flavors as well. This is food-as-entertainment at its finest.

STIR-FRIED PORK WITH WALNUTS

For today's hustling, bustling people, this is classic convenience food, which is not a contradiction in terms when done by Hong Kong chefs. The walnuts add rich flavor and crunchiness to the savory seasoned pork. Quick and easy, as well as nutritiously sustaining, it reflects the best of both the old and the new cooking styles.

1 pound pork fillet or lean boneless pork chops

MARINADE
1 tablespoon cornstarch
2 teaspoons light soy sauce
2 teaspoons rice wine
½ teaspoon salt
1 teaspoon sesame oil

½ cup walnuts
½ cup peanut oil
1 tablespoon light soy sauce
1 tablespoon Rich Chicken Stock (page 221)
½ teaspoon salt
½ teaspoon cornstarch mixed with ½ teaspoon water

Cut the pork into ½-inch dices, add it to a medium-sized bowl with the marinade ingredients, and refrigerate for 20 minutes.

Blanch the walnuts in a small pot of boiling water for 5 minutes. Drain and dry with paper towels.

Heat a wok or large skillet until it is hot and add the oil. Fry the walnuts for 2 minutes and drain off all but 1½ tablespoons oil. Reheat and stir-fry the pork for about 2 to 3 minutes or until lightly browned. Add the soy sauce, chicken stock, salt, and cornstarch mixture. Stir to mix well and add the walnuts. Mix and serve immediately.

YIELD: SERVES 4 TO 6

STIR-FRIED PORK WITH SALTED FISH

1 pound lean pork tenderloin or boneless pork chops

MARINADE
1 egg white
1 tablespoon cornstarch
1 tablespoon light soy sauce
2 teaspoons sesame oil

1 cup peanut oil
2 tablespoons finely chopped salted fish in oil
1 tablespoon finely chopped fresh ginger
2 tablespoons finely chopped whole scallions
1 tablespoon rice wine

Place the pork in the freezer for about 20 minutes or until it is firm to the touch. Then cut it, against the grain, into slices. Place the meat in a large bowl with the marinade ingredients and refrigerate for 20 minutes.

Heat a wok or large skillet until it is hot and add the oil. When the oil is hot, add the pork and stir-fry for 2 minutes. Drain the meat in a colander set inside a stainless steel bowl, reserving 2 tablespoons oil.

Return the drained oil to the wok and when it is hot, add the salted fish and ginger and stir-fry for 2 minutes. Return the pork to the wok, add the scallions, and stir-fry another minute. Finally add the rice wine, give the mixture several stirs, and serve at once.

YIELD: SERVES 4 TO 6

NOTE: Salted fish is treated in two ways: dried or dried and packed in oil. The dried variety needs to be soaked before it can be used. I prefer the type packed in oil because the taste and aroma are more fragrant and it is easier to handle.

What goes around comes around. Many years ago, when I was growing up in Chicago, my mother used to serve salted fish regularly. It was nutritious and cheap. I was surprised to discover recently in Hong Kong that this prosaic food has become a fashionable and fairly expensive food item, partly due to the overfishing of the South China Sea. To make up for the demand of the huge Hong Kong market, salt fish is being sold by small entrepreneur fishers in the region who lack the capital required to freeze the fish. The Cantonese heritage also plays a role here: many of the new generation, I am sure, recollect the dish that their mothers served, as I do. Making a virtue out of the necessity and seeing the latent demand for the salted fish, Hong Kong chefs have revived old and created new recipes that make the best of it. I particularly like the variety that is preserved in oil. It has an attractive aroma, like that of good anchovies. It goes very well with pork, as in this recipe, because the pork has more than enough character to bear the distinctive flavor of the fish.

FRIED SPARERIBS WITH SPICED SALT

Stir-fried seafood with spiced salt and pepper is a very popular item in Hong Kong. What's new is that Hong Kong chefs are applying the technique and the seasonings to foods such as spareribs, as here. The result is a dish of new and richer dimensions. The three-step cooking process should not put you off. The first simmering tenderizes the meat and can be done hours in advance. The second step in which the ribs are coated with batter (for extra crispness) and deep-fried is also quick and easy. This makes the ribs crusty on the outside and soft and moist on the inside. Finally, just before serving, the ribs are stir-fried in the salt and spices. The multi-step cooking and the seasonings turn the ordinary into something quite special.

1½ pounds pork spareribs
3 unpeeled fresh slices ginger
4 whole scallions, cut into 3-inch pieces
2 teaspoons salt

BATTER
3 tablespoons cornstarch
1 tablespoon flour
1 teaspoon baking powder
Pinch of salt
3 tablespoons water

2 cups peanut oil, for deep-frying

SPICE MIXTURE
2 tablespoons coarsely chopped garlic
2 teaspoons coarse salt
1 teaspoon Sichuan peppercorns, roasted and ground
½ teaspoon five-spice powder
½ teaspoon sugar

GARNISH
2 tablespoons finely chopped whole scallions

Have your butcher cut the spareribs into small, bite-size pieces. Combine the ribs with the ginger, scallions, and salt in a pot of water and bring the mixture to a boil. Skim the surface and reduce the heat, cover, and simmer for about 40 minutes or until the ribs are tender. Drain thoroughly and allow to cool.

In a small bowl, mix the batter ingredients until a thick paste is formed. Let stand for at least 20 minutes. Add the cooked ribs and mix well. Let the mixture sit for 5 minutes.

Heat the oil in a wok or large skillet. Deep-fry the spareribs in several batches for about 5 minutes or until they are golden brown. Drain off all but 2 tablespoons of oil. Reheat the wok, stir-fry the spice mixture for 30 seconds. Return the fried spareribs and continue to stir-fry for 2 minutes until the ribs are thoroughly coated with the mixture. Garnish with the scallions and serve at once.

YIELD: SERVES 4 TO 6

BRAISED BEEF SHANK

1½ to 2 pounds beef shank

BRAISING LIQUID
4 cups Rich Chicken Stock (page 221)
6 star anise
2 tablespoons whole unroasted Sichuan peppercorns
4 tablespoons rock sugar
3 tablespoons dark soy sauce
1½ tablespoons light soy sauce
4 pieces dried ginger (galangal)
3 cinnamon bark pieces or cinnamon sticks
2 teaspoons five-spice powder

Blanch the beef shank in a pot of boiling water for about 20 minutes. Drain well and discard the liquid.

Bring all the braising-liquid ingredients to a boil in a large clay pot or heavy casserole. Add the beef shank and lower the heat to a simmer. Braise slowly for 2 hours or until the meat is quite tender. Remove the meat, strain the liquid, and then return the meat to the liquid. Allow the meat and liquid to cool thoroughly and then refrigerate. When you are ready to serve, remove the meat from the jellied braising sauce, and thinly slice. Carefully cut the jellied sauce into cubes and serve with the sliced meat.

YIELD: SERVES 4

Northern Chinese cuisine is quite distinct in many ways from the Cantonese–Hong Kong style. As this recipe shows, however, there are no real barriers between the two; it perfectly illustrates the amalgamation of regional cuisines. The beef shanks, a northern favorite, are rendered lighter and less greasy, and when treated with traditional seasonings are quite popular. The rather inexpensive shanks are thus transformed into a delicious meal. This dish can be made even days ahead of time, making it easy to prepare for dinner guests. It is a fine first course or, alternatively, an exotic picnic item. Serve at room temperature with the rich jelly, redolent of the seasonings, that results from the cooking liquid.

CURRIED BEEF STEW

Traditional and hearty food has not been forgotten in Hong Kong's receptivity to new cuisines. This stew is among the many old favorites you can still find there in homes and restaurants. The curry influence comes from India via Southeast Asia, but it is in a mild form, unlike some of the hot and spicy curries of Indonesia or India. The Western influence, however, can be seen in the use of potatoes and carrots, both of which are relative newcomers in Chinese cuisine. This is food that is always welcome, but particularly in cool weather.

3 pounds beef brisket
3 tablespoons peanut oil
2 tablespoons finely chopped garlic
2 tablespoons finely chopped fresh ginger
3 tablespoons light soy sauce
6 tablespoons Madras curry powder or paste
3 tablespoons bean sauce
3 tablespoons finely chopped whole scallions
2 tablespoons rice wine
2 tablespoons sugar
1½ pounds carrots, peeled and roll-cut (page 267) into 2-inch pieces
1½ pounds potatoes, peeled and cut into large cubes

Cut the brisket into large chunks and blanch for 15 minutes in a large pot of boiling water. Drain well and blot dry with paper towels.

Heat a wok or large skillet until it is hot and add the oil. Brown the meat for 10 minutes, then add the rest of the ingredients except for the carrots and potatoes. Turn the mixture into a large clay pot or casserole. Cover and simmer for 1 hour.

Meanwhile, prepare the carrots and potatoes. Leave them in cold water until you are ready to use them. Add the vegetables to the clay pot and continue to cook for another 35 to 40 minutes or until the meat is very tender.

This dish reheats extremely well. It can be made days ahead and refrigerated.

YIELD: SERVES 6 TO 8

VEGETABLES

STIR-FRIED PICKLED GINGER WITH BEAN CURD

FRIED BEAN CURD WITH CHIVE DIPPING SAUCE

CHINESE GREENS WITH OYSTER SAUCE

BRAISED BEAN CURD AND CHINESE GREENS WITH SHRIMP ROE

SHREDDED EGGPLANT IN FISH-FLAVOR SAUCE

VEGETARIAN BEAN-CURD CASSEROLE

BEAN CURD WITH SPICY BEEF SAUCE

PAN-FRIED BEAN CURD WITH YELLOW CHIVES

STIR-FRIED ASPARAGUS WITH GARLIC

STIR-FRIED ASPARAGUS WITH CORN

FRESH ASPARAGUS IN CRABMEAT SAUCE

FRESH MUSHROOMS IN SHRIMP ROE SAUCE

PEPPER STIR-FRY

BRAISED YOUNG CABBAGE IN OYSTER SAUCE

FRIED MILK WITH PINE NUTS

DEEP-FRIED MILK DIAMONDS

One of the first things that struck me when I first visited the colorful markets of Hong Kong was the vast variety of green vegetables. These, along with soy bean curd and more recently introduced products such as tomatoes, lettuce, corn, and asparagus are scattered throughout the markets and are now staples of Hong Kong cooking. Balance—of foods, flavors, textures, colors, and nutrients—is the cardinal virtue of this cuisine, with vegetables playing a most important role. Chefs thus accord them respect and imaginative treatment. They are used as edible garnish, stuffed, stir-fried, and braised. Many of these vegetable dishes are thoroughly enjoyable served by themselves.

STIR-FRIED PICKLED GINGER WITH BEAN CURD

Frequently in Hong Kong, pickled ginger is eaten freshly pickled and thinly sliced as a treat with preserved eggs or just as a refreshing condiment at the table. However, I have enjoyed it just as much when it is cooked with meats or, as in this case, with bean curd. The bean curd is pan-fried, giving it a golden crust, and then stir-fried with the young pickled ginger. The result is a very nutritious, fresh, and tasty vegetable side dish, or it can be served in a large quantity as a main vegetarian course.

1 pound firm bean curd
½ cup peanut oil
¼ cup pickled young ginger or Sichuan preserved vegetable
2 tablespoons finely chopped whole scallions
½ teaspoon salt
2 tablespoons rice wine
1 tablespoon light soy sauce
1 tablespoon dark soy sauce
2 teaspoons sugar
1 teaspoon sesame oil

Cut the bean curd into 2-inch squares and blot dry with paper towels. Heat a wok or large skillet until it is hot and add the oil. Gently pan-fry the bean curd until it is golden brown. Drain on paper towels and set aside, reserving 1 tablespoon oil.

Cut the pickled ginger into thin slices and set aside.

Reheat the wok, and when the oil is hot, add the pickled ginger slices and stir-fry for 30 seconds, then add the rest of the ingredients except the sesame oil. Continue to stir-fry for another minute. Return the bean curd to the wok and stir-fry another minute. Finally add the sesame oil and give the mixture a final stir. Pour onto a serving platter and serve at once.

YIELD: SERVES 4

FRIED BEAN CURD WITH CHIVE DIPPING SAUCE

Bean curd or tofu is the protein food of the future, according to many nutritionists and food experts. If that is so, bean curd Hong Kong–style will surely lead the way. The variety and high quality of the bean curd dishes featured in the new Hong Kong

1 pound firm bean curd
2 cups peanut oil, for deep-frying

CHIVE DIPPING SAUCE
2 teaspoons finely chopped garlic
3 tablespoons coarsely chopped Chinese green or yellow chives or whole scallions
1 teaspoon salt
¼ cup Rich Chicken Stock (page 221)
½ teaspoon cornstarch mixed with ½ teaspoon water

Drain the bean curd and cut it into 4 equal slices. Cut each slice diagonally into halves to form triangles. Blot dry with paper towels.

Heat a wok or large skillet and add the oil. When the oil is hot, deep-fry the triangles for 3 minutes on each side or until they are golden and crisp. Remove them with a slotted spoon and drain on paper towels.

Drain off all but 1 tablespoon of oil from the wok and reheat. When it is hot, add the garlic and stir-fry for 10 seconds. Then add the chives, salt, and chicken stock and simmer for 1 minute. Stir in the cornstarch mixture and, when the sauce has slightly thickened, serve on the side with the bean curd triangles.

YIELD: SERVES 4

cuisine are astonishing. Hong Kong chefs are imaginative and creative in their recipes for this bland but adaptable food. In this recipe, the bean curd is slowly pan-fried, giving it a crisp surface texture while maintaining a soft creamy core. It is then dipped in a savory sauce, making a most enjoyable meal indeed. The key here is not to overcook the bean curd, which dries it out. Gentle pan-frying is the proper way to do it.

CHINESE GREENS WITH OYSTER SAUCE

1 pound young Chinese white cabbage (bok choy)

SAUCE
3 tablespoons oyster sauce
2 teaspoons peanut oil

If you are using a large cabbage, separate the leaves and stalks and cut the leaves into 2-inch pieces. Peel the stems, cut them into thin diagonal slices, and wash them well in several changes of water. If you are using the small, young variety, simply rinse them very well in several changes of water.

Blanch the cabbage for 1 minute in a large pot of salted boiling water. Remove with a slotted spoon and arrange on a platter. Mix the oyster sauce and oil in a small bowl, pour this over the vegetables, and serve at once.

Note: There is one variety of bok choy (white cabbage), but it comes in two forms. The larger, leafy type is often available in supermarkets — commercially grown and less tasty — and is better for soup. The younger variety has smaller stalks, is less fibrous and tastier.

YIELD: SERVES 2 TO 4

This is a simple, straightforward dish of universal appeal. Fresh, young, tender bok choy, that wonderful Chinese green (not the large mature stalks), are gently blanched. They are then served lightly flavored with oyster sauce. The result is a quick-and-easy, wholesome, and appealing vegetable dish. It shows the finesse of Hong Kong chefs in their preparation of greens.

BRAISED BEAN CURD AND CHINESE GREENS WITH SHRIMP ROE

A new and unusual taste I discovered in Hong Kong was dried shrimp roe. As you can imagine, it has a pungent aroma and strong taste not unlike shrimp paste. It is certainly an acquired taste. Cooked in relatively bland bean curd, it really gives the whole dish a kick. Here, the bean curd is paired with the flowering variety of bok choy that is sweet but has a slight mustard taste. Like the flowering cabbage, the shrimp roe can be found in Asian specialty markets, but you may substitute shrimp paste.

1 pound firm bean curd
1 cup peanut oil, for deep-frying
1 pound Chinese flowering cabbage (choi sum) or
    Chinese white cabbage (bok choy)
1 tablespoon finely chopped fresh ginger
1 tablespoon finely chopped garlic
2 tablespoons finely chopped whole scallions
1½ tablespoons dried shrimp roe
    or 2 teaspoons shrimp paste
2 teaspoons light soy sauce
1 tablespoon oyster sauce
1 tablespoon rice wine
½ cup Rich Chicken Stock (page 221)
1 teaspoon cornstarch mixed with 1 teaspoon water
2 teaspoons sesame oil

Cut the bean curd in half and then diagonally in half again to make triangles. Blot dry with paper towels. Heat a wok or large skillet until it is hot and add the oil. Deep-fry the bean curd in two batches and drain on paper towels.

Separate the flowering cabbage leaves and stalks and cut the leaves into 2-inch pieces. Peel the stalks and cut them into thin diagonal slices. Wash well in several changes of water.

Blanch the flowering cabbage in a pot of boiling water for 1 minute. Drain and arrange on a platter.

Combine the rest of the ingredients except the sesame oil in a wok and bring the mixture to a boil. Return the bean curd and cook for 1 minute. Finally, add the sesame oil and give the mixture a final stir. Pour this over the bok choy and serve.

YIELD: SERVES 4

SHREDDED EGGPLANT IN FISH-FLAVOR SAUCE

1½ pounds (about 5) Chinese eggplants
2 tablespoons peanut oil

SAUCE
1 teaspoon finely chopped fresh ginger
2 teaspoons finely chopped garlic
2 teaspoons chili bean sauce
1 tablespoon rice wine
1 tablespoon finely chopped fresh coriander
1 fresh red chili pepper, seeded and finely chopped
3 whole scallions, cut into diagonal pieces
½ teaspoon salt
2 tablespoons Rich Chicken Stock (page 221)
2 teaspoons black vinegar

Preheat the oven to 350° F. Place the eggplants on a baking tray and bake for 15 minutes. When the eggplants are cool peel and shred into long pieces.

Heat a wok or large skillet until it is hot and add the oil. Add the ginger, garlic, and chili bean sauce and stir-fry for 30 seconds. Then add the rest of the sauce ingredients and the shredded eggplant and continue to cook for another 3 minutes.

Serve immediately or at room temperature.

YIELD: SERVES 2 TO 4

The eggplant is a native of southeastern Asia, probably India, where it is believed to have been cultivated more than four thousand years ago. Eggplants are found in abundance in Hong Kong's food markets. They are inexpensive and versatile — often cooked with black beans, braised, or steamed. A popular method is this Sichuan inspiration called "fish flavor" because the sauce was originally developed for fish dishes, but has no fishy taste itself whatsoever. The sauce is also wonderful to use with meats but is especially fine with eggplants. In Hong Kong, eggplants are cooked richly with lots of oil — perhaps too richly. I have found a better method by precooking the eggplants in the oven so that they absorb less oil. This dish is wonderful cold and makes a good vegetable salad.

VEGETARIAN BEAN-CURD CASSEROLE

It is a bit surprising to me that there are very few vegetarian restaurants in Hong Kong. However, vegetarian cuisines are often found in the New Territories at Buddhist or Taoist temples. In my many visits there, I sampled a vegetarian casserole, and this is my interpretation of that wonderful dish. The vegetables are savory and have contrasting tastes and textures — for me, a key element in the success of a vegetarian dish.

1 small package (2 ounces) bean thread noodles
½ cup dried Chinese black mushrooms
½ pound bok choy
1 cup peanut oil, for deep-frying
½ pound Chinese eggplant, roll-cut (page 267)
½ pound firm bean curd, cut into cubes
½ pound Chinese silk squash or zucchini, peeled and
    roll-cut
1 tablespoon finely chopped fresh ginger
2 teaspoons finely chopped garlic
2 tablespoons red fermented bean curd
1 teaspoon salt
2 cups Rich Chicken Stock (page 221) or water
1 tablespoon cornstarch mixed with 1 tablespoon water
2 tablespoons rice wine
2 teaspoons sesame oil

Soak the bean thread noodles in a medium-sized bowl of warm water for about 20 minutes and drain in a colander.

Soak the mushrooms in a bowl of warm water for about 20 minutes or until they are soft and pliable. Squeeze out the excess water and cut off and discard the woody stems.

Separate the bok choy leaves and stalks and cut the leaves into 2-inch pieces. Peel the stems and cut them into thin diagonal slices. Wash well in several changes of water.

Heat a wok or large skillet until it is hot and add the oil. When it is quite hot, deep-fry the eggplant for 3 minutes, remove with a slotted spoon, and drain on paper towels. Reheat the wok and deep-fry the bean curd cubes until they are golden brown, about 5 minutes. Remove with a slotted spoon and drain on paper towels.

Pour off all but 1½ tablespoons oil and reheat the wok. Stir-fry the silk squash for 1 minute, then add the ginger, garlic, fermented bean curd, salt, chicken stock, and cornstarch/water mixture. Mix and turn the contents of the wok into a clay pot or casserole. Add the eggplant, bean curd, bean thread noodles and mushrooms, cover again, and cook over high heat for 2 minutes. Add the bok choy, cover, and cook an additional 2 minutes. Stir in the rice wine and sesame oil and serve at once.

YIELD: SERVES 2 TO 4

BEAN CURD WITH SPICY BEEF SAUCE

1 pound soft bean curd, drained
2 tablespoons peanut oil
1 tablespoon finely chopped fresh ginger
1 tablespoon finely chopped garlic
1 tablespoon chili bean sauce
1 teaspoon bean sauce
½ pound ground beef
2 teaspoons sugar
¼ cup Rich Chicken Stock (page 221)
2 tablespoons rice wine
1 teaspoon cornstarch mixed with 1 teaspoon water

GARNISH
2 teaspoons sesame oil
2 tablespoons finely chopped whole scallions

Gently cut the bean curd into 1½-inch cubes and set aside. Heat a wok or large skillet until it is hot and add the oil. Add the ginger, garlic, chili bean sauce, and bean sauce and stir-fry for 30 seconds. Add the ground beef and stir-fry for another 2 minutes. Then add the sugar, chicken stock, and rice wine and continue to cook for another 2 minutes. Stir in the cornstarch mixture and bring to a boil. When the sauce has slightly thickened, carefully add the bean curd and cook for 2 minutes or until the bean curd is heated through.

Drizzle with sesame oil, sprinkle with scallions, and serve at once.

YIELD: SERVES 2 TO 4

A bright new interpretation of a classic Sichuan dish is this version from the Sichuan Garden restaurant in Hong Kong. In this case, beef is used instead of the usual pork, altering the flavor slightly. The soft, bland bean curd nicely balances the sauce — the custardy texture of the bean curd is delicate and light compared with the heavier meat and spicy flavors. This is another example of the updating of classic dishes — with a modern and Cantonese touch — that makes the food in Hong Kong so unique and delicious.

PAN-FRIED BEAN CURD WITH YELLOW CHIVES

A typical Cantonese–Hong Kong blend of spices and seasonings that is nonetheless global in its palatability makes this tofu dish very popular. Yellow chives, ginger, chilies, and garlic combine to make a centerpiece as flavorsome as it is nutritious.

1 pound firm bean curd
1 cup peanut oil, for deep-frying
1 tablespoon finely chopped garlic
2 teaspoons finely chopped ginger
1 tablespoon coarsely chopped fresh red chili pepper
2 teaspoons salt
4 tablespoons Rich Chicken Stock (page 221)
1 teaspoon sugar
1 tablespoon rice wine
6 tablespoons coarsely chopped yellow chives or whole
  scallions

Cut the bean curd diagonally to form triangular wedges and blot dry with paper towels.

Heat a wok or large skillet until it is hot and add the oil. When oil is hot, deep-fry the bean curd wedges until they are golden brown. It is best to do this in two batches. Drain the bean curd thoroughly on paper towels and arrange them on a serving platter.

Drain off all but 1 tablespoon oil and reheat the wok. Add the garlic and ginger and stir-fry for 30 seconds. Then add the chili and salt and stir-fry another 30 seconds. Stir in the chicken stock, sugar, rice wine, and yellow chives. Pour the sauce over the bean curd and serve at once.

YIELD: SERVES 2 TO 4

STIR-FRIED ASPARAGUS WITH GARLIC

No doubt asparagus was introduced to Hong Kong by Westerners who first served the vegetables in hotel dining rooms. Today, asparagus is a favorite

1 pound fresh asparagus
1½ tablespoons peanut oil
1 teaspoon salt
2 teaspoons finely chopped garlic
½ cup Rich Chicken Stock (page 221)
2 teaspoons sesame oil

Cut the asparagus into diagonal slices, about 2 inches in length.

Heat a wok or large skillet until it is hot and add the oil. Then add the salt and garlic and stir-fry for 30 seconds. Add the asparagus and continue to stir-fry for another minute. Add the chicken stock and continue to cook over high heat for 2 minutes or until the asparagus is tender. Stir in the sesame oil and serve at once.

YIELD: SERVES 4

vegetable, and it is most often prepared in the simplest way — that is, stir-fried with garlic, which allows the natural flavors of the wonderful vegetable to dominate. This recipe is quick and easy and works well when served cold. A simple dish, this is a perfect match to accompany something more complicated.

STIR-FRIED ASPARAGUS WITH CORN

1 pound fresh asparagus
½ cup fresh or canned baby corn
1½ tablespoons peanut oil
½ cup Rich Chicken Stock (page 221)
½ teaspoon salt
2 teaspoons sesame oil

Cut the asparagus into ½-inch rounds. If you are using fresh baby corn, blanch in boiling water for 2 minutes. Drain and set aside. If you are using canned baby corn, rinse well in cold running water, drain, and set aside.

Heat a wok or large skillet until it is hot and add the oil. Add the asparagus and stir-fry for 1 minute. Then add the chicken stock and salt. Continue to stir-fry for 2 minutes. Add the baby corn and continue to stir-fry another 2 minutes or until all the liquid has evaporated. Add the sesame oil, give the mixture a couple of turns, and serve at once.

YIELD: SERVES 4 TO 6

This recipe is a splendid example of the new cooking of Hong Kong. Western asparagus and Southeast Asian baby corn have been absorbed into the Cantonese tradition, creating a dish at once innovative and traditional. In this delightful vegetable dish we have an example of the creative blend of East and West.

FRESH ASPARAGUS IN CRABMEAT SAUCE

The Chinese in Hong Kong prefer large asparagus because they are meatier and are believed to have more taste. The restaurants there serve the asparagus with a sauce made from crabmeat and crab roe. This is a rich and tasty dish, a perfect combination of two exotic and unusual foods.

¾ cup Rich Chicken Stock (page 221)
1 tablespoon finely chopped ginger
1 tablespoon finely chopped garlic
Salt to taste
1½ pounds large asparagus, tough ends trimmed

CRABMEAT SAUCE
½ cup Rich Chicken Stock
1 tablespoon rice wine
2 teaspoons sugar
½ teaspoon salt
Freshly ground white pepper to taste
¼ pound fresh crabmeat
1 egg white
1 tablespoon sesame oil
1 teaspoon cornstarch mixed with 1 teaspoon water

GARNISH
2 tablespoons finely chopped green scallion tops

In a wok or large skillet, combine the chicken stock, ginger, garlic, and salt. Bring to a boil, add the asparagus and cook over high heat for about 4 minutes or until the asparagus is barely tender. Remove the asparagus with a slotted spoon, arrange on a serving platter, and keep warm. Most of the liquid should have evaporated from the wok.

Wipe the wok clean and add the chicken stock, rice wine, sugar, salt, and pepper and cook for 30 seconds over high heat. Add the crabmeat, and reduce the heat to simmer. In a small bowl, combine the egg white with the sesame oil and add this mixture to the wok in a slow, steady stream, stirring constantly. Then add the cornstarch mixture and give the sauce a final stir. Arrange the sauce along the stem ends of the asparagus in a half-moon pattern. Garnish with scallion tops and serve at once.

YIELD: SERVES 4 TO 6

FRESH MUSHROOMS IN SHRIMP ROE SAUCE

1 pound fresh mushrooms
1½ tablespoons peanut oil
3 cloves peeled garlic, crushed
3 large slices unpeeled ginger
1 teaspoon dried shrimp roe
½ teaspoon salt
1 teaspoon sugar
1 teaspoon light soy sauce
1 teaspoon dark soy sauce
1 tablespoon oyster sauce
1 teaspoon sugar
2 teaspoons rice wine
1½ teaspoons sesame oil
3 tablespoons Rich Chicken Stock (page 221)
1 teaspoon cornstarch mixed with 1 teaspoon water

Fresh straw mushrooms found in the marketplaces in Hong Kong are a treat. Although they are not available here, I found this dish tastes almost as good with our fresh domestic mushrooms. The technique is to blanch the mushrooms quickly; they absorb moisture that they later give up as they cook. The shrimp roe gives this dish a distinctive flavor, but you can substitute shrimp paste if shrimp roe is not available.

Blanch the mushrooms in a pot of boiling water for 30 seconds. Drain and set aside.

Heat a wok or large skillet until it is hot and add the oil, garlic, and ginger. Stir-fry the garlic and ginger for 30 seconds, then remove and discard. Add the mushrooms and the rest of the ingredients and stir-fry for 5 minutes until the mushrooms are cooked. Serve at once.

YIELD: SERVES 2 TO 4

PEPPER STIR-FRY

For those seeking a good vegetable dish with plenty of textures, this Hong Kong favorite fits the bill. It is simple to make once the preparations are done. The colors of the dish are festive, and it is equally delicious cold. If you like, serve the peppers in lettuce cups with hoisin sauce.

1 cup dried Chinese black mushrooms

EGG MIXTURE
2 eggs, beaten
1 teaspoon sesame oil
¼ teaspoon salt

1 tablespoon plus 2 teaspoons peanut oil
1 tablespoon finely chopped whole scallions
1 tablespoon finely chopped ginger
1 tablespoon finely chopped garlic
1 fresh red chili pepper, seeded and finely shredded
2 medium-sized red, yellow, or green peppers, seeded and finely shredded
2 tablespoons rice wine
1 tablespoon light soy sauce
1 teaspoon chili bean sauce
1 teaspoon sugar
Salt and freshly ground black pepper to taste
½ pound bean sprouts (both ends plucked, optional)
2 tablespoons Rich Chicken Stock (page 221) or water
2 teaspoons sesame oil

GARNISH
2 tablespoons finely chopped whole scallions

Soak the mushrooms in a bowl of warm water for about 20 minutes or until they are soft and pliable. Squeeze out the excess water and cut off and discard the woody stems. Finely shred the caps.

Combine the egg mixture in a small bowl. Heat a wok or large skillet until it is hot and add 2 teaspoons of oil. Add the egg mixture and spread over the surface of the wok until it forms a thin crepelike pancake. Remove it and when it cools, shred, and set it aside.

Reheat a wok and add the remaining tablespoon of oil. Add the scallions, ginger, garlic and chili and stir-fry for 30 seconds. Add the peppers, mushrooms, rice wine, soy sauce, chili bean sauce, sugar, salt, and black pepper. Stir-fry for 2 minutes or until the peppers are soft. Then add the bean sprouts, shredded egg pancake, and chicken stock. Stir-fry gently for another 2 minutes, add the sesame oil, and give it one final stir.

Remove the mixture to a serving platter and garnish with the chopped scallions. Serve at once.

YIELD: SERVES 4 TO 6

BRAISED YOUNG CABBAGE IN OYSTER SAUCE

1½ pounds Shanghai (baby bok choy) young greens
1 tablespoon peanut oil
2 teaspoons peeled finely minced fresh ginger
2 teaspoons finely minced whole scallions
½ cup Rich Chicken Stock (page 221)
3 tablespoons oyster sauce
1 tablespoon rice wine
1 teaspoon sugar
1 teaspoon cornstarch mixed with 1 teaspoon water

Wash the greens well in cold water, trimming the bottoms as needed. Cut them in half.

Heat a wok or large skillet until it is hot and add the oil. When the oil is hot, add the ginger and scallions and stir-fry for 20 seconds. Add the greens and stir-fry for 1 minute, then add the rest of the ingredients except the cornstarch mixture. Reduce the heat to a simmer, cover the wok, and gently braise for 5 minutes. Remove the vegetables to a serving platter with a slotted spoon. Slowly stir the cornstarch mixture into the sauce. Bring to a boil, pour over the vegetables, and serve at once.

YIELD: SERVES 4

These "baby" bok choy are called cabbages but they really are a variety of the mustard green family, a popular vegetable in Hong Kong. Braising is the appropriate cooking technique for them because they have a delicate flavor and texture. The oyster sauce is nicely absorbed and the resulting combination is a tasty treat. It goes well with plain rice and can serve as a side vegetable dish to any meal.

FRIED MILK WITH PINE NUTS

A scholar has noted that "the Chinese and other eastern and Southeast Asian peoples do not merely have an aversion to the use of milk, they loathe it intensely, reacting to the prospect of gulping down a nice, cold glass of the stuff much as Westerners might react to the prospect of a nice, cold glass of cow saliva. Less than 5 percent of adult Chinese can absorb milk lactose." It is therefore quite surprising to find many popular milk dishes in Hong Kong. The chefs there have ingeniously combined fresh and evaporated milk (which has less of a milk taste and smell) and incorporated them into dishes in which milk is featured. When the ingredients are stir-fried, the milk curdles and its chemistry changes into something digestible by — and palatable to — Chinese; it also results in a new flavor and taste. The milk is combined with egg white and the result is a light and fluffy mixture — enhanced by the crunchy pine nuts, the salty, smoky flavor of ham, and the textural quality of the crisp noodles. Altogether it is an unusual dish, a wonderful combination of tastes and textures.

1⅓ cups milk
¾ cup unsweetened evaporated milk
7 egg whites
1 tablespoon cornstarch
2 teaspoons salt
1 small package (2 ounces) bean thread noodles
1½ cups peanut oil
¼ cup pine nuts

GARNISH
2 tablespoons finely chopped fresh coriander
1 tablespoon finely chopped Smithfield ham

In a medium-sized bowl, combine the milk and evaporated milk with the egg whites, cornstarch, and salt. Beat the mixture with a wire whisk until it is slightly frothy and set aside.

Separate the bean thread noodles inside a paper bag to prevent them from scattering. Heat a wok or large skillet until it is hot and add the oil. Deep-fry the noodles for 10 to 15 seconds until they have puffed up and are crisp but not brown. Remove them with a slotted spoon, drain on paper towels, and place on a serving platter.

Drain off all the oil leaving 2 tablespoons in the wok. Reheat the wok until it is very hot, add the pine nuts, and stir-fry for 30 seconds until they are golden brown. Remove them immediately. Quickly add the milk mixture and stir-fry until it forms small curds. Add the pine nuts and give the curds a final gentle stir to mix well. Pour the contents of the wok into a colander to drain off any excess liquid.

Place the stir fried milk on top of the noodles, garnish with the coriander and ham, and serve immediately.
YIELD: SERVES 4 TO 6

DEEP-FRIED MILK DIAMONDS

1½ cups milk
¾ cup evaporated milk
½ teaspoon salt
½ teaspoon freshly ground white pepper
5 tablespoons cornstarch
2 tablespoons finely chopped Smithfield Ham

BATTER
¾ cup flour
4 tablespoons cornstarch
2 teaspoons baking powder
¾ cup water
1 teaspoon salt

1 cup peanut oil, for deep-frying
Sugar, for dipping

Combine the two milks, salt, pepper, cornstarch, and ham in a medium-sized saucepan and mix until smooth. Simmer over low heat for about 10 minutes or until the mixture has thickened. Pour the cooked milk mixture into an oiled baking pan and allow it to cool thoroughly. Cover with plastic wrap and refrigerate. This can be done the night before.

In a medium-sized bowl, mix the batter ingredients and allow to sit at room temperature for 30 minutes. Cut the milk curd into diamond-shaped, 3-inch pieces.

Heat a wok or deep skillet until it is hot and add the oil. When it is slightly smoking, dip some of the milk pieces into the batter with a slotted spoon and deep-fry them for 3 minutes or until they are golden and crisp. Drain them on paper towels and repeat the process until you have fried all the milk pieces.

Serve the fried "milk" with a small dish of sugar for dipping.
YIELD: SERVES 4 TO 6

One of the most interesting and fascinating dishes I have encountered in Hong Kong is the so-called deep-fried milk. Milk custard is lightly battered and deep-fried. The result is a crisp exterior with a creamy, custardy interior, a combination of textures that appeals to the Chinese taste. How milk got into Hong Kong cuisine is an intriguing question. The most plausible theory is that the Western-influenced milk dishes started with the Portuguese of Macao in the sixteenth century and later spread to Hong Kong. In this recipe, the contrast between the slightly salty ham and sweet sugar is also striking. In Hong Kong, deep-fried milk is served with spareribs or simply dipped in sugar, as in this dish.

RICE
AND
NOODLES

~~~~~~~~~~~~~~~~~~~~~~~~~~~~~

FRIED RICE WITH PINEAPPLE

FRIED RICE WITH EGG AND SALTED FISH

RICE NOODLE SOUP WITH SHREDDED MEAT AND PRESERVED VEGETABLE

SHREDDED CHICKEN ON CRISP THIN NOODLES

SINGAPORE NOODLES

FRIED RICE WITH BEEF

SICHUAN GARDEN'S *DAN DAN* NOODLES

YANGZHOU-STYLE FRIED RICE

CHIU CHOW FRIED RICE

BRAISED *YI FU* NOODLES WITH SHRIMP

BEAN THREAD NOODLES WITH SHREDDED PORK

NOODLES WITH CRABMEAT IN BROTH

STIR-FRIED RICE NOODLES WITH BEEF AND CHILI BEAN SAUCE

CHIU CHOW NOODLES IN SESAME SAUCE

CHINESE PANCAKES

Although rice, cooked in various ways, is the staple of most Chinese cooking, noodles also play an important role. In northern Chinese cuisine, wheat in the form of rolls and pancakes is customarily eaten but these recipes have not penetrated southern Chinese regional cooking. So, rice and rice noodles dominate in Hong Kong cuisine. (Though for those who prefer them, many kinds of northern Chinese or Western-style pancakes and breads are readily available.) The recipes here give an indication of the imaginative uses to which rice may be put, whether boiled, fried, or as a noodle.

FRIED RICE WITH PINEAPPLE

Fried rice is often served at meals that include many dishes. Generally, it is meant as an extra dish, to be sure that even the hungriest guest is satisfied. But fried rice lends itself to many variations. This is a popular and unusual rice dish in Hong Kong that I suspect is of Thai origin. Thai cooks commonly hollow out the pineapple and fill it with fried rice or some other tasty stuffing, and it is often presented this way in Hong Kong restaurants. Southeast Asian influences in Hong Kong have always been strong, especially since the mid-1970s when Southeast Asian immigrants escaping war and persecutions streamed into Hong Kong. Although many who arrived were ethnic Chinese, they brought with them the flavors of their former country. Because many of the countries of Southeast Asia are also eager to sell their food products to an affluent Hong Kong, there is a vast variety of fruits available in Hong Kong. This recipe demonstrates one use to which the fruit is put. The result is a refreshing and piquant finish to any meal.

2 tablespoons peanut oil
½ cup ground pork
1 teaspoon light soy sauce
½ teaspoon salt
1 tablespoon finely chopped fresh ginger
2 tablespoons finely chopped whole scallions
3 cups cooked rice
2 cups chopped fresh pineapple

Heat a wok or large skillet until it is hot and add the oil. Stir-fry the ground pork for 2 minutes, then add the soy sauce, salt, ginger, and scallions; continue to stir-fry for another minute. Add the rice, stirring to mix well. Finally, add the pineapple and continue to stir-fry for another 3 minutes or until the pineapple is heated through. Serve at once.
YIELD: SERVES 4

FRIED RICE WITH EGG AND SALTED FISH

3 tablespoons peanut oil
2 tablespoons finely chopped salted fish
3 cups cooked rice
3 tablespoons finely chopped fresh ginger
2 eggs, beaten

Heat a wok or large skillet until it is hot and add the oil. Add the salted fish and stir-fry for 10 seconds. Stir in the rice and ginger and stir-fry for 2 minutes over high heat. Add the eggs and continue to stir-fry for another minute. Serve at once.

YIELD: SERVES 4

The good news is, rice is still cheap; the bad news, salted fish is now expensive. When I was a child, rice was the mainstay of my diet. My mother would imaginatively enliven the rice dishes and stretch our food budget by adding small portions of other foods to the rice. Sometimes she would add a little chopped salted fish to a little ground pork and, after steaming the blend, would serve it with the rice. Or she would serve the salted fish alone, gently steamed. In either case, it was a cheap way "to make the fan (rice) go down," and very nutritious as well.

Today, it has even become rather chic to serve salted fish in fancy restaurants. This recipe, for example, is offered at some of the best Hong Kong eating places. It is derived from the popular style of Chiu Chow, a small fishing village and area in southern China, and Hong Kong has absorbed the best features of that style. When rice is fried with the salted fish, it becomes pleasantly aromatic. The distinctive ginger flavor nicely balances any assertiveness on the part of the fish. The eggs add mildness and lightness to the dish.

RICE NOODLE SOUP WITH SHREDDED MEAT AND PRESERVED VEGETABLE

In Hong Kong, any time is food time and every hour, day or night, food is being prepared and eaten. The number of restaurants and food stalls is staggering. One of the great pleasures of walking in the streets of Hong Kong is the smell of delicious aromas wafting from food stalls. This popular and quick soup is typical of the style; it uses dried rice noodles that are light and quick to make. Fast food, yes, but tasty and nutritious as well.

½ **pound thin, flat, dried rice noodles**
½ **pound lean pork**

MARINADE
2 **teaspoons light soy sauce**
1 **teaspoon rice wine**
1 **teaspoon cornstarch**

4 **cups Rich Chicken Stock (page 221)**
2 **tablespoons peanut oil**
3 **tablespoons finely chopped Sichuan preserved vegetable**
2 **teaspoons salt**
½ **teaspoon freshly ground black pepper**
2 **teaspoons sesame oil**

Soak the rice noodles in a medium-sized bowl of warm water for about 20 minutes and then drain in a colander.

Place the pork in the freezer for about 20 minutes or until it is firm to the touch. Cut into thin slices and then finely shred the slices. Add the pork to a medium-sized bowl with all the marinade ingredients and refrigerate for 20 minutes.

Bring the chicken stock to a simmer in a medium-sized pot. Add the rice noodles and simmer for 2 minutes.

Meanwhile heat a wok or large skillet until it is hot and add the peanut oil. When the oil is smoking, stir-fry the pork for 30 seconds; add the preserved vegetables. Continue to stir-fry for another minute. Add the salt, pepper, and sesame oil. Give the mixture one final stir and add to the soup and noodles. Serve immediately.

YIELD: SERVES 4 TO 6

SHREDDED CHICKEN ON CRISP THIN NOODLES

½ **pound chicken breasts**

COATING
1 **egg white**
2 **teaspoons cornstarch**
1 **teaspoon salt**

½ **pound thin fresh Chinese egg noodles**
3 **tablespoons peanut oil**

½ **cup peanut oil, for velveting (page 271)**

SAUCE
1 **cup Rich Chicken Stock (page 221)**
2 **tablespoons rice wine**
1 **teaspoon salt**
1 **teaspoon cornstarch mixed with 1 teaspoon water**

GARNISH
3 **tablespoons finely chopped whole scallions**

Place the chicken in the freezer for about 20 minutes or until it is firm to the touch. Then cut it into thin slices and finely shred it. Combine the chicken with the coating mixture and refrigerate for 20 minutes.

Blanch the noodles for 2 minutes in a large pot of boiling water. Drain well.

Heat a frying pan and when it is hot, add 1½ tablespoons of oil. Evenly spread the noodles out, turn down the heat, and brown slowly. This should take about 5 minutes. When the noodles are browned, flip them over and brown the other side, adding the other 1½ tablespoons oil if needed. When both sides are browned, remove the noodles to a round serving platter, and keep warm.

Heat a wok or large skillet until it is hot and add the ½ cup of oil. When the oil is moderately hot, add the chicken and stir quickly to separate. When the chicken turns white, remove immediately, and drain in a colander.

Add the sauce ingredients to the wok and bring to a simmer. Return the chicken to the sauce and give the mixture a few turns. Pour over the noodles, garnish with the scallions, and serve at once.

YIELD: SERVES 4

This "pasta" dish is a great favorite of many dim sum diners in Hong Kong. Pan-fried, so that thin fresh egg noodles are crisply browned on both sides, and then served with a soft-textured, mild-flavored shredded-chicken sauce, it makes a wonderful finale to any dim sum meal. It also makes an ideal appetizer or the main dish of a luncheon. As with noodles in general, this dish is enjoyable anytime, and one can see people eating it throughout the day, not just after dim sum. In this recipe, the chicken shreds are velveted, that is, coated with egg white and cornstarch, to keep them moist and tender. The result is a home-style dish elevated to a simple culinary delight.

SINGAPORE NOODLES

Another noodle favorite in Hong Kong is thin rice noodles, which are lighter than wheat noodles, and lend themselves to dishes that are subtle, delicate, yet full of flavor. Singapore-style rice noodles are just such a treat. Whenever I visit Hong Kong, I love to sample them whether in a food stall in the streets or in any of a number of "quick-noodle" fast-food restaurants. The dish is invariably well made and I am never disappointed. Here, the noodles are paired with tiny fresh shrimp and shredded ham or Chinese barbecued pork, but the real secret to this tasty dish is the curry sauce which must be made with Madras curry paste or powder. I often like to eat these noodles as a one-dish meal or served as a first course in a multi-course dinner party. This dish is also wonderful cold and would be lovely and unusual for a picnic.

½ pound (½ package) thin dried rice noodles
2 ounces dried Chinese black mushrooms

CURRY SAUCE
1 tablespoon finely chopped garlic
2 teaspoons finely chopped fresh ginger
2 tablespoons light soy sauce
3 tablespoons Indian Madras curry paste or powder
2 tablespoons rice wine
1 tablespoon sugar
1 teaspoon salt
1 cup fresh or canned coconut milk
1 cup Rich Chicken Stock (page 221)

3 tablespoons peanut oil
¼ pound Chinese barbecued pork or Smithfield ham, finely shredded
6 fresh red chili peppers, seeded and finely shredded
4 whole scallions, finely shredded
¼ pound cooked small bay shrimp
½ cup fresh sweet peas (½ pound of pods), blanched
4 fresh or canned water chestnuts, peeled and thinly sliced
4 eggs, beaten
1 tablespoon sesame oil

GARNISH
Fresh coriander leaves
Fresh basil leaves

Soak the rice noodles in a medium-sized bowl of warm water for about 25 minutes or until soft. Drain in a colander and set aside. Soak the mushrooms in a bowl of warm water for about 20 minutes or until they are soft and pliable. Squeeze out the excess water and cut off and discard the woody stems.

In a small pan, combine all the curry sauce ingredients and simmer for 2 minutes. Set aside.

Heat a wok or large skillet until it is hot and add the oil. Stir-fry the mushrooms, pork or ham, chilies, and scallions for 30 seconds. Then add the rice noodles, shrimp, peas, and water chestnuts and stir-fry for 1 minute more. Add the curry sauce and stir-fry, mixing all the while, for about 4 minutes or until most of the liquid has evaporated. Mix the eggs with the sesame oil in a small bowl and add this to the mixture, stirring constantly. Ladle the dish onto a platter and garnish with the coriander and basil leaves. Serve at once.

YIELD: SERVES 4 TO 6

FRIED RICE WITH BEEF

2 tablespoons peanut oil
1 cup ground beef
2 teaspoons light soy sauce
½ teaspoon salt
1 tablespoon finely chopped fresh ginger
2 tablespoons finely chopped whole scallions
3 cups cooked rice

Heat a wok or large skillet until it is hot. Add the oil and stir-fry the ground beef for 2 minutes. Then add the soy sauce, salt, ginger, and scallions and continue to stir-fry for another minute. Add the rice, stirring to mix well. Stir-fry for another 3 minutes and serve at once.

YIELD: SERVES 4

This dish is easily enlivened with a small amount of beef that adds body and flavor to the dependable but bland rice. Traditionally such fried rice dishes are served as a finish to a banquet or dinner but today they are served more and more as a rice dish to accompany an entrée.

SICHUAN GARDEN'S *DAN DAN* NOODLES

Even Sichuan cooking succumbs to the Hong Kong style. The Sichuan Garden, for example, is a popular restaurant in Hong Kong and its chefs were trained by master chefs from Sichuan. Although many of the dishes remain authentic and delicious, there is a subtle Hong Kong touch. For example, unlike the traditional execution of dan dan noodles, at Sichuan Garden they are lighter and less oily. Moreover, instead of using the thicker, traditional noodle of western China, Sichuan Garden uses the thin, dried egg noodles so characteristic of southern Chinese cooking. Here one gets the full bite of chilies, garlic, and other seasonings without the heaviness. These noodles are usually served at the close of a meal to make a tasty finale. This dish can be a delicious part of any meal or a simple luncheon dish in itself.

1 tablespoon peanut oil
4 tablespoons (4 ounces) Sichuan preserved vegetable, thoroughly rinsed and finely chopped
1 tablespoon finely chopped garlic
2 teaspoons finely chopped fresh ginger
2 tablespoons Chinese rice wine or dry sherry
2 tablespoons chili bean sauce
1 tablespoon sesame paste or peanut butter
1 tablespoon dark soy sauce
1 tablespoon sugar
2 cups Rich Chicken Stock (page 221)
½ pound fresh flat or thin Chinese wheat noodles or thin, dried Chinese egg noodles

Heat a wok or large skillet over high heat and add the oil. Add the preserved vegetables, garlic, and ginger and stir-fry for 1 minute. Add the rice wine, chili bean sauce, sesame paste, soy sauce, sugar, and chicken stock. Reduce the heat and simmer for 3 minutes over low heat.

Cook the noodles in a large pot of boiling water for 2 minutes if they are fresh or 5 minutes if they are dried. Drain them well in a colander. Divide the noodles into individual bowls and ladle the sauce over them. Serve at once.

YIELD: SERVES 4

YANGZHOU-STYLE FRIED RICE

2 eggs, beaten
1 teaspoon sesame oil
½ teaspoon salt
Freshly ground white pepper to taste
4 tablespoons peanut oil
1 pound fresh peas, shelled and blanched,
    or 1 cup frozen peas
2 tablespoons finely chopped garlic
3 cups cooked rice
½ cup diced Smithfield ham or bits of Chinese barbecued
    pork
½ cup cooked bay shrimp
4 tablespoons finely chopped whole scallions
1 tablespoon light soy sauce
2 tablespoons Rich Chicken Stock (page 221)
½ teaspoon salt
Freshly ground white pepper to taste

Mix together the eggs, sesame oil, salt, and pepper. Heat a wok or large skillet and add 1 tablespoon of the oil.

When it is hot, add the egg mixture and swirl it in the wok until it forms a large egg crepe. Once it sets, remove immediately and allow to cool. When it is cool, finely slice into thin shreds and set aside.

Blanch the peas in a saucepan of boiling water for about 5 minutes if they are fresh or 2 minutes if they are frozen. Drain them in a colander.

Add the oil to a wok or large skillet, and when it is hot, add the garlic and stir-fry for 30 seconds. Add the cooked rice and stir-fry for 1 minute.

Mix in the ham, peas, bay shrimp, and scallions and stir-fry for 2 minutes. Then add the soy sauce, chicken stock, salt, and pepper and continue to stir-fry another minute. Finally add the shredded cooked eggs and cook for another 2 minutes, stirring constantly. Serve at once or allow it to cool and serve at room temperature as a rice salad.

YIELD: SERVES 4 TO 6

This universally popular rice dish is familiar to Americans because it has been for so long a staple item on the menus of Chinese restaurants here. It is also popular in Hong Kong since it arrived from Eastern China, brought by the Shanghainese (Yangzhou is an area near Shanghai).

This fried rice is a good example of the cross-regional influences that make Hong Kong cooking so unique. The ham often used comes from Yunnan (southwest China) or Zhejiang (eastern China) or sometimes I use barbecued pork, a traditional southern Chinese ingredient. Combine this with fresh small shrimp, typical of southern China, and a very Western adoption, peas. Its diverse origins and ingredients demonstrate the many roots of the Hong Kong cuisine.

CHIU CHOW FRIED RICE

*The peasant Chiu Chow cooking
of southern China that is so
popular in Hong Kong is
characterized by the use of shrimp
paste. It is not difficult to see why
shrimp paste is so widely used by
the Chiu Chow people, as they are
seafaring people from the
Shantou port district of the
Guangdong province. Their
cuisine has been influenced by
that of the Fujianese people in the
adjacent province. Seafood in
many forms is evidence of these
coastal people's seafaring
tradition. Their food is bold and
hearty, as this recipe readily
illustrates. Shrimp paste is akin
to anchovy paste in European
cookery. Its acquired taste is
addicting for anyone who loves the
strong flavors of the sea.*

3 tablespoons peanut oil
3 cups cooked rice
3 tablespoons shredded fresh ginger
½ cup cooked bay shrimp or raw small shrimp cut in half
1 cup fresh sweet peas (1 pound of pods), blanched
2 eggs, beaten
2 teaspoons shrimp paste

Heat a wok or large skillet until it is hot and add the oil.
Stir in the rice, ginger, shrimp, and peas and stir-fry for
2 minutes over high heat. Add the eggs and continue to stir-
fry for another minute. Finally add the shrimp paste and stir
to mix well. Serve at once.
YIELD: SERVES 4 TO 6

BRAISED *YI FU* NOODLES WITH SHRIMP

2 tablespoons salt
1 pound medium shrimp, peeled and deveined
½ pound or 6 cakes of dried *Yi Fu* noodles or dried or
    fresh thin egg noodles
½ cup dried Chinese black mushrooms
2 tablespoons peanut oil
1 tablespoon finely shredded peeled fresh ginger
½ cup Chinese yellow or green chives, cut into
    2-inch pieces

SAUCE
2 tablespoons light soy sauce
1 tablespoon oyster sauce
2 teaspoons dark soy sauce
1 teaspoon sesame oil
1 teaspoon sugar
½ cup Rich Chicken Stock (page 221)

Fresh noodles of all shapes and sizes abound in the markets of Hong Kong. They are eaten at home and in restaurants at all hours of the day or night. This particular recipe is very popular because it is both easy to make and deliciously wholesome. The dried thin egg noodles are readily available.

Fill a large bowl with cold water and 1 tablespoon of salt; gently wash the shrimp in the salt water. Drain and repeat the process. Rinse the shrimp under cold running water, drain, and blot dry with paper towels.

In a large bowl of boiling water, blanch the noodles for 2 minutes or until they are soft. Drain well and dry with paper towels.

Soak the mushrooms in a bowl of warm water for about 20 minutes or until they are soft and pliable. Squeeze out the excess water and cut off and discard the woody stems. Finely shred the mushroom caps.

Heat a wok or large skillet until it is hot and add the oil. Add the shredded ginger and shrimp and stir-fry for 2 minutes, then remove with a slotted spoon. Add the mushrooms, chives, and sauce ingredients and cook over high heat for 1 minute. Return the noodles to the wok and cook in the sauce for about 2 minutes or until the sauce is absorbed into the noodles. Return the shrimp to the wok and mix well until they are heated through. Serve at once.

YIELD: SERVES 4 TO 6

BEAN THREAD NOODLES WITH SHREDDED PORK

This common noodle dish is a staple offering of the many small restaurants and food stalls that service the vast population of Hong Kong. The "noodles" are actually made from green soy beans (with a little starch and water). They are quite nutritious and acquire a velvety, light, and appealing texture that allows them to absorb the flavors of a sauce, as in this dish. The bits of pork add a rich dimension to the simple noodles. This is tasty, sustaining food and easy to make; small wonder it is so popular.

3 small packages bean thread noodles (12 ounces)
½ pound lean pork tenderloins or boneless pork chops

MARINADE
2 teaspoons light soy sauce
1 teaspoon cornstarch mixed with 1 teaspoon water

1 tablespoon peanut oil

SAUCE
2 tablespoons light soy sauce
1 teaspoon salt
2 tablespoons sesame paste
1 tablespoon fish sauce
2 teaspoons rice wine
1 teaspoon sugar
1 cup Rich Chicken Stock (page 221)

GARNISH
2 tablespoons finely chopped whole scallions

Soak the bean thread noodles in a medium-sized bowl of warm water for about 20 minutes and drain in a colander.

Place the pork in the freezer for about 20 minutes or until it is firm to the touch. Cut the meat into slices and then into shreds. Mix together the marinade ingredients and add to the pork. Allow the pork to marinate for 20 minutes.

Heat a wok or large skillet until it is hot and add the oil. When the oil is hot, stir-fry the pork shreds for 1 minute. Add the sauce ingredients, bring to a boil, and add the noodles. Stir well and continue to cook for about 5 minutes or until most of the liquid has been absorbed by the noodles. Garnish with the scallions and serve at once.

YIELD: SERVES 4 TO 6

NOODLES WITH CRABMEAT IN BROTH

½ pound thin, dried Chinese egg noodles
4 cups Rich Chicken Stock (page 221)
1 teaspoon salt
2 teaspoons sesame oil
½ pound crabmeat

GARNISH
2 tablespoons finely chopped whole scallions

Blanch the noodles in boiling water for about 4 minutes. Drain immediately and divide into four serving bowls.

Meanwhile, heat the chicken stock in a medium-sized pot and add the salt and sesame oil. Add crabmeat to each bowl and ladle the hot stock over. Garnish with scallions and serve at once.

YIELD: SERVES 4

As I have noted elsewhere, hotel restaurants in Hong Kong offer some of the best and most innovative cooking. The Rainbow Room of the Lee Gardens Hotel in Causeway Bay is an example. One year, the chef there prepared an outstanding meal for my cooking group. It included such imaginative delectables as Fried Fresh-Milk Prawns and Pan-Fried Chicken with Lemon Juice. The dinner closed with this marvelous noodle and crab soup, a tour de force, coming as it did after so many other treats. The subtle but distinct crab flavor made a perfect marriage with the noodles and the broth — light, refreshing, and impressive enough to stand by itself. I was surprised to learn that once you have the fresh crabmeat — the key ingredient — this dish is actually quite easy to make. I have since served it often myself, offering it, however, as an opening course to a formal dinner, for which it serves splendidly. I also have found that dried, rather than fresh, noodles work very well.

STIR-FRIED RICE NOODLES WITH BEEF AND CHILI BEAN SAUCE

People in Hong Kong habitually eat late meals. With a mild climate for much of the year and restaurants open all night, they live a very Mediterranean type of life. Being in Hong Kong reminds me of my stays in Naples, where at eleven in the evening, you can easily satisfy your urge for a quick pasta dish. Southern Chinese choose something filling but lighter, such as rice noodles, which are satisfying and easy to digest. This popular Hong Kong noodle dish is one of my favorites. It is nutritious and full of flavor. You may substitute pork for beef if you wish. Delicious served at room temperature, this dish is wonderful for a buffet or picnic.

½ pound (½ package) thin, flat, dried rice noodles
¾ to 1 pound market steak, beef fillet, or New York steak

COATING
1 egg white
2 teaspoons light soy sauce
2 teaspoons rice wine
1 teaspoon sesame oil
½ teaspoon salt
1 teaspoon cornstarch

1 cup peanut oil
1 tablespoon finely chopped garlic
2 teaspoons finely chopped fresh ginger
3 fresh red chili peppers, seeded and shredded
2 teaspoons chili bean sauce
2 teaspoons dark soy sauce
¼ cup Rich Chicken Stock (page 221)
1 teaspoon sugar
1 teaspoon rice wine
1 teaspoon sesame oil

GARNISH
3 tablespoons finely chopped scallion tops

Soak the noodles in a bowl of warm water for 20 minutes or until they are soft and pliable. Drain and set aside.

Place the steak in the freezer for about 20 minutes or until it is firm to the touch. Then cut it, against the grain, into slices. Add it to a bowl with all the coating ingredients and refrigerate for 20 minutes.

Heat a wok or large skillet until it is hot and add the oil. Add the meat, stir-fry for 1 minute, and immediately drain into a colander set inside a bowl, reserving 1 tablespoon oil.

Reheat the wok and return the drained oil. Add the garlic, ginger, chilies, chili bean sauce, and dark soy sauce and stir-fry for 30 seconds. Add the drained rice noodles and the chicken stock, mix well, and continue to stir-fry for 1 minute. Return the drained meat to the mixture and stir-fry

for 1 more minute. Add the sugar, rice wine, and sesame oil
and give the mixture a final stir. Ladle the dish onto a platter,
garnish with the scallion tops, and serve.
YIELD: SERVES 4 TO 6

CHIU CHOW NOODLES IN SESAME SAUCE

½ **pound (about 6 cakes) dried** *Yi Fu* **noodles or dried or
   fresh thin egg noodles**
2 **tablespoons sesame oil**

SESAME SAUCE
4 **tablespoons sesame paste**
1 **tablespoon dark soy sauce**
2 **tablespoons light soy sauce**
2 **teaspoons sugar**
1 **cup Rich Chicken Stock (page 221)**
½ **teaspoon salt**

Blanch the noodles for 2 minutes, or until they are barely
soft, in a large pot of boiling salted water. Drain well and
toss immediately with sesame oil and arrange on a serving
platter.

   Meanwhile, mix the sesame sauce ingredients together
in a small pot and bring to a simmer. Allow the sauce to cool
slightly and toss with the noodles. Serve at once.
YIELD: SERVES 4 TO 6

*Overpopulation in southern
China forced many of the natives
of Chiu Chow to emigrate to other
regions in Southeast Asia, and
this produced poor economic
conditions. Those who remained
managed on meager food supplies
but used them imaginatively.
Later, many came to Hong Kong,
where Chiu Chow cuisine thrives
today with lesser-known southern
Chinese cooking styles, such as
those of the Hakka, Tanka and
Hoklo people. Here, a savory
sesame sauce transforms a simple
noodle dish into a special meal.
This simple dish can be served
directly from the stove or at room
temperature and is excellent
either way.*

CHINESE PANCAKES

*These pancakes are a northern
Chinese traditional classic. In
Hong Kong, they are most
frequently served in restaurants
that specialize in Peking Duck.
As you will see when you make
them yourself, the pancakes play
an essential role in the enjoyment
of that treat, and of many other
sumptuous foods. Persevere in
your efforts to make these
correctly — they are well worth the
trouble since homemade pancakes
are always so much better than
the commercial variety. And with
practice you will find it easier and
easier.*

2 cups all-purpose unbleached flour
1 cup very hot water
2 tablespoons sesame oil
Flour, for dusting

In a large bowl, combine the flour and hot water, stirring constantly with chopsticks or a fork until the water is fully incorporated. Add more hot water if the mixture seems dry. The dough should just hold together in coarse lumps. Remove and knead it with your hands until it is smooth. Return the dough to the bowl, cover it with a clean, damp towel, and set it aside for about 30 minutes.

Take the dough out of the bowl and knead it again for about 5 minutes, dusting with a little flour if it is sticky. Then form it into a roll about 18 inches long and about 1 inch in diameter. Cut the roll into about 18 pieces.

Roll each piece into a ball. Dip one side of one ball into the sesame oil and place the oiled side on top of another ball. Take a rolling pin and roll the two together into a circle about 6 inches in diameter. Rolling two pieces together keeps the dough moist inside, allows you to make thinner pancakes, and keeps them from drying out in cooking.

Heat an unoiled frying pan or wok over a very low flame. Put the double pancake into the wok or pan and cook it until it has dried on one side. Flip it over and cook the other side briefly in the same way. Remove the pancakes, peel them apart, and set them aside. Repeat this process until all the dough is used up.

When you are ready to serve the pancakes, simply steam them. To set up a steamer, put a rack inside a wok or deep pan. Fill the pan with about 2 inches of water. Bring the water to a boil, then reduce the heat to a low simmer. Place the pancakes on a heat-proof plate and put the plate on the rack. Cover and steam for 8 minutes. Or wrap them in plastic wrap and heat them in a microwave oven for 35 seconds to 1½ minutes or until they are warm through.

Note: Do not reheat the pancakes in the oven because this will dry them too much. If you want to freeze the cooked pancakes, wrap them tightly in plastic wrap. When using pancakes that have been frozen, let them thaw, still wrapped, in the refrigerator before reheating them.

YIELD: MAKES 18 PANCAKES

DESSERTS

~~~~~~~~~~~~~~~~~~~~

COLD HONEYDEW MELON AND COCONUT SOUP

"DOUBLE-STEAMED" BIRD'S NEST WITH COCONUT

SWEET ALMOND SOUP

CUSTARD TARTLETS

SWEET WALNUT CREAM

MANGO PUDDING

ORANGE CREAM PUDDING

ALMOND PUDDING WITH FRESH FRUIT

HONEYDEW PUDDING

STEAMED MILK WITH GINGER JUICE

~~~~~~

Traditionally, the concept of dessert has not had very high status in Chinese cuisine and sweets in general are relatively unusual. This has changed somewhat recently, with refined sugar becoming cheap and plentiful. The traditional Chinese finale to a meal generally involves something naturally sweet such as fruit, very small amounts of honey, or coconuts. Hong Kong chefs continue this tradition and consciously avoid the introduction of too much refined sugar. Human palates are quite sensitive and the addictive power of white sugar can be overwhelming, to the destruction of a fine cuisine. The recipes here are for sweet but never cloying dishes.

COLD HONEYDEW MELON AND COCONUT SOUP

Banquets in Hong Kong are usually followed by rich pastries, and invariably dessert includes this sweet cold "soup." No doubt of Southeast Asian inspiration, this soup gives a sweet and refreshing finish to any meal. I use tapioca to thicken the soup here, as a substitute for sago, which is a starch obtained from the stem of the Southeast Asian sago palm. Tapioca is prepared from the tuberous roots of the tropical cassava or manioc shrub and is a good substitute for sago, which is less available here. The melons should be very ripe and full of flavor. I think you will find this soup a perfect ending to any meal, especially during the warm-weather season.

¼ cup small pearl tapioca
½ cup water
2 cups fresh or canned coconut milk
6 tablespoons sugar
1 cup cold milk
1 or 2 ripe honeydew melons, about 3 pounds

GARNISH
Fresh mint leaves

Combine the tapioca and water in a small bowl and let sit for 45 minutes. Drain the tapioca and set aside.

In a medium-sized saucepan combine the coconut milk, sugar, and tapioca and simmer for 10 minutes or until the mixture begins to thicken. Add the cold milk and allow the mixture to cool thoroughly, then cover with plastic wrap and refrigerate.

Cut the honeydew melon into quarters, remove the seeds, and cut off the peel. Cut the melon into large pieces and purée in a blender or food processor until it is a thick liquid. Pour into a medium-sized bowl, cover with plastic wrap, and refrigerate.

When you are ready to serve the soup, combine the two mixtures in the following manner: In a soup tureen, add the coconut-tapioca mixture on one side, then add the honeydew mixture on the other side, letting them run together to form a yin-yang pattern. Garnish with the mint leaves and bring to the table and serve after a few stirs.

YIELD: SERVES 6 TO 8

"DOUBLE-STEAMED" BIRD'S NEST WITH COCONUT

½ cup loosely packed dried bird's nest
2 cups fresh or canned coconut milk
½ cup sugar
1 cup water

Soak the bird's nest overnight in warm water. Drain and rinse under cold running water. Blanch the bird's nest in boiling water for 5 minutes. Drain thoroughly and set aside.

Combine the bird's nest with the coconut milk, sugar, and water. Simmer for 25 minutes. Ladle the mixture into individual bowls or a soup tureen and serve at once.

YIELD: SERVES 4 TO 6

Whenever you desire an unforgettable close to a very special dinner party, consider this reasonable facsimile of one of the really exotic Cantonese–Hong Kong desserts. A bird's nest inside a hollowed-out coconut shell and, if possible, set within a coconut-shaped tureen, will certainly make an impression. The silky soft texture of the bird's nest in the sweet, fragrant coconut milk is indeed a grand finale to your meal. This recipe is, as I have noted, a facsimile that omits the long double-steaming process and the laborious carving out of the coconut. I simply combine the coconut milk, sugar, and water with the bird's nest and simmer them together. The result is not as spectacular as the original but it is a close version, still quite exceptional and very much easier to make. Give it a try; you won't forget it.

SWEET ALMOND SOUP

I remember my mother grinding almonds into a purée with water, then adding sugar and heating it until it was a rich, thick, milky, fragrant, warm "soup." We would have it as a snack with cookies during the day or as a dessert. Such sweet soups are a traditional Cantonese favorite. Sometimes they are made with black sesame seeds or with red beans. The almond soup has always been my favorite, and I am pleased to find it experiencing renewed popularity in Hong Kong. Almonds are usually ground by hand in stone mortars — blenders and food processors for some reason make them bitter, at least to my taste. But unless you like to grind things by hand, substitute commercially made almond paste. It tastes just like Mother-used-to-make, and it certainly saves time. The result is a warm, sweetly delicious dessert that evokes the fragrance of Hong Kong.

1 cup almond paste
1 cup milk
2 cups water

Combine the almond paste, milk, and water together in a medium-sized pot and simmer for 15 minutes. Serve at once.

YIELD: SERVES 4 TO 6

CUSTARD TARTLETS

PASTRY INGREDIENTS
1 cup flour
4 tablespoons butter, cut into small pieces
2 tablespoons sugar
2 tablespoons heavy cream
½ teaspoon salt

3 cups dried beans, for weighting down pastry shell
½ cup water
4 tablespoons sugar
3 eggs, beaten

These custard tartlets are a well-known part of dim sum luncheons. In Hong Kong, lard is generally used to make the pastry, which results in a flaky but heavier pastry with an oily flavor. I have reworked the idea to suit my own taste, using butter. Butter is an ingredient familiar to the people of Hong Kong, and though not widely used, its use is growing. The custard should be light and silky.

Mix all the pastry ingredients together in a bowl or a food processor until well mixed. Roll the pastry into a ball, wrap it with plastic wrap, and refrigerate for at least 30 minutes.

Preheat the oven to 375° F. Roll out the pastry to about ⅛ inch thick and press into 6 small 3-inch tartlet molds. Place a sheet of foil over the sides and surface of the pastry and pour enough dried beans on the foil to weight it down. Bake for about 10 to 12 minutes or until the dough is lightly browned.

Remove the beans and the foil from the tartlet molds. Lightly pierce the pastry surface with a fork. Return the tartlets to the oven and bake for 5 minutes longer or until the bottom crust is dry.

In a saucepan, boil together the water and sugar for 5 minutes to make a light syrup. Let the syrup cool thoroughly and combine it with the eggs. Pour an equal amount of custard into each pastry shell.

Reduce the oven heat to 325° F and bake for 15 minutes or until the custard just sets.
YIELD: MAKES 6 TARTLETS

SWEET WALNUT CREAM

Americans and other Westerners
are at first surprised to see soup
served as a dessert. They soon
discover that it works very well.
Walnut soup has made its way
onto the menus of some of Hong
Kong's best restaurants.
Although my favorite is almond
soup, I never turn down this
version either. It is a deliciously
different way to close out a nice
dinner.

1 cup walnuts
2 cups water
1 cup evaporated milk
1 cup sugar

Blanch the walnuts for 5 minutes in a small pot of boiling
water. Drain and rinse well in warm water. Allow them
to dry.

Preheat the oven to 350° F, place the walnuts on a baking tray, and bake for 15 minutes or until they are light
brown and crisp. Allow them to cool.

In a blender, combine the walnuts and water and blend
into a fine purée. Strain the purée through a fine sieve.

Combine the walnut purée and milk in a medium-sized
pan and simmer for 1 minute. Beat in the sugar and simmer
for 1 minute. Serve immediately or when cool.

YIELD: SERVES 4

MANGO PUDDING

Ripe mangoes are marvelous. In
season, their aroma haunts the
air of Hong Kong's fruit stalls.
And Hong Kong gets the best of
the Asian crop: mangoes from
Thailand and the Philippines.
Hong Kong chefs have concocted
this basically Western dessert,
using milk and gelatin to make
the most of the taste, fragrance,

2 mangoes (about 14 ounces each)
1 cup low-fat milk
1 cup water
1 package unflavored gelatin
1 cup sugar

Skin the mangoes. Remove the flesh and purée in a food
processor. Put the purée through a strainer and set aside.

Combine the milk, water, gelatin, and sugar in a medium-sized pot and bring to a simmer. Stir well with a whisk
to dissolve the gelatin. In a separate pot, bring the mango

purée to a simmer and cook over low heat for 5 minutes. Combine the contents of the 2 pots together in a lightly oiled medium-sized (4 cup) copper mold or heat-proof pyrex glass bowl, which needs no oiling. Cool to room temperature and then refrigerate for at least 2 hours.

YIELD: SERVE 4 TO 6

and texture of the mango. Use the ripest mangoes you can find for this superb dessert.

ORANGE CREAM PUDDING

2 cups strained orange juice
1 package unflavored gelatin
½ cup milk
½ cup sugar
2 eggs
1 cup heavy cream

Bring the orange juice to a simmer. Place it in a blender, add the gelatin, and blend for 15 seconds until smooth.

Add the milk, sugar, and eggs and blend for 10 seconds. Add the cream and continue to blend for another 20 seconds.

Spoon into individual serving dishes, cover with plastic wrap, and chill for at least three hours before serving.

YIELD: SERVES 4 TO 6

Fruits are the preferred close to most traditional Chinese meals, but gelatin and ice cream desserts are popular too. To my taste, many of the gelatin desserts are rather rubbery in texture, perhaps reflecting the Chinese passion for textured foods. But I have taken an orange-fruit dessert that I have had in Hong Kong restaurants and reduced the amount of gelatin in the recipe. The result is a silky custardlike dessert, only slightly firm but textured enough. A bonus is that it takes about five minutes to make.

ALMOND PUDDING WITH FRESH FRUIT

Puddings made with gelatin are a popular offering in many homes and restaurants in Hong Kong. The light texture of gelatin is a soothing finish to meals in which strong flavors such as garlic, shrimp paste, oyster sauce, or black beans are used to flavor meats or vegetables. Here, an almond inspiration is combined with fresh oranges to make a typical light dessert. You can easily use other seasonal fruits, such as raspberries, strawberries, or fresh peaches.

½ cup sugar
1 package unflavored gelatin
½ cup evaporated milk
1½ cups fresh or canned coconut milk
1 teaspoon almond extract
2 oranges, peeled

Mix the sugar and gelatin together in a large stainless bowl.

Combine the two milks in a medium-sized saucepan, bring to a simmer, and add the almond extract. Pour the mixture in a steady stream into the gelatin mixture, stirring constantly with a whisk. Pour the mixture back into the pan and continue to cook over low heat for 2 minutes, stirring all the while. Remove from the heat and if the mixture is lumpy, strain it. When cool, pour into a 3-cup mold, cover with plastic wrap, and refrigerate for 4 hours or until it has set.

Separate the orange segments by cutting down both sides between the flesh and the membrane. Save any juice and set aside.

To unmold, dip the bottom of the mold in warm water briefly, being careful not to let any of the water inside the mold. Hold the mold firmly against a serving plate and invert.

Garnish the pudding with the fresh orange segments and juice. Serve at once.

YIELD: SERVES 4

HONEYDEW PUDDING

1 package unflavored gelatin
¼ cup cold water
2 cups honeydew melon purée
4 egg yolks
½ cup sugar
Pinch of salt
¾ cup milk
1 cup heavy cream

Combine the gelatin and water and set aside. Remove the flesh of the honeydew and purée in a blender until it yields 2 cups.

In a large bowl, beat the egg yolks, sugar, and salt together until fluffy and light yellow in color. Bring the milk to a boil, remove, and slowly pour in a steady stream into the egg mixture, beating all the while. Return the mixture to the stove and cook over medium heat, constantly stirring until the mixture thickens. Remove from the heat, stir in the gelatin mixture, and allow to cool.

Fold in the honeydew purée.

Beat the cream until it is stiff and fold this into the mixture. Turn the mixture into a mold or into individual dishes. Chill for at least two hours.

YIELD: SERVES 4 TO 6

Traditionally, Chinese dinners and banquets have no proper dessert course. Instead, fresh fruits may be offered, sometimes presented dramatically, with the fruits elaborately carved and set on dry ice which sends off smokelike vapors, a cooling, refreshing contrast to the highly seasoned, hot dishes that had comprised the dinner. However, dessert courses are now making their appearance on a regular basis in Hong Kong restaurants. Still linked to tradition, they tend to make use of fruit as this recipe shows. Sweet honeydew melon in a rich, creamy pudding very much like a Bavarian cream provides a cooling, sweet close to any meal. It is easy to make, can be done hours ahead of time, and is thus perfect for entertaining.

STEAMED MILK WITH GINGER JUICE

Milk is not a common item in the Chinese diet but when it does appear, you may be sure it has been somehow modified or is meant to be consumed in small portions. In Hong Kong, there are many shops that specialize in either bean-curd custard or this dish. The whole milk is mixed with the flavoring and then steamed briefly, transforming the milk into a delicate custard, with a refreshing ginger bite, a sweet-and-spicy dessert to serve by itself or with fruit or cookies.

3 cups whole milk
6 tablespoons sugar
2 tablespoons ginger juice
Sliced oranges and mangoes (optional)

Combine the milk, sugar, and ginger juice. Mix well. Pour the mixture into a heat-proof casserole. Set up a steamer. Place the casserole inside the steamer and slowly steam for 20 minutes.

Allow to cool slightly. Gently drain off the excess liquid from the surface of the milk and serve warm with fresh fruit slices.

YIELD: SERVES 4

STOCKS
AND
SAUCES

~~~~~~~~~~

STOCKS:

RICH CHICKEN STOCK

HAM AND CHICKEN STOCK

SAUCES:

SWEET-AND-SOUR SAUCE

VINEGAR–CHILI BEAN DIPPING SAUCE

VINEGAR-GINGER SAUCE

GINGER SAUCE

GINGER-SCALLION SAUCE

CHILI BEAN–SCALLION SAUCE

MUSTARD SAUCE

SOY-SCALLION CHILI DIPPING SAUCE

GARLIC-VINEGAR DIPPING SAUCE

SALT-AND-PEPPER DIP

~~~~~~

It cannot be repeated too often: Good cooking requires good stocks. Without good stocks, no proper blendings can occur, no sauces will delight the palate, no cuisine can achieve its desired goals. Think of stocks as fundamental. Give them your attention. Use them as your points of departure. With a solid basis in your good stocks, you will never find yourself out on a limb with a failed recipe.

STOCK

Stock is the foundation of all good cooking. I emphasize this because it is so important a principle. Good stock, especially chicken stock, is necessary for the cuisine of Hong Kong, whose subtle flavors, fresh ingredients, and fast cooking techniques require very good stock. Light, flavorful, and versatile chicken stock should be considered a staple, to set beside salt, cooking oil, or soy sauce.

There are commercially prepared canned or cubed stocks but many of them are of inferior quality, being either too salty or containing additives and colorings that adversely affect your health as well as the natural taste of good foods. Make your own, it is the best. You can make a big batch and freeze it for your own use when needed. In making a good stock, here are a few rules to remember:

- It is best to use about 50 percent bones and 50 percent meat. Without meat, the stock will not have the necessary body or richness or depth of flavor and will taste watery. Stewing old hens is best if you can find them, because they are inexpensive and full of flavor.
- Stock should simmer. Never let the stock come to a boil because that will result in a cloudy and heavy stock. Flavors and digestibility come with a clear stock.
- Use a tall heavy pot so the liquid covers all the solids and evaporation is slow.
- Simmer on low heat and gently skim the stock every now and then to remove any impurities.
- Strain the stock slowly through several layers of cheesecloth or a fine mesh strainer.
- Allow the stock to cool thoroughly before storing in the refrigerator or freezer.

RICH CHICKEN STOCK

7½ pounds whole chicken and parts, such as backs,
    feet, wings
6 quarts cold water
8 slices unpeeled fresh ginger
8 whole scallions, cut into pieces
2 teaspoons salt

Cut up the chicken and put the pieces and parts together into a very large pot. Cover them with the cold water and bring the stock to a simmer. Using a large, flat spoon, gently skim off the scum as it rises from the bones. Watch the heat as the stock should *never* boil. Keep skimming until the stock looks clear. This can take from 30 to 40 minutes. Do not stir or disturb the stock.

Turn the heat down to a low simmer and add the ginger, scallions, and salt. Simmer the stock on a very low heat for at least 3 hours, skimming any fat off the top at least twice during this time. Strain the stock through several layers of dampened cheesecloth or through a very fine mesh strainer, and then let it cool thoroughly. Remove any fat that has risen to the top. It is now ready to be used or transferred to containers and frozen for future use.

YIELD: 6 QUARTS

If you make a habit of saving your uncooked chicken bones and carcasses, you will have the essential ingredient for stock in no time. It makes good economical sense also.

The stock should be rich and full-bodied, which is why it needs to be simmered for such a long time. This way the stock (and any soup you make with it) will have plenty of taste. With a good stock, you will also get good sauces for a true taste of Hong Kong!

HAM AND CHICKEN STOCK

Some of the special dishes of Hong Kong cuisine require a stronger stock, in which case, the one to use is this ham and chicken stock. It is primarily used with shark's fin or bird's nest soup, exotic foods that are prized for their texture but need additional strong flavors. This rich stock will more than suffice.

½-pound piece of Smithfield ham
3½ quarts (14 cups) Rich Chicken Stock (page 221)
4 whole scallions, cut into pieces
6 slices fresh ginger

Blanch the ham in boiling water for 10 minutes. Remove with a slotted spoon.

Bring the chicken stock to a simmer, add the ham, scallions, and ginger. Simmer uncovered for about 2 hours.

Strain the stock through a fine sieve. The ham can be used for garnish or flavoring soups. Allow the stock to cool thoroughly. Remove any fat that has risen to the top. It is now ready to be used or transferred to containers and frozen for future use.

YIELD: 3½ QUARTS

SWEET-AND-SOUR SAUCE

Unlike carelessly made sweet-and-sour sauces found in mediocre restaurants, this one, inspired by several I have had in Hong Kong, has just the right balance. You may very well use it as a barbecue sauce, as well as for dipping crisp wontons.

½ cup white rice vinegar
½ teaspoon salt
5 tablespoons sugar
¼ cup tomato paste or tomato ketchup
1 tablespoon dark soy sauce
1 teaspoon cornstarch mixed with 1 teaspoon water

Combine all the ingredients in a small saucepan and simmer for about 5 minutes.

Cool before serving.

YIELD: ¾ CUP

VINEGAR–CHILI BEAN DIPPING SAUCE

1 tablespoon chili bean sauce
2 tablespoons white rice vinegar
1 tablespoon light soy sauce

Put the chili bean sauce into a small dish, then mix in the vinegar and gradually beat in the soy sauce to taste. This sauce should be made just before serving.
YIELD: ½ CUP

This is a sauce you can adjust to your taste. In fact, it is usually mixed by the individual diner. It is used for dipping dumplings, such as Preserved Vegetable Dumplings (page 30).

VINEGAR-GINGER SAUCE

¼ cup red rice vinegar
4 tablespoons finely shredded peeled fresh ginger

Combine the vinegar and ginger in a small deep dish. Allow to sit for at least 5 minutes or up to 1 hour before serving.
YIELD: ¼ CUP

A delicious and refreshing sauce used with rich meat dumplings such as Steamed Shanghai Dumplings (page 31). The bite of fresh ginger is a wonderful counterpoint to the meat; the fresh ginger should be shredded as finely as possible.

GINGER SAUCE

This gingery sauce can be used for Cold Drunken Chicken (page 115) or other cold meats. If you are a real lover of ginger, it can be used as a dip for anything you wish. This is easy to make.

3 tablespoons finely chopped fresh ginger
2 teaspoons salt
1½ tablespoons peanut oil

Combine the ginger and salt together in a small dish. Heat the oil in a small pan or wok until it is smoking; pour over the ginger-salt mixture. Allow to sit for 5 minutes before serving. Use immediately. Do not reheat.
YIELD: ¼ CUP

GINGER-SCALLION SAUCE

This childhood favorite of mine is very popular in Hong Kong. I have often wondered how such a southern Chinese sauce made it across the Pacific to Chicago. No matter; it is delectable wherever one may be.

2 teaspoons finely chopped ginger
2 tablespoons finely chopped whole scallions
½ teaspoon salt
2 teaspoons light soy sauce
1 tablespoon peanut oil

Combine the ginger, scallions, salt, and soy sauce in a small, dipping-sauce plate. Heat the oil in a saucepan or wok and when it is smoking, pour it over the mixture. Use at once.
YIELD: ¼ CUP

CHILI BEAN–SCALLION SAUCE

2 tablespoons chili bean sauce
2 tablespoons finely chopped whole scallions
1 tablespoon peanut oil
1 teaspoon sesame oil

Mix the chili bean sauce and scallions together in a small dish. Heat the peanut oil and sesame oil together in a small pan until almost smoking. Pour this hot oil over the chili mixture. Allow to sit for 5 minutes before serving.
YIELD: ¼ CUP

A perfect sauce for chili lovers who want to add an extra spicy note to their foods, this can be used for meats, noodles, or poultry.

MUSTARD SAUCE

2 tablespoons dry, ground yellow mustard (sometimes referred to as "English style")
2 tablespoons hot water
2 teaspoons peanut oil

Place the mustard in a small mixing bowl and gradually stir in the hot water until it is thoroughly mixed. Allow the sauce to sit for 2 minutes, then pour the peanut oil over the surface to cover. It is now ready to serve.
YIELD: ¼ CUP

This yellow mustard sauce is a familiar sight to Americans because its origin is Western. It nevertheless became quite popular in Hong Kong, having been brought there by the British over a hundred years ago. Using hot water intensifies the mustard flavor. The thin film of oil prevents the sauce from crusting and keeps it smooth.

SOY-SCALLION CHILI DIPPING SAUCE

You will find this very popular sauce frequently served throughout meals in Hong Kong. Since the chili is mild, the bite is less strong. It is used for dipping cooked fresh shrimps, as well as cooked poultry or meats. I find it delicious with almost any dish.

1 fresh, mild red chili pepper, seeded and finely shredded
¼ cup finely shredded whole scallions
2 tablespoons light soy sauce
1 tablespoon dark soy sauce
1½ tablespoons peanut oil

Combine the chili pepper, scallions, and soy sauces in a dish. Heat the oil in a small pan until it is almost smoking and pour this over the chili-scallion mixture. Allow the sauce to sit for 10 minutes before serving. This sauce can be made at least 2 hours in advance.

YIELD: ¼ CUP

GARLIC-VINEGAR DIPPING SAUCE

This rather strong sauce is used for Braised Chiu Chow Duck (page 39) or for Pigs' Feet Cooked in Wine and Vinegar (page 36). The zesty bite of the raw garlic is mellowed by the vinegar and provides a strong counterpoint to those rich dishes.

1 tablespoon finely chopped peeled garlic
3 tablespoons white rice vinegar

Combine the garlic and vinegar in a small dish and allow to sit for at least 10 minutes before serving.

YIELD: ¼ CUP

SALT-AND-PEPPER DIP

1 tablespoon Sichuan peppercorns, roasted and finely
   ground
3 tablespoons coarse salt

Heat a wok or large skillet until it is hot and add the ground peppercorns and salt. Stir-fry for 1 minute, remove, and allow to cool. Then mix in a blender for 1 minute. The dip is now ready to be used or can be saved for future use.

YIELD: ¼ CUP

This dip is a favorite condiment on Hong Kong tables. It is frequently used to add a spicy and salty note to fried foods, but it may be added to any dish, as you prefer.

GLOSSARY

INGREDIENTS

~~~~~~

Fresh ingredients are, of course, essential to good cooking, especially in the case of Hong Kong cuisine. People in Hong Kong often shop daily, often up to three times a day. This is due partially to small refrigerators and lack of storage space. But the chief cause is the desire to get food as fresh as possible. These fresh foods are further enhanced by seasonings, spices, and sauces that complement and add subtle nuances to dishes. Thus fresh foods and the proper ingredients are essential to duplicating the taste of Hong Kong. The recipes in this book draw upon special ingredients that provide a distinctive taste to the foods, making them authentic versions of the originals.

All the ingredients used in these recipes can be obtained not only in Chinese and Asian supermarkets, but also in ordinary metropolitan supermarkets, in the ethnic food sections.

At the end of this introduction, I list all the special ingredients I have used in this book, their uses, how to store them, and what to look for.

One ingredient commonly used throughout Asia, but less in good Hong Kong restaurants and homes, and which you will *not* find mentioned here is monosodium glutamate (also known as MSG, Ve Tsin, Accent, seasoning or taste powder). This is a white crystalline extract of grains and vegetables widely used to tenderize and enhance the natural flavor of certain foods. Some people have an adverse reaction to it, experiencing symptoms such as headaches, excessive thirst, and heart palpitations. This allergic response is sometimes known as "Chinese restaurant syndrome." All good chefs maintain that the freshest and finest ingredients need no enhancing, and I agree with them wholeheartedly.

Hong Kong food markets are full of exotic vegetables that unfortunately are difficult or impossible to find here: wild rice shoots, fresh straw mushrooms, fresh bamboo shoots, smoked garlic, pea shoots, and yellow cucumbers are among ingredients impossible to find in the West. The good news, however, is that *most* ingredients, seasonings, and vegetables *are* available and becoming increasingly so with expanding trade and the spread of an international style of cuisine. Today, with a little effort, you can duplicate many of the culinary wonders of Hong Kong quite easily. All the recipes included in this book were tested with ingredients that are found here.

BAMBOO SHOOTS

Bamboo shoots are the young edible shoots of certain kinds of bamboo belonging to the grass family. There are as many different types of bamboo shoots as there are kinds of bamboo — and at least ten of the possible hundred or so are marketed. They generally fall into two broad categories: spring shoots and winter shoots, the winter being smaller and more tender than the spring ones, which tend to be quite large.

Fresh bamboo shoots are prepared by first stripping off all their leaves and then trimming the hard base. Only the center core is edible. It is then cut and blanched for at least five minutes to remove its bitterness. Then the shoots are ready to be stir-fried or cooked.

Although you can occasionally find fresh bamboo shoots in Hong Kong food markets, they are nevertheless expensive and not as available as those that are canned, which is the only way you can find them in the West. Canned bamboo shoots tend to be pale yellow with a crunchy texture and, in some cases, a slightly sweet flavor. They come peeled and either whole or thickly sliced. You can find them not only in Asian specialty markets but also in many supermarkets. Rinse them thoroughly before use and transfer any leftover shoots to a jar, cover them with fresh water, and keep in the refrigerator. If the water is changed daily they will keep two to three days.

BEAN CURD

Bean curd is also known by its Chinese name, *dou fu,* or by its Japanese name, tofu. It has played an important part in Chinese cookery for over a thousand years because it is highly nutritious, rich in protein, and works well with other foods. Bean curd has a distinctive texture but a bland taste. It is made from yellow soybeans that are soaked, ground, mixed with water, and then cooked briefly before being solidified. It is usually sold in two forms: as firm cakes or in a soft, custardlike variety, but it is also available in several dried forms and in a fermented version. The soft bean curd (sometimes called silken tofu) is used for soups and other dishes, while the solid type is used for stir-frying, braising, and deep-frying. Solid bean-curd cakes are white in color and are sold in many supermarkets or Asian specialty markets. They are packed in water in plastic containers and may be kept in this state in the refrigerator for up to five days, provided the water is changed daily. To use solid bean curd, cut the amount required into cubes or shreds using a sharp knife. Do this with care as bean curd is delicate; it also needs to be cooked gently as too much stirring can cause it to disintegrate (although this does not affect its nutritional value).

In Hong Kong markets, you can find bean curd stalls that specialize in assorted forms of bean curd.

DRIED BEAN CURD STICKS

Dried bean curd sticks are made by boiling soybean milk, which results in a film forming. This film is then lifted off and dried. This comes in many forms. Especially common is the dried long "stick" form. It must be soaked for about 30 minutes in warm water before it can be used. These sticks are inexpensive and can be found in many Chinese markets. They usually come wrapped in cellophane and can be stored in a dry, cool place. They last indefinitely.

FERMENTED BEAN CURD (RED, CHILI, AND REGULAR)

This is a cheeselike form of bean curd preserved in rice or with wine, brine with rice, or with chilies, and sold in glass jars at Asian specialty markets. It is used as a flavoring agent, especially with vegetables. A little adds zest to any vegetable dish. Once it begins to cook, it produces a fragrant odor that enriches the vegetables. It comes in several forms: the red fermented bean curd has been cured in a brine with red rice, the chili version has flecks of crushed chili peppers, and the regular one is plain. It can be eaten plain with rice also. Once the jar is opened, it will keep indefinitely when well sealed in the refrigerator. There is no substitute for this unique ingredient.

PRESSED AND SEASONED BEAN CURD

When water is extracted from fresh bean-curd cakes by pressing them with a weight, the bean curd becomes firm and compact. Simmered in water with soy sauce, star anise, and sugar, the pressed bean curd acquires a smooth, resilient texture that is quite unusual. Cut into small pieces, it can be stir-fried with meat or vegetables; when cut into larger pieces, it can be simmered. In China, pressed bean curd is a popular offering at many food stalls. Here, it can be found at Asian specialty markets. If it is unavailable, substitute fresh, firm bean curd.

BEAN SPROUTS

Bean sprouts are now widely available in supermarkets and Asian specialty markets. They are the sprouts of the green mung bean, although some Chinese markets also stock yellow soybean sprouts that are much larger. Bean sprouts should always be very fresh and crunchy. They will keep for several days loosely wrapped in paper towels, inside a plastic bag stored in the vegetable compartment of a refrigerator.

BEAN THREAD NOODLES. *SEE* NOODLES

BIRD'S NEST

One of the most sought-after, great delicacies in Hong Kong, these are literally birds' nests, constituted from regurgitated spittle by birds of the swift family from the East Asian tropics (Thailand, Vietnam, Java, and the Philippines). Their nests are found in large caverns where workers climb on long bamboo scaffolding to retrieve them; it is dangerous work. Bird's nest is said to be good for the complexion and, because it is almost pure protein, is prescribed for those recovering from long illnesses. There are shops in Hong Kong that specialize in bird's nest of all grades. The top ones are the "white nests" and "pink or blood nests" that are literally complete cups. The nests are expensive and are usually sold precleaned — that is, all feathers and other debris are hand-plucked from the nests. They are sold dried and must be soaked before using as instructed in the recipes. The result, like shark's fin, is a tasteless, soft, crunchy jelly that relies for flavor on whatever sauce or broth it is served with. Bird's nest is an acquired taste.

~~~~~~

BITTER MELON

A controversial vegetable with an acquired taste that has as many fans as it does detractors. Even Chinese people must learn to love it. It is abundant in Hong Kong food markets. It has a warty-looking, dark- to pale-green skin. In Hong Kong, it is often stir-fried with meats and used in soups or braised. It has a slightly bitter quinine flavor that leaves a cooling effect in the mouth. In China it is often dried and used as medicine. The greener the melon the more bitter its taste, and many cooks look for the milder, yellow-green-skinned melon. To use, cut in half, seed, and discard interior membrane. Then to lessen its bitter taste, either blanch or salt it, according to the instructions in the recipe. Store in the bottom of your refrigerator in a loose plastic or paper bag. It can keep there for about three to five days, depending on the condition in which it was bought.

Bitter melon is available in many Chinese and Asian supermarkets, especially in large urban areas or wherever Asian grocers are found.

BLACK BEANS

These small black soybeans, also known as salted black beans or fermented black beans, are preserved by being fermented with salt and spices. They have a distinctive, slightly salty taste and a pleasantly rich smell and are used as a seasoning, often in conjunction with garlic or fresh ginger. Black beans are among the most popular flavors of Hong Kong where their appetizing aroma wafts through the narrow streets. The black beans are inexpensive and often people buy only what they need at the market. They are easy to find in America, even in supermarkets. Although you can find them in cans marked "black bean sauce," you may also see them packed in plastic bags — these are preferable. In Hong Kong, the black beans are usually used whole or coarsely chopped. Although some recipes say to rinse them before using, I notice that most chefs in Hong Kong do not bother with this. The beans will keep indefinitely if stored in the refrigerator or in a cool place.

BOK CHOY. *SEE* CHINESE WHITE CABBAGE

CAUL FAT

Caul fat is a lacy membrane often used by European and Chinese cooks to encase stuffings and to keep food moist while cooking. Actually the lower stomach of a pig or cow, caul fat melts during cooking and keeps meats and fillings moist and delicious. It is highly perishable, so buy it in small quantities and use quickly. For longer storage, wrap the caul fat carefully and freeze. To defrost, rinse in cold water. You can order caul fat from your butcher. I find that soaking it in cold water helps to separate the fat without tearing its fragile webs.

~~~~~~

CHILI BEAN SAUCE. *SEE* SAUCES AND PASTES

CHILIES, DRIED RED

Although dried red chilies are used less frequently in Hong Kong dishes, they are used in Sichuan-inspired dishes. Some are small, thin, and about a half-inch long. They are used to season oil for stir-fried dishes, or split and used in sauces, as well as for braising. They are normally left whole or cut in half lengthwise with the seeds left in. Unlike the Sichuanese, the Chinese of Hong Kong do not like the chilies blackened, and they cut down the amount normally used. Dried chilies can be found in most supermarkets and at Asian markets, and they will keep indefinitely in a tightly covered jar in a cool place.

CHILIES, FRESH

Fresh chilies — the seed pods of the capsicum plant — are used extensively and are popular in Hong Kong cuisine. However, the type of chili most often found (var. *Longum Bailey*, known as *ngau kok tsiu* or cow's-horn pepper) are oblong, about four- to five-inches long and usually pointed. Although they are spicier than sweet red pepper, they are not as pungent or spicy as the ones found in many parts of Southeast Asia or other regions of China such as Sichuan or parts of the United States. Although relatively new to Hong Kong cuisine, chilies are now always available in Hong Kong markets. Though seldom found in traditional Cantonese cooking, they are widely used in the *new* Hong Kong cuisine, not only for color and presentation as garnishes but also chopped and used in many dishes and sauces. They can be obtained fresh, dried, or ground.

   Throughout this book, I have used the variety most frequently found in the United States (Anaheim and Fresnos), using the red ones wherever possible. I have cut down the amounts to compensate for the slightly hotter ones found here. Look for fresh chilies that are bright, with no brown patches or black spots. Use red chilies wherever possible; they are generally milder than green ones because they sweeten as they ripen.

   To prepare fresh chilies, first rinse them in cold water. Then using a small sharp knife, slit them lengthwise. Remove and discard the seeds. Rinse the chilies well under cold running water, and then prepare them according to the instructions in the recipe. Wash your hands, knife, and chopping board before preparing other foods, and be careful not to touch your eyes until you have thoroughly washed your hands with soap and water.

CHILI OIL/CHILI DIPPING SAUCE

Chili oil is sometimes used as a dipping condiment in Hong Kong. It is slightly less hot than the commercially made ones from the Sichuan province in China, and certainly never as hot as the ones from Southeast Asia. This is to be expected inasmuch as the Cantonese like strong but more subtle flavors and taste. You can purchase chili oil from Chinese markets. The Thai and Malaysian versions are especially hot; the Hong Kong, Taiwanese, and Chinese versions are a bit milder. Such commercial products are quite acceptable, but I include this recipe because the homemade version is the best. Remember that chili oil is too dramatic to be used directly in cooking; it is best used as part of a dipping sauce or as a condiment. I include pepper and black beans for additional flavors.

Once made, put the chili oil in a tightly sealed glass jar and store in a cool, dark place where it will keep for months.

⅔ **cup peanut oil**
2 **tablespoons chopped dried red chilies**
1 **tablespoon whole unroasted Sichuan peppercorns**
2 **tablespoons whole black beans**

Heat a wok over a high heat and add the oil and the rest of the ingredients. Cook over a low heat for about ten minutes. Allow the mixture to cool undisturbed and then pour it into a jar. Let the mixture sit for two days, and then strain the oil. The sauce will keep indefinitely.

CHINESE BROCCOLI

Chinese broccoli is not like Western broccoli. It is very crunchy and slightly bitter and resembles Swiss chard in flavor; it is quite delicious with an earthy, green taste. It has deep olive-green leaves and sometimes white flowers. It is usually only available at Chinese markets but is well worth the search. If you can find it, look for stems that are firm and leaves that look fresh and green. Chinese broccoli is prepared in exactly the same way as Western broccoli and should be stored in a plastic bag in the vegetable compartment of the refrigerator where it will keep for several days. If you cannot find Chinese broccoli, substitute ordinary broccoli.

CHINESE CHIVES

Chinese chives are related to common chives and belong to the garlic family. Their taste is much stronger and garliclike than our chives and, like Western chives, flowers can be used as well as the blades. These chives are extremely popular and widely used in Hong Kong. They have an earthy onion taste and are delicious by themselves or cooked with other foods. Chinese chives can be found in Chinese markets, but they are very easy to grow in home herb gardens. Look for wide, flat blades and sprays of white, star-shaped flowers. They can be substituted for regular chives but adjust the quantity to allow for their stronger flavor. Rinse and dry the chives, store them in a plastic bag with a slightly damp paper towel in the refrigerator and use as soon as possible.

Chinese yellow chives are Chinese chives that have been grown in the dark and are pale yellow in color; they have a rich, earthy taste that is more subtle than that of the green ones. They also are harder to find and highly perishable. In Hong Kong, they are used extensively, especially in restaurants. Select fresh leaves with no signs of decay; they keep for only one or two days in the refrigerator. Trim any decaying parts. Wash and dry thoroughly and store between paper towels in the lower part of your refrigerator.

CHINESE FLOWERING CABBAGE

Chinese flowering cabbage is part of the large, mustard green–cabbage family and is found frequently in dishes in Hong Kong where it is usually known by its more familiar Cantonese name, *choi sum.* Many in Hong Kong consider this the best of the Chinese cabbages. It has green leaves and may have small yellow flowers that are eaten along with the leaves and stems. In Hong Kong this is one of the most common and popular leafy vegetables and is delicious as a stir-fry dish. Look for it in Chinese food markets.

CHINESE LONG BEANS

These beans are popular in Hong Kong and can be found in great abundance in the markets there. They are also known as yard-long beans and can grow to three feet in length. They are not related to green beans, the long beans having originated in Asia. Buy beans that are fresh and bright green, with no dark marks. There are two varieties: the light pale green ones and the dark green and thinner ones. You will usually find these beans sold in looped bunches; there is no need to string them. In Hong Kong, they are stir-fried with meats or with fermented bean curd. They have a crunchy texture like string beans but cook faster. You will find them in some supermarkets and in many Chinese markets. Store the fresh beans in a plastic bag in the refrigerator and use within four days.

CHINESE WHITE CABBAGE

Chinese white cabbage is more popularly known as bok choy; it has been grown in China for centuries and has a light, fresh, slightly mustardy taste and requires little cooking. Although there are many varieties, the most common and best known is the one with a long, smooth, milky-white stem and large, crinkly, dark-green leaves. The size of the plant indicates how tender it is. The smaller the better, especially in the summer, when the hot weather toughens the stalks. In Hong Kong, bok choy is used in soup or stir-fried. It is now widely available in supermarkets. Store in the bottom level of your refrigerator. Look for firm, crisp stalks and unblemished leaves.

SHANGHAI (BABY BOK CHOY)

Shanghai bok choy is the small, light green, miniature version of the commonly available Chinese bok choy or white cabbage. It has grown in popularity in Hong Kong due to the large

Shanghainese population. It can, on occasion, be found in many Chinese markets. Ordinary bok choy can be substituted.

CHINESE WHITE RADISH

Chinese white radish is also known as Chinese icicle radish or daikon, its Japanese name. It is long and white and rather like a carrot in shape but usually very much larger. It is a winter radish or root and can withstand long cooking without disintegrating. It thus absorbs the flavor of sauce yet retains its distinctive radish taste and texture. In Hong Kong, these radishes are usually found in home dishes, treated like potatoes or carrots are in the West. Chinese white radish must be peeled before it is used. Look for firm, heavy, solid unblemished ones. Inside they should be solid and not fibrous. You can find them in some supermarkets and almost always at Chinese or Asian markets. They should be slightly translucent inside and not tough. Store in a plastic bag in the vegetable compartment of your refrigerator where they will keep for over a week.

CINNAMON STICKS OR BARK

Cinnamon sticks are curled, thin pieces of the bark of the cinnamon tree. The Chinese version is rather thick, highly aromatic, and more pungent than the common cinnamon sticks, but the latter are an adequate substitute. They add a robust taste to braised dishes and are an important ingredient of five-spice powder. Store cinnamon sticks or bark in a tightly sealed jar to preserve their aroma and flavor. Ground cinnamon is too strong and not a satisfactory substitute.

CITRUS PEEL (DRIED TANGERINE PEEL, DRIED ORANGE PEEL)

Often you will find in the markets of Hong Kong all different types of oranges from China, Southeast Asia, and the United States. A popular one used for home cooking is immature oranges that are green because of the chlorophyll in their skin. They are slightly sour and their skins are often dried and used in cooking, as the Chinese believe they are good for digestion. You can often see them already peeled and stacked in mounds at the market.

CLOUD EARS. *SEE* MUSHROOMS: CHINESE TREE EARS

COCONUT MILK

Widely used throughout Asia, coconut milk is more important than cow's milk in cooking. It has the properties of cow's milk: the cream rises to the top when it sits; it must be stirred as it comes to a boil; and the saturated fat is chemically closer to butterfat than to vegetable fat. Coconut milk is not the liquid inside the coconut but rather the liquid created from the grated and soaked meat. It can be found frozen or in cans from Thailand. In Hong Kong, coconut milk is used in Southeast Asian–inspired dishes and in some popular desserts.

You can make your own coconut milk according to this recipe:

1 small coconut
3 cups low-fat milk
6 tablespoons sugar

To prepare the coconut, pierce two of the "eyes" in the shell and drain and discard the liquid inside. Place the drained coconut in an oven preheated to 350° F. for about twenty minutes. If this does not crack the shell, split it by rapping it with a hammer along the center until the coconut breaks apart. Wrap the coconut in a towel while cracking to prevent the small pieces from flying about. Pry off any meat that sticks to the shell with a knife. Cut the coconut into small pieces and place in a medium-sized saucepan. Cover the meat with two cups of the milk and simmer for ten minutes. Remove from the heat and allow it to cool. Process the coconut mixture in a blender on high speed for one minute. Let the coconut milk stand for fifteen minutes and then pour it through a strainer into a bowl. Using the back of a wooden spoon, press the chopped coconut against the strainer to squeeze out all the liquid. Return the coconut milk to the saucepan; add the sugar and the remaining cup of milk. Simmer for five minutes until the mixture thickens. Allow it to cool and refrigerate until you are ready to use it.

Or you can use the canned variety. I have found the canned version quite acceptable and certainly a lot less work. Look for the ones from Thailand or Malaysia. You can find them at Asian specialty markets, usually in 14- or 15-fluid-ounce cans. Be sure to shake the cans well before opening to use. Place any remainder in a glass jar and store in the refrigerator no longer than a week.

CORIANDER (CHINESE PARSLEY, CILANTRO)

Fresh coriander is one of the relatively few herbs used in Chinese cookery; it is widely used in southern China and, of course, quite extensively in Hong Kong. It looks like flat-leaved parsley but its pungent, musky, citruslike flavor gives it a distinctive character that is unmistakable. Its feathery leaves are often used as a garnish, or it is chopped and then mixed into sauces and stuffings. You can find it in many supermarkets now. When buying fresh coriander, look for deep-green, fresh-looking leaves. Yellow and limp leaves indicate age and should be avoided.

To store coriander, wash it in cold water, drain it thoroughly or spin-dry in a salad spinner, and put it in a clean plastic bag with a couple of sheets of moist paper towels. Store it in the vegetable compartment of your refrigerator; it will keep for several days.

~~~~~~

CORNSTARCH

In China and Asia there are many types of flour and starch — water-chestnut powder, taro starch, and arrowroot, for example — that are used to bind and thicken sauces and to make batter. Traditional cooks used a bean flour because it thickened faster and held longer. In Hong Kong, sauces are light and barely coat the food. Food is never swimming in thick sauce.

Cornstarch also is now widely used in the new Hong Kong cooking. As part of a marinade, cornstarch helps to coat the food properly, and it gives dishes a velvety texture. It also protects food during deep-frying by helping to seal in the juices, and gives a crisper coating than flour. It can be used as a binder for minced stuffings. Cornstarch is invariably blended with cold water until it forms a smooth paste and added at the last moment when used in sauces. It will look milky at first, but when the sauce is done, turns clear and shiny and thickens.

EGG NOODLES. *SEE* NOODLES

EGGPLANT

This pleasing, purple-skinned vegetable ranges in size from the huge, fat ones that are easy to find in all produce stores to the small, thin variety that the Chinese prefer because of its more delicate flavor. Look for those with smooth, unblemished skin.

Asians normally do not peel eggplant because the skin preserves its texture, shape, and taste. Large eggplants should be cut according to the recipe, sprinkled with a little salt, and left to sit for twenty minutes. They should be rinsed and blotted dry with paper towels. This process extracts bitter juices and excess moisture from the vegetable before it is cooked, giving a better taste to the final dish. The eggplant also absorbs less moisture after this process. This procedure is unnecessary if you are using Chinese eggplants.

EGG WHITE

Egg whites are often used in Hong Kong food as ingredients of batters and coatings. They seal in flavor and juices and make a light and protective coating for foods when plunged into warm oil, especially for velveting. Egg whites freeze well; a good method is to freeze them in an ice-cube tray.

FISH SAUCE

Fish sauce has been used in southern China for a long time but has recently experienced renewed popularity with the influx of Vietnamese immigrants who came to Hong Kong in the mid-1970s and '80s. It is also known as fish gravy or *nam pla*, a thin brownish sauce made from the fermentation of salted fresh fish. Fish sauce is sold bottled and has a very fishy odor and salty taste. Cooking greatly diminishes the "fishy" flavor and the sauce adds a special flavor. Fish sauce can be bought at many Chinese food stores; it adds a special richness and flavor to dishes.

FIVE-SPICE POWDER

Five-spice powder, less commonly known as five-flavored powder or five-fragrance-spice powder, is available in the spice section of many supermarkets and in Chinese markets. In Hong Kong, chefs are using this traditional spice in innovative ways, such as marinating the inside of a Peking Duck. This brownish powder is a mixture of star anise, Sichuan peppercorns, fennel, cloves, and cinnamon. A good blend is pungent, fragrant, spicy, and slightly sweet at the same time. The exotic fragrance it gives to a dish makes the search for a good mixture well worth the effort.

FLOUR

GLUTINOUS RICE FLOUR

This flour is made from glutinous rice and is often used in making pastries; it gives a chewy texture to doughs and is widely used in Hong Kong dim-sum pastries. Glutinous rice flour is not an acceptable substitute for regular rice flour. It can be found in Chinese markets.

RICE FLOUR

This flour is made from raw rice and is used to make fresh rice noodles. Store it as you would plain flour. You can find it in Chinese markets.

FUNGUS. *SEE* MUSHROOMS

GARLIC

The pungent flavor of garlic is part of the fabric of Hong Kong's cuisine. It would be inconceivable to cook without this distinctive, highly aromatic ingredient. Garlic is used in numerous ways: whole, finely chopped, crushed, and pickled. And in Hong Kong I have even found it smoked. It is used to flavor oils as well as spicy sauces and is often paired with other equally pungent ingredients, such as spring onions, black beans, curry, shrimp paste, or fresh ginger. In Hong Kong, cooks often add a smashed clove of garlic to the hot oil. The garlic becomes fragrant and is said to have "sweetened" the oil; it is then removed and discarded.

Select fresh garlic that is firm and heavy, the cloves preferably pinkish in color. It should be stored in a cool, dry place, but not in the refrigerator where it can easily become mildewed or begin sprouting.

GARLIC SHOOTS

Together with scallions and various forms of Chinese chives, you frequently see garlic shoots in Hong Kong's markets. These are young shoots of garlic before they begin to form a bulb. Harvested early in the spring, they add a mild and delicate perfume to food that is highly prized among Hong Kong's discerning diners. Garlic shoots look a bit like scallions; their green tops may also be used as a garnish or flavoring. It can be found in some supermarkets and in some Chinese markets.

GINGER

Fresh ginger in traditional Cantonese cooking is as ancient and essential as the wok. It is said that ginger from Canton is the most aromatic. Like garlic, it is an indispensable ingredient of Hong Kong cookery. Its pungent, spicy, and fresh taste adds a subtle but distinctive flavor to soups, meats, fish, sauces, and vegetables. These rhizomes are golden-beige in color with a thin, dry skin. They vary in size and range from small pieces to large knobby "hands." In Hong Kong you can find peeled ginger at the markets and older, more shriveled ginger that is used for medicinal broths. Look for ginger that is firm and clear-skinned with no signs of shriveling.

YOUNG STEM GINGER

Young stem ginger often makes its appearance in the markets of Hong Kong. These are knobby in shape and moist pink; they look naked. This is the newest spring growth of ginger and is usually stir-fried and eaten in dishes or commonly pickled in Hong Kong. Because it is young and tender, it does not need peeling and can be eaten as a vegetable. A popular way to eat pickled young ginger is with preserved Thousand-Year Duck Eggs as a snack; it is often served in Hong Kong restaurants as an hors d'oeuvre.

Ginger wrapped in plastic wrap will keep in the refrigerator for up to two weeks. Fresh ginger is widely available at many food stores, supermarkets, and in most Chinese markets. Young stem ginger is hard to find but is well worth the search. Peeled ginger stored in a glass jar covered in rice wine or dry sherry will last for several months. This has the added benefit of producing a flavored wine that can be substituted for rice wine in some recipes.

DRIED GINGER (GALANGAL)

Dried ginger or dried galangal is a member of the ginger family and is used by the Chinese for medicinal as well as culinary purposes. In Hong Kong, it is used in braised meat dishes, especially exotic "game" dishes to counter the strong odor of the meat. It can be found in many Chinese and Asian markets and often comes in plastic or cellophane bags. Keep it in a jar at room temperature and they will last indefinitely.

~~~~~~

GINGER JUICE

Ginger juice is made from fresh ginger and is used in marinades to give a subtle ginger taste without the bite of the fresh chopped pieces. Here is a simple method to extract ginger juice invented by my cooking associate, Gordon Wing: Cut unpeeled fresh ginger into one-inch chunks and drop the chunks into a running food processor. When the ginger is finely chopped, pour the contents into a linen towel and squeeze out the juice into a small bowl. Or you can use your hands. If a food processor is not available, mash the ginger with a kitchen mallet or the side of a cleaver or knife until most of the fibers are exposed. Then with a linen towel or your hands, simply squeeze out the juice.

KOSHER SALT. *SEE* SALT

LEEKS

This vegetable is grown and used primarily in northern China. The Cantonese of Hong Kong treat it as an onion and stir-fry it with meats. The leeks found in Hong Kong are large and cylindrical, resembling a giant scallion with a white husk like garlic. Leeks found in the United States are a good substitute. Leeks have a mild, slightly sweet onion flavor. To use, cut off and discard the green tops and roots and slice the leeks in half lengthwise. Wash them well. Store them as you would scallions.

LEMONGRASS

This aromatic tropical grass is widely used in Southeast Asian cooking to impart a lemony fragrance to dishes. It has made its way into Hong Kong cuisine since the arrival of Southeast Asian immigrants in the 1970s and early '80s. It can be found occasionally in food markets but is used more in restaurants than in homes in Hong Kong. Lemongrass looks like dried, over-sized scallions that are slightly gray or pale green in color. The bulb base of the stalk is used, either sliced or coarsely shredded, for the exquisite flavor it imparts to broths and sauces. It can be found fresh in Chinese markets. Look for pale green tops and make sure the lemongrass is not dried out. Cut off the fibrous base and peel off the outside layers. Trim off the tops but save them to flavor oils or soups. Lemongrass can be sliced and frozen for future use. Use lemon juice or lemon zest as a substitute.

LILY BUDS

Also known as tiger-lily buds, golden needles, or lily stems, dried lily buds are an ingredient in *mu shu* dishes and hot-and-sour soups. They add texture as well as an earthy taste. Soak the buds in hot water for about thirty minutes or until soft. Cut off the hard ends and shred or cut in half according to the recipe directions. You can find lily buds in Chinese markets; they are quite inexpensive. Store them in a jar in a dry place.

MALTOSE SUGAR. *SEE ALSO SUGAR*

This type of malt sugar is a liquid syrup that adds a wonderful richness to stews and sauces without a cloying sweetness. It may be stored at room temperature and is found in Chinese markets. Light-flavored honey may be used as a substitute.

MUSHROOMS

CHINESE TREE EARS

These tiny leaflike, dried black fungi are also known as cloud ears because, when soaked, they look like little clouds. Soak the dried fungus in hot water for twenty to thirty minutes until soft. Rinse them well. Cut away any hard portions. Fungi are valued for their crunchy texture and slightly smoky flavor. You can find them in Chinese markets usually wrapped in plastic or cellophane bags. They keep indefinitely in a jar stored in a cool, dry place.

CHINESE WOOD EARS

These fungi are the larger variety of the above-described fungus. Prepare and soak them in the same manner. Rinse them well. Once soaked, they will swell up to four or five times their size. Rinse well and cut away any hard portions. Sold in Chinese markets, they keep indefinitely when stored in a cool, dry place.

DRIED CHINESE MUSHROOMS

These wonderful mushrooms are said to have been cultivated for more than a thousand years in southern China, and there are many grades of them. Black or brown in color, they add a particular flavor and aroma to Chinese dishes. The best are very large with a light color and a highly cracked surface; they are usually the most expensive. As you can imagine, they are very popular in Hong Kong, and dried-food shops there carry every grade heaped in mounds, with the more expensive grades elaborately boxed. Here, they can be bought in boxes or plastic bags or cellophane from Chinese markets and are expensive. Keep dried mushrooms stored in an airtight jar in a cool, dry place. Fresh mushrooms of a similar variety are Japanese shiitake but they are not an adequate substitute as Chinese cooks never use them fresh, preferring the distinct, robust, smoky flavors and succulent texture of the dried variety. In Hong Kong, they are used as seasonings, finely chopped and combined with meats, fish, and shellfish.

To use Chinese dried mushrooms, soak the mushrooms in a bowl of warm water for about twenty minutes or until they are soft and pliable. Squeeze out the excess water and cut off and discard the woody stems — only the caps are used.

The soaking water can be saved and used in soups and for cooking rice. Strain the water through a fine sieve to discard any sand or residue from the dried mushrooms.

~~~~~~

NAPA CABBAGE. *SEE* PEKING CABBAGE

NOODLES

In Hong Kong, you will see people eating noodles of all kinds, day and night, in restaurants and at food stalls. They provide a nutritious, quick, light snack and usually are of good quality. Several styles of Hong Kong noodles and dishes have now made their way here, such as the thin, fresh egg noodles that are browned on both sides, thin rice noodles, and fresh noodles that can be readily found in Chinese markets. Below is a listing of the major types of noodles that can be found in Hong Kong and are available here.

BEAN THREAD NOODLES
These noodles, also called cellophane noodles, are made from ground mung beans and not from a grain flour. They are available dried and are very fine and white. Easy to recognize, packed in their neat, plastic-wrapped bundles, they are stocked by most Chinese markets and some supermarkets. They are never served on their own, but are added to soups or braised dishes or are deep-fried and used as a garnish. They must be soaked in warm water for about five minutes before use. As they are rather long, you might find it easier to cut them into shorter lengths after soaking. If you are frying them, do not soak them before using, but they must first be separated. A good technique is to separate the strands in a large paper bag to keep them from flying all over the place.

RICE NOODLES
Rice noodles, which are called "fun noodles," are popular in southern China and through-out Hong Kong. They can be found either dried or fresh in Chinese markets here. If fresh they must be cooked immediately. They are white and come in a variety of shapes, from hair-thin strands that are dry and brittle to thin, flat varieties that resemble fettucine. They are known by all sorts of names: rice-stick noodles, rice vermicelli, rice pasta. They can also vary in thickness and are about the length of a chopstick. Use the type called for in the recipes or you can substitute, as they can be used interchangeably. Rice noodles are very easy to use. Simply soak them in warm water for ten to twenty minutes, depending on the thickness, until they are soft. Drain them in a colander or a sieve and they are then ready to be used in soups or stir-fried.

The Chinese make large sheets of fresh rice noodles that are soft and fragile from a basic mixture of rice flour, wheat starch (*not* flour), and water. This batter is then poured onto a hot steamer plate and then steamed in sheets for about two minutes; when they are finally cooked, they are cut into noodles to be eaten immediately, as no further cooking is necessary. A very popular street snack in Hong Kong, the freshly cooked rice noodles are most often served with a sauce.

~~~~~~

WHEAT NOODLES AND EGG NOODLES

These are made from hard or soft wheat flour and water. If egg has been added, the noodles are usually labeled as egg noodles. They can be bought dried or fresh from Chinese markets, and many supermarkets and gourmet shops also stock both the dried variety and the fresh. Flat noodles are usually used in soups and rounded noodles are best for stir-frying or pan-frying. The fresh ones freeze nicely if they are well wrapped. Thaw them thoroughly before using.

Noodles are very good blanched and served with main dishes instead of plain rice. I think dried wheat or fresh egg noodles are best for this.

If you are using fresh noodles, immerse them in a pot of boiling water and cook them for three to five minutes or until you find their texture done to your taste. If you are using dried noodles, either cook them according to the instructions on the packet or cook them in boiling water for four to five minutes. Then drain and serve.

If you are cooking noodles ahead of time before using them or before stir-frying them, toss the cooked drained noodles in two teaspoons of sesame oil and put them into a bowl. Cover this with plastic wrap and refrigerate. The cooked noodles will remain usable for about two hours. Add them at the last moment to reheat in the sauce or blanch in hot water for thirty seconds.

OIL

Oil is the most commonly used cooking medium in Hong Kong, and the favorite is peanut oil. Animal fats, usually lard and chicken fat, are also used in some areas, particularly in some parts of mainland China, but I have never seen chicken fat used in Hong Kong. On all counts, the preferred oil is peanut oil, as many in Hong Kong find animal fats too heavy.

Throughout this book I have indicated a few instances in which oil can be reused. Where this is possible, simply cool the oil after use and filter it through cheesecloth or a fine strainer into a jar. Cover it tightly and keep in a cool, dry place. If you keep it in the refrigerator it will become cloudy, but it will clarify again when the oil returns to room temperature. I find oils are best reused just once, which is healthier since constantly reused oils increase in saturated-fat content. However, for clarity of flavors, I prefer *not* to reuse oil. In the finest restaurants in Hong Kong, the oil is *always* fresh, which helps account for the consistently high-quality results.

CORN OIL

Corn oil is a healthful, mostly polyunsaturated oil that is good for cooking. It has a high heating point, although I find it rather heavy, with a distinctive smell and taste. Its qualities make it ideal for deep-frying. Though it is found in Hong Kong, it is not very popular.

PEANUT OIL

This is the preferred oil used in Hong Kong cookery because it has a pleasant, mild taste that is unobtrusive. Its ability to be heated to a high temperature without burning makes it perfect for stir-frying and deep-frying. The peanut oils found in Hong Kong are cold-pressed and have the fragrance of freshly roasted peanuts. Some Chinese supermarkets stock the Hong Kong brands, their names written just in Chinese characters; they are well worth the search. But if you cannot find it, use domestic or French peanut oil.

SESAME OIL

This amber-colored oil is made from roasted sesame seeds and has a strong nutlike flavor and aroma. It is widely used in Hong Kong cooking in limited amounts as a final seasoning or in marinades but is not normally used as a cooking oil with other oils, as it is in northern China. As a final seasoning, it is added to subtly enrich a dish without overwhelming its basic flavor. Dark sesame oil is sold in bottles in many supermarkets and in Chinese markets.

OTHER VEGETABLE OILS

Some of the cheaper vegetable oils, such as soybean, safflower, and sunflower oils, are available in Hong Kong. They are light in color and taste and can also be used in cooking. In Hong Kong, they are used mainly by cheap food stalls and cheap restaurants.

OYSTERS, DRIED

Like other kinds of dried seafood found in Hong Kong, these oysters are frequently used in finely minced form to enhance dishes. They come in all grades and sizes. Use dried oysters carefully as they can overwhelm a dish with their assertive flavor. Soak them in a bowl of warm water for at least one hour or more until soft, or as long as overnight. If you wish, you may substitute canned smoked oysters, which come packed in oil.

OYSTER SAUCE

From the fishing villages in the New Territories, this important sauce is an essential taste of the Hong Kong cuisine. It is thick and brown and is made from a concentrate of oysters cooked in soy sauce, seasonings, and brine. It does not taste fishy but has a rich flavor, and it is used not only in cooking but also as a condiment, diluted with a little oil, for vegetables, poultry, and meats, which is very popular in Hong Kong. Oyster sauce is usually sold in bottles and can be bought in Chinese markets and some supermarkets. Look for the most expensive ones, as they are of the highest quality.

PEANUTS

Raw peanuts are used in Chinese cooking to add flavor and a crunchy texture, and in Hong Kong they are especially popular when stir-fried before being added to dishes. The thin, red skins need to be removed before you use the nuts. To do this, simply immerse them in a pot of boiling water for about two minutes. Drain them and let them cool, and the skins will come off easily. Raw peanuts can be found at health-food shops, good supermarkets, and Chinese markets.

PEKING CABBAGE

Peking cabbage is popularly known as Napa cabbage, as it was first grown in the Napa Valley in California. It comes in various sizes from long, compact, barrel-shaped types to fat, squat ones. They are tightly packed with firm, pale green, in some cases slightly yellow, crinkled leaves. This versatile vegetable is used in Hong Kong for soups or stir-fried with meats. Its spongelike ability to absorb flavors and its sweet pleasant taste and texture make it a favorite for chefs who match it with foods that have rich flavors. It is now widely available in supermarkets as well as Chinese markets. This is a delicious, crunchy vegetable with a mild but distinctive taste. Store it as you would ordinary cabbage.

PRESERVED MUSTARD GREENS

Preserved mustard greens are light green Chinese mustard greens which are preserved in a brine of water, salt, and sugar. In Hong Kong, they are eaten by themselves, or stir-fried or braised with meat. They have a wonderful, sweet and sour taste which contrasts nicely with meat. They can be found in cans or in vacuum-packed plastic bags and are widely available in Chinese markets. Once out of the can, put them in a jar and they will keep indefinitely in the refrigerator.

RED BEAN CURD. *SEE* BEAN CURD

RED-IN-SNOW

This is Chinese pickled cabbage that can be bought in cans at Asian specialty markets. It adds a pungent, slightly sour taste to dishes when used as a flavoring, or it can be used as an interestingly textured ingredient when added to stir-fried dishes.

RICE

GLUTINOUS RICE

Glutinous rice is also known as sweet rice or sticky rice. It is short, round, and pearl-like and is used in Hong Kong for stuffings and dessert pastries. It has more gluten than ordinary rice, and when cooked is stickier and sweeter. It is used for rice dishes wrapped in lotus leaves or served sometimes in Hong Kong at the end of banquets. Glutinous rice is also used for making Chinese rice wine and vinegar. It must be soaked for at least two hours but preferably overnight before cooking. Most Chinese markets and some supermarkets stock it.

LONG-GRAIN RICE

This is the most popular rice for cooking in Hong Kong. You will find rice shops offering a variety of long-grain white rice from all over the world, including the United States and Australia; among the favorites are the fragrant long-grain rice of Thailand. The aromatic long-grain Thai rice is now available at many Chinese and Southeast Asian markets. It has a pleasing fragrance similar to Indian basmati rice.

SHORT-GRAIN RICE

Short-grain rice, which is slightly stickier than long-grain white rice, is not frequently found in Hong Kong, though it may be used in making the popular morning rice porridge so often found there in the food stalls. Varieties known as "American Rose" or "Japanese Rose" are suitable and can be found in many Chinese markets, some supermarkets, or in shops that carry Japanese food products. Short-grain rice is more often found in northern parts of China where it is lightly milled and looks slightly browned; it has a strong grain flavor similar to brown rice. Hong Kong Chinese find this type of rice distasteful and associate it with poverty and rationing. It tends to be heavy and coarse.

TO WASH RICE

An optional step, if you wish to do as Chinese cooks do. Put the required amount of rice into a large bowl. Fill the bowl with cold water and swish the rice around with your hands. Carefully pour off the cloudy water. Repeat this process several times until the water is clear.

RICE NOODLES. *SEE* NOODLES

RICE PAPERS

These Vietnamese rice papers (Banh Tran brand or variety) are often beautifully textured by the imprint of the bamboo trays they dry on. They are very thin dried sheets, made from rice flour and water, usually round, and they are used as wrappers for a Vietnamese-style spring roll. The dried sheets are very briefly soaked in water to soften them and then rolled around a filling and deep-fried to a light and crisp texture. Unlike the Chinese wrappers, the filled rice papers can be stored in the refrigerator for up to three hours before frying. Once they are fried, they can be kept crisp in a low oven for up to two hours. The influx of Vietnamese immigrants of Chinese origin into Hong Kong created the popularity for Vietnamese-style food, with a Hong Kong flair.

~~~~~~

RICE WINE

An important element in the flavors of Hong Kong, rice wine is made from glutinous rice, yeast, and spring water. This wine is used extensively for cooking and drinking throughout China; the finest variety is believed to be from Shaoxing in Zhejiang province in eastern China. In Hong Kong, many varieties can be found and chefs frequently use it for not only cooking but in marinades and for sauces. A good quality, dry pale sherry can be substituted but cannot equal the rich, mellow taste of Chinese rice wine. Do not confuse this wine with sake, which is the Japanese version of rice wine and quite different. Western grape wines are not an adequate substitute. Chinese rice wine is now readily available here from Chinese markets and some wine shops. Once open, it should be kept tightly corked at room temperature.

ROSE WINE (MEI KUEI LU CHIEW)

This very strong liqueur is made from a blending of *gaoliang* liqueur and rose petals, not to be confused with Western rosé wine. It is used in many Hong Kong recipes, adding a very special fragrance to sauces that cannot be duplicated. Rice wine can be substituted. Rose wine is found usually in earthenware crocks in Chinese markets.

SALT

Salt was formerly expensive and available only in soy sauce and preserved foods in ancient China. In Hong Kong, several forms can be found. Table salt is the finest grind of salt and is less frequently used. Many chefs and cooks use sea salt (much like our kosher salt), which has a grayish cast and coarser texture than fine table salt. This sea salt is frequently found in bins at the Hong Kong markets. Rock salt is most often known for its role in freezing ice cream, and the larger crystals make an excellent medium of heat conduction. Rock salt is often used in certain kinds of Hong Kong–Hakka cooking, such as with chicken or squab.

SATAY SAUCE. *SEE* SAUCES AND PASTES: CHILI BEAN SAUCE

SAUCES AND PASTES

Hong Kong cookery involves a number of thick, tasty sauces and pastes. They are essential to the authentic taste of the food, and it is well worth the effort to obtain them. Most are now easy to find in bottles or cans in Chinese markets and some supermarkets. Canned sauces, once opened, should be transferred to screw-top glass jars and kept in the refrigerator where they will last indefinitely.

BEAN SAUCE

This thick, spicy, aromatic sauce is made with yellow beans, flour, and salt that are fermented together. It is quite salty but adds a distinctive flavor to Chinese dishes and is frequently used in Hong Kong cookery. There are two forms: whole beans in a thick sauce; and mashed or puréed beans, also sold as crushed yellow bean sauce. I prefer the whole bean variety because it is slightly less salty and has a better texture. It keeps indefinitely in the refrigerator and can be found in Chinese markets.

CHILI BEAN SAUCE (SATAY SAUCE)

This is a thick dark sauce or paste made from soybeans, chilies, and other seasonings; it is very hot and spicy. Widely used in cooking in western China, it is now also used in Hong Kong; it is usually available here in jars in Chinese markets. Be sure to seal the jar tightly after use and store in the refrigerator. Do not confuse chili bean sauce with chili sauce, which is a red, hot, thinner sauce made without beans and used mainly as a dipping sauce for cooked dishes. There are Southeast Asian versions of chili bean sauce called Satay sauce, and they are very spicy and hot. Use them if you can find them; they are called for in some of the recipes in this book.

CHILI SAUCE

Chili sauce is a bright red hot sauce that is made from chilies, vinegar, sugar, and salt. It is sometimes used for cooking, but more frequently in Hong Kong as a dipping sauce. There are various brands available in many supermarkets and Chinese markets, and you should experiment with them until you find the one you like best. If you find it too strong, dilute it with hot water. Do not confuse this sauce with the chili bean sauce.

CURRY PASTE

Curry flavors have been widely adopted by Hong Kong cooks. However, they are prepared in the French style, achieving the fragrant aroma of curry but avoiding the overwhelming pungent spiciness of Indian and Thai dishes. The most frequently used curry is in the form of prepared paste. It has a better curry flavor than the powdered variety because the spices are mixed with oil and chilies. Be sure to get the Indian variety, often labeled Madras, which is generally the best. You can find it at some supermarkets and at many Chinese markets. Kept refrigerated after opening, the curry paste keeps indefinitely.

HOISIN SAUCE

Widely used in Hong Kong, this is a thick, dark-brownish red sauce that is made from soybeans, vinegar, sugar, spices, and other flavorings. It is sweet and spicy and is widely used in southern Chinese cookery. In the West, it is often used as a sauce for Peking Duck instead of the traditional sweet bean sauce. Hoisin sauce is sold in cans and jars (it is sometimes also called barbecue sauce) and is available in Chinese markets and some supermarkets. When refrigerated, it keeps indefinitely.

SESAME PASTE

This rich, thick, creamy brown paste is made from toasted sesame seeds and is used in both hot and cold dishes; it is particularly popular in northern and western China but is used on a limited basis also in Hong Kong. It is sold in jars at Chinese markets. If the paste has separated in the jar, empty the contents into a blender or food processor and mix well. If you cannot obtain Chinese sesame paste use a smooth peanut butter instead, but do not confuse it with Middle Eastern tahini.

SHRIMP PASTE

Used extensively in Hong Kong cookery, this ingredient adds an exotic fragrance to dishes. Made from shrimp that are ground and fermented, it has an odor much stronger than its taste; once cooked, it is somewhat like anchovy paste. Shrimp paste can be found in Chinese markets usually in glass jars. Refrigerated, it will keep indefinitely.

SESAME SEEDS

These are dried seeds of an Asian annual herb. Unhulled, the seeds range from grayish-white to black in color, but once the hull is removed, the sesame seed is cream-colored, tiny and flat, and pointed at one end. Sesame seeds are valued throughout Asia as a flavoring agent and as a source of oil and paste. Sesame seeds can be found in supermarkets and Chinese markets. Keep them in a glass jar in a cool, dry place. They will last indefinitely.

To toast sesame seeds: Heat a sauté pan or skillet over a burner until hot. Add the sesame seeds and stir occasionally. Watch them closely, and when they begin to lightly brown, in about three to five minutes, stir them again, and pour them onto a plate. When they have thoroughly cooled, store them in a glass jar in a cool, dark place. Or, preheat the oven to 325° F. Spread the sesame seeds on a baking tray. Roast them in the oven for about ten to fifteen minutes until they are lightly browned. Cool before storing in a glass jar.

SHALLOTS

Shallots are mild-flavored members of the onion family. They are small, about the size of pickling onions, with copper-red skins, and a distinctive onion taste that is not as strong as ordinary onions. They are an excellent substitute for Chinese shallots, which can sometimes be found in Chinese markets. In Hong Kong, you will find them fresh and pickled, to be served with preserved eggs as a snack. Shallots are expensive but a few go a long way. They are readily available in supermarkets. Keep them in a cool, dry place (not the refrigerator) and peel them as you would an onion.

SHARK'S FIN

Besides bird's nests, shark's fin is the other exotic delicacy of Hong Kong, so important that it is now a multi-billion dollar business with every important restaurant in Hong Kong offering it, often with a long list of preparations to choose from. A symbol of extravagance, to which Hong Kong is no stranger, it can be extremely expensive. Shark's fin is found in many dry-food shops in Hong Kong. The fin refers to the dorsal "comb fin" or the two ventral fins of any of a variety of sharks; indeed, in Hong Kong, shark's fins are imported from all over the world.

Like bird's nest, shark's fin has little flavor but is prized for its clear, gelatinous strands and texture. It is usually served with a rich stock, as in the Double-Steamed Shark's Fin Soup (page 52) or stuffed in poultry or scrambled with eggs and crab.

Preparation usually involves an elaborate process of soaking and boiling in several changes of water and stocks. However, thanks to modern technology, you can now purchase prepared shark's fin in the freezer section of a Chinese market. This convenience brings shark's fin within the scope of today's home cooking.

SHRIMP, DRIED

Seafood of all forms — fresh or dried — is a favorite of Hong Kong people. Dried shrimp are used to perk up fried rice or mixed with meat dishes to give an added dimension to the overall dish. Dried shrimp are sold in packages in Asian specialty markets. Look for the brands with the pinkest color and avoid grayish-colored ones. They will keep indefinitely when sealed in a glass container and stored in a cool, dry place. When cooked, the dried shrimp add a delicate taste to sauces quite unlike the fishy taste indicated by their smell.

SHRIMP ROE

These tiny red beads are the dried roe of shrimp. Most often used in braising dishes, they are very pungent and add a very special taste to dishes. Look for this ingredient in Chinese markets. Substitute shrimp paste if you cannot obtain shrimp roe.

SICHUAN PEPPERCORNS

Sichuan peppercorns are known throughout China and Hong Kong as "flower peppers" because they look like flower buds opening. They are reddish-brown in color with a strong, pungent odor that distinguishes them from the hotter black peppercorns. They are actually not from peppers at all, but are the dried berries of a shrub that belongs to the citrus family. Their smell reminds me of lavender, and their taste is sharp and mildly spicy. Sichuan peppercorns are roasted and then can be ground in a conventional pepper mill. They are sold wrapped in cellophane or plastic bags in Chinese stores and are inexpensive. They will keep indefinitely if stored in a well-sealed container.

To roast Sichuan peppercorns: Heat a wok or heavy frying pan to a medium heat. Add the peppercorns (you can cook up to about a quarter cup at a time) and stir-fry them for about five minutes until they slightly brown and start to smoke. Remove the pan from the heat and cool.

Grind the peppercorns in a pepper mill, clean coffee grinder, or with a mortar and pestle. Seal in a screw-top jar to store or keep the whole roasted peppercorns in a well-sealed container and grind them as needed.

SICHUAN PRESERVED VEGETABLE

There are many types of Chinese pickled vegetables. One of the most popular is Sichuan preserved vegetable, a specialty of Sichuan province. This is the root of the mustard green that is pickled in salt and hot chilies. It is sold in tins in Chinese markets and gives a pleasantly crunchy texture and spicy taste to dishes. Before using it, rinse in cold water and then slice or chop as required. Any unused vegetable should be transferred to a tightly covered jar and stored in the refrigerator where it will keep indefinitely.

SILK SQUASH (CHINESE OKRA)

A popular vegetable frequently found in Hong Kong markets, this is a long, thin, cylindrical squash, tapering at one end with deep narrow ridges. Choose firm, unblemished dark-green ones. Peel the ridges. If the squash are young, you can leave some of the green; if they are older, it is best to peel all the skin. The inside flesh turns soft and tender as it cooks, like a cross between a cucumber and zucchini. Absorbent, it readily picks up flavors of the sauce or food it is cooked with.

SMITHFIELD HAM

In Hong Kong you will see whole preserved Yunnan or Jinhua hams in many food shops. It is a popular staple, used as seasoning or in many Hong Kong dishes as an ingredient. Unfortunately, it is not obtainable here. Smithfield ham is an acceptable substitute for these wonderfully rich, smoky-flavored Chinese hams. Sold in Chinese markets in slices or large pieces, Smithfield ham will keep for months tightly wrapped in the refrigerator. If a small amount of mold appears on the skin, simply scrape it off. Westphalian ham may be used as a substitute.

SNOW PEAS

Smaller varieties of snow peas are found in the Hong Kong markets than those found here. But like the ones in Hong Kong, this familiar vegetable combines a tender, crisp texture and a sweet, fresh flavor. In Hong Kong, snow peas are simply stir-fried with a little oil and salt and bits of garlic and ginger. Frequently, they are combined with meats. Snow peas are readily available at supermarkets. Look for pods that are firm with very small peas, which means they are tender and young. They keep for at least a week in the vegetable compartment of the refrigerator.

SOY SAUCE

Soy sauce is an essential ingredient in Hong Kong cooking. It is made from a mixture of soybeans, flour, and water, which is then fermented naturally and aged for some months. The distilled liquid is soy sauce. The ones most frequently used in Hong Kong are the Amoy brand or the Pearl River brand from China. There are two main types of soy sauce:

LIGHT SOY SAUCE

As the name implies, this is light in color, but it is full of flavor, saltier than dark soy sauce, and the best to use for most marinating and cooking. Light soy sauce is known in Chinese markets as Light Soy Sauce, Thin Soy Sauce or Superior Soy. This type of soy sauce is used extensively in Hong Kong.

DARK SOY SAUCE

This sauce is aged for much longer than light soy sauce, hence its darker, almost black color. It is slightly thicker and stronger than light soy sauce and is more suitable for braising and richer sauces. I prefer it to light soy as a dipping sauce, though both can be used for dipping. It is known in Chinese markets as Dark Soy Sauce and Soy Superior Sauce. Although used less, it is nevertheless important to have on hand.

SPINACH

Spinach is popular in Hong Kong; however, the Western varieties of spinach are quite different from those used in Hong Kong. Nevertheless, they make satisfactory substitutes for the Chinese variety. Spinach is most commonly stir-fried, so frozen spinach is obviously unsuitable. Chinese water spinach *(Ipomoea aquatica)* is most frequently cooked in Hong Kong and is available in Chinese markets here. It has hollow stems and delicate, pointed leaves, lighter in color than common spinach and with a milder taste. It should be cooked when it is very fresh, preferably on the day it is bought.

STAR ANISE

The star anise is the hard, star-shaped seedpod of the anise bush, also known as Chinese anise or whole anise. It is similar in flavor and fragrance to common aniseed but is more robust and licoricelike. Star anise is an essential ingredient of five-spice powder and is widely used in braised dishes to which it imparts a rich taste and fragrance. Star anise is sold in plastic packs at Chinese markets, and should be stored in a tightly covered jar in a cool, dry place.

SUGAR

Sugar has been used sparingly in the cooking of savory dishes in China for a thousand years. Properly used, it helps balance the various flavors of sauces and other dishes. Chinese sugar comes in several forms: as rock or yellow lump sugar, as brown sugar slabs, and as maltose or malt sugar. I particularly like to use rock sugar because it is rich and has a more subtle flavor than that of refined granulated sugar. Chinese rock sugar also gives a good luster or glaze to braised dishes and sauces. You can buy it in Chinese markets where it is usually sold in packages. You may need to break the lumps into smaller pieces with a wooden mallet or rolling pin. If you cannot find rock sugar, use white sugar or coffee-sugar crystals (the amber, chunky kind) instead.

TIANJIN PRESERVED CABBAGE

This is a northern Chinese celery cabbage that is pickled with salt and garlic. It is used with rice porridge and as a condiment in braised dishes.

VINEGAR

Chinese vinegars are widely used in Hong Kong as dipping sauces and for cooking. Unlike Western vinegars, they are usually made from a rice base. There are many varieties, ranging in flavor from strong and spicy and slightly tart to mild, sweet, and pungent. Their color ranges from red to yellow, and white and black varieties also exist.

All these vinegars can be bought from Chinese markets. They are sold in bottles and will keep indefinitely. If you cannot get Chinese vinegar, use cider vinegar. Malt wine vinegars cannot be substituted because their taste is too strong.

BLACK RICE VINEGAR

Black rice vinegar is very dark in color and rich though mild in taste. It is used for braised dishes, noodles, and sauces.

RED RICE VINEGAR

Red rice vinegar is sweet and spicy in taste and is usually used as a dipping sauce for seafood.

WHITE RICE VINEGAR

White rice vinegar is clear and mild in flavor. It has a faint taste of glutinous rice and is used for sweet-and-sour dishes.

WATER CHESTNUTS

Water chestnuts, which do not belong to the chestnut family at all, are a sweet root vegetable or bulb about the size of a walnut and have been eaten in China for centuries. They are especially popular in the South, where they are sometimes grown in paddies between rice plants, which is why they are often muddy. White and crunchy, they are eaten in Hong Kong as a snack, after they have been boiled in their skins or peeled and simmered in rock sugar. They are also used in many cooked dishes.

Here, fresh water chestnuts can be obtained from Chinese markets or some supermarkets. When buying fresh ones, look for a firm, hard texture. The skin should be taut, not wrinkled. If they are mushy, they are too old. Feel them all over for soft, rotten spots. If you peel them in advance of cooking, cover them with cold water to prevent browning, and store them in the refrigerator. They will keep unpeeled in a paper bag in the refrigerator for up to two weeks.

Canned water chestnuts are sold in many supermarkets and Chinese markets. A pale version of the fresh ones, they have a good texture but the flavor for the most part is lost in the canning process. Rinse them well in cold water before you use them and store any unused ones in a jar of cold water. They will keep for several weeks in the refrigerator if you change the water daily. Fresh jicama is a suitable substitute for water chestnuts and is preferable to the canned.

WHEAT NOODLES. *SEE* NOODLES

WHEAT STARCH

Wheat starch is a flourlike powder left after the protein is removed from wheat flour to make wheat gluten, a doughy substance used by Chinese vegetarian cooks. It is mainly used as a wrapping for dumplings in Hong Kong. It can be purchased in Chinese markets, usually in one pound bags. It will keep indefinitely if tightly sealed and kept in a cool, dry place. There is no acceptable substitute for this ingredient.

WONTON WRAPPERS

Wonton wrappers are made from egg and flour and can be bought fresh or frozen in Chinese markets. They are thin, pastrylike wrappings that can be stuffed with minced meat and fried, steamed, or used in soups. They are sold in little piles of three-inch squares or sometimes a bit larger, wrapped in plastic. The number of squares or skins in a package varies from about thirty to thirty-six, depending upon the supplier. Fresh wonton skins will keep for about five days if stored in plastic wrap or a plastic bag in the refrigerator. If you are using frozen wonton wrappers, just peel off the number you need and thaw them thoroughly before you use them.

WOOD EARS. *SEE* MUSHROOMS: CHINESE WOOD EARS

EQUIPMENT

Although technique is primary, good equipment is necessary in cooking the recipes of Hong Kong. Though not absolutely essential for cooking Chinese food, there are a few items that will make it very much easier. Most are inexpensive and are serviceable for a long time. Look for authentic implements from a Chinese or Asian market or in specialty gourmet stores that feature good cooking equipment.

CAMPHOR WOOD CHIPS

Camphor wood chips are aromatic wood chips used for smoking poultry, like duck, squab, or chicken. They are popular in Hong Kong, though not available outside of Hong Kong. I found that hickory wood chips, widely available, are an acceptable substitute.

CHOPPING BOARD

The Chinese traditionally use a soft wood block for chopping. Such a block is not only difficult to maintain, however, but also accumulates bacteria. I prefer a board made of hardwood or white acrylic. These are strong, easy to clean, and last indefinitely. There is so much chopping and slicing to be done when preparing food for Asian-style cooking that it really is essential to have a large, steady cutting board. For health reasons never cut cooked meat on a board that you have also used for chopping raw meat or poultry. Keep a separate board for this purpose. And always properly clean your cutting boards after use. Vinegar or lemon works well, but you may prefer to use a stronger bleach solution.

CHOPSTICKS

Chopsticks are not just used for eating but also for cooking — for stirring, beating, and whipping. Special long chopsticks are available for these purposes, but it is not necessary to purchase them. Any long spoon, spatula, or fork and, in many cases, regular chopsticks will suffice. They can be bought at many department stores, Asian specialty markets, and in the ethnic food section of supermarkets, as well as from many Chinese restaurants.

CLAY POTS

These attractive, lightweight clay pots are also known as sandy pots or sand pots because their unglazed exteriors have a sandy texture. They are made from a mixture of clay and sand with glazed interiors that help conduct heat and hold moisture in. They come in a variety of shapes and sizes and are equipped with tight-fitting lids that have a small steam vent. They sometimes are encased in a wire frame. The pots are designed to be used on the stove top (most people in Hong Kong do not have ovens) and are used for braised dishes and soups, and for cooking rice. The chefs of Hong Kong have given new meaning to these pots. Instead of merely for braising, they are often used to finish a stir-fried dish. The stir-fried ingredients are put in a clay pot, covered, and cooked over high heat for a very short period of time. This technique intensifies flavors, resulting in highly aromatic dishes.

Clay pots are well worth the investment and many recipes in this book call for their use.

To use, never put an empty sand pot onto the heat or put a hot sand pot onto a cold surface; in other words, avoid drastic temperature changes or the pot is likely to crack. However, the pots can be used over high gas heat. If you are using a sand pot on an electric stove, be sure to use a heat-diffusing plate to insulate it from the electric coils. The pot should always have some liquid in it when in use.

Any good enamelware casserole or seasoned cast-iron pot can be used as a substitute.

Because of the intense steam heat that can rise when you raise the lid off the pot, always open it *away* from you.

The pots are quite attractive and have a rustic charm. You can serve directly from the stove to the table, with a heat-proof pad or towel underneath to protect your table. It is wonderful to open your clay pot and have superb aromas grace the table.

CLEAVERS

No self-respecting Chinese cook would be seen with a knife instead of a cleaver. These heavy choppers serve many purposes. They are used for all kinds of cutting, ranging from fine shredding to chopping up bones. A Chinese cook would usually have three types of cleaver: lightweight, with a narrow blade for cutting delicate foods, including vegetables; medium-weight, for general cutting, chopping, and crushing purposes; and heavy, for heavy-duty chopping. Of course, you can prepare Chinese food using good sharp knives, but if you decide to buy a cleaver, you will be surprised at how easy it is to use. Choose a good quality stainless steel one and keep it sharp. I have found a medium-sized, all-purpose, stainless steel cleaver is the best kind to have around.

RICE COOKERS

Electric rice cookers are widely used in Hong Kong homes and are very popular. They cook rice perfectly and keep it warm throughout a meal. A rice cooker also has the advantage of freeing a burner, thus making for a less cluttered stove top, an important consideration in Hong Kong's small apartments. They are relatively expensive, however, so unless you eat rice frequently, they may not be worth the investment.

STEAMERS

Bamboo steamers are among the most ancient of Chinese cooking utensils. These attractive, basketlike bamboo steamers come in several sizes of which the ten-inch is the most suitable for home use. Bamboo steamers can be filled with food and placed on top of a pot or over a wok of boiling water. Clean, damp cheesecloth is sometimes placed over the open slats of the bamboo steamer to prevent the food from falling through. One of the advantages of the design is that several steamers can be stacked on top of one another for multiple cooking. Bamboo steamers can be bought at Asian specialty markets and at cookware and department stores. Before using a bamboo steamer for the first time, wash it and steam it empty for about 5 minutes. Any wide, metal steamer can also be used.

WOK

The most useful piece of equipment is the wok. It allows you to stir-fry, while quickly moving the food without spilling all over the place. You will find the wok useful for cooking bulky vegetables such as spinach or large quantities of any food, whatever the cuisine. When used for deep-frying, the wok saves cooking oil because the base is smaller, requiring less oil, but delivers depth, which is important. Another advantage is that the shape of the wok allows the heat to spread evenly over its surface, thus facilitating the rapid cooking that is fundamental to stir-frying.

After many years of teaching and demonstrating, I have found the most appropriate wok for a Western-type stove has one long wooden handle, about twelve to fourteen inches in length. I also prefer a wok that has a slightly flattened bottom, which allows it to rest securely on the stove top. Originally adapted for use on electric ranges, it works extremely well with gas. Although these innovations and design changes seem to go against the purpose of the traditional design, which is to concentrate intense heat at the center, I have found the flat-bottomed wok made of good carbon steel to be perfect for a Western-type stove. In Hong Kong, most homes have intensive gas burners, allowing for the all-important, extremely high heat; if you allow the wok to heat up properly without adding too much food at once, you can come fairly close to doing it the way people in Hong Kong do.

CHOOSING A WOK

Choose a medium-sized wok, preferably about twelve to fourteen inches in diameter, with good deep sides. Some woks on the market are too shallow or too flat on the bottom, making them no better than a large skillet. It is better to cook a small quantity in a medium-sized wok than to try to accommodate a large quantity in a small one. Select one that has heft to it. If possible, choose one made of carbon steel rather than of light, stainless steel or aluminum — these tend to scorch and do not withstand the required hot heat. I do not like nonstick woks; not only are they more expensive, but they cannot be seasoned like an ordinary wok, and that detracts from the flavor of the food. I also dislike electric woks, because I find they do not heat up to a sufficiently high temperature and tend to be too shallow.

SEASONING A WOK

All woks (except nonstick or stainless steel) need to be seasoned. Many need to be scrubbed first as well to remove the machine oil that is applied to the surface by the manufacturer to protect it in transit. This is the only time you will scrub your wok — unless you let it rust. Scrub it with kitchen cleanser and water to remove as much of the machine oil as possible. Dry the wok and place it over low heat. Add two tablespoons of cooking oil (peanut, corn oil, or vegetable oil). Rub all over the inside of the wok using paper towels until the entire surface is lightly coated. Heat the wok slowly for ten to fifteen minutes and then wipe it thoroughly with more clean paper towels. Your paper should be blackened from the remaining machine oil. Repeat this process of coating, heating, and wiping until the paper towel comes out clean. Your wok, once seasoned, will darken with use. This is a good sign because this means your wok is properly seasoned like a good omelet or crêpe pan.

CLEANING A WOK

Do not scrub a seasoned wok. Just wash it in plain water without detergent. Dry it thoroughly, preferably by placing it over a low heat for a few minutes before putting it away. This should prevent the wok from rusting, but if it does rust, scrub it off with kitchen cleanser and repeat the seasoning process. If you wish to store it for a long while or if you live in a humid climate, rub the inside of the wok with one tablespoon of cooking oil for added protection before storing.

WOK ACCESSORIES

WOK STAND

This is a metal ring or frame designed to keep a conventionally shaped wok steady on the burner, and is essential *only* if you are using a wok with the traditional round bottom. And if you have this type of wok and wish to use it for steaming, deep-frying, or braising, you will need a wok stand. Most woks of this type usually come with a stand.

WOK LID

A wok lid is a domelike cover, usually made from aluminum, that is used when steaming. Normally it comes with the wok, but it may be purchased separately from a Chinese or Asian market. Any large, domed pot lid that fits snugly over the top of the wok can be used instead. Aluminum wok lids are inexpensive.

~~~~~~

SPATULA

A long-handled metal spatula shaped like a small shovel is ideal for scooping and tossing food in a wok. Any good long-handled spoon may be used instead.

RACK

If you use your wok or a large pot as a steamer, you will need a wooden or metal rack or trivet that stands above the water level and supports the plate of food to be steamed. Some woks are sold with a metal stand, but most Asian specialty markets, department stores, and hardware shops stock triangular wooden stands or round metal stands for this purpose. You can improvise a stand by using an empty, inverted tin can of suitable size.

MISCELLANEOUS EQUIPMENT

A good colander and several stainless steel bowls are indispensible in cooking the recipes in this book. Many of the methods call for oil to be drained from the wok, so a good colander or sieve, to be set inside a stainless steel bowl, can facilitate the method.

A fairly large-size strainer or slotted spoon is also helpful for removing food from the wok or oil.

TECHNIQUES

More than any other cuisine, preparation of ingredients for Chinese-style food before beginning to cook is of paramount importance. All the recipes in this book assume proper preparation, as the actual cooking time is a matter of minutes. Since the heat must be very hot and the cooking fast, everything *must* be prepared in advance. There is no time for last-minute chopping. Once the cooking process starts, you must move quickly and confidently. This comes with experience. You will find that foods prepared in this Hong Kong style will retain their natural textures and tastes, which is why Hong Kong has been described as the "capital of Chinese gastronomy" and a "paradise of delicious food" by Chinese food critics Doreen Leung and Willie Mark. Careful preparation also enhances the visual appeal of a dish. This eye appeal is greatly prized by the Hong Kong people and all who care for good food properly prepared and served. A Chinese cook always uses a cleaver for cutting, slicing, and chopping tasks, wielding it with skill and dexterity.

Chinese cooking is a sophisticated cuisine involving a number of cooking methods that are relatively uncommon in the West. Sometimes, several different cooking techniques are used in the preparation of a single dish; for example, stir-frying crab with seasonings and then finishing it in a clay pot over high heat for a short time. Most of these techniques can be easily mastered with a little practice. When you are planning a meal, be sure to select dishes that entail a reasonable range of techniques; limit yourself to one stir-fried dish per meal until you have become used to this important method of cooking.

CUTTING TECHNIQUES

DIAGONAL SLICING

This technique is used for cutting vegetables such as asparagus, carrots, or scallions. The purpose is to expose more of the surface of the vegetable for quicker cooking. Angle the knife or cleaver at a slant and cut.

DICING

This is a simple technique of cutting food into small cubes or dice. The food should first be cut into slices. Stack the slices and cut them again lengthwise into sticks, just as you would for shredding. Stack the strips or sticks and cut crosswise into evenly sized cubes or dice.

ROLL-CUTTING

This is rather like diagonal slicing but is used for larger, rounder vegetables such as zucchini, carrots, eggplant, or silk squash. As with diagonal slicing, this technique allows more of the surface of the vegetable to be exposed to the heat, thereby speeding up the cooking time. Begin by making one diagonal slice at one end of the vegetable. Then roll it 180 degrees and make the next diagonal slice. Continue in this way until you have chopped the entire vegetable into evenly sized, somewhat diamond-shaped pieces. This method also gives the vegetable an attractive shape that enhances the visual appeal of the dish.

SCORING

This is a technique used to pierce the surface of foods to help them cook faster and more evenly. It also gives them an attractive appearance. Use a cleaver or sharp knife and make cuts into the food at a slight angle to a depth of about one-eighth of an inch. Take care not to cut all the way through. Make cuts all over the surface of the food, cutting crisscross to give a wide, diamond-shaped pattern. This is particularly useful when steaming whole fish — scoring the fish before steaming allows the heat to penetrate the thicker portions. When the sizzling hot sauce is poured over the cooked fish, the taste penetrates through the scored flesh.

SHREDDING

This is the process by which food is cut into thin, fine, matchsticklike shreds. First cut the food into slices and then pile several slices on top of one another and cut them lengthwise into fine strips.

To shred raw meat or poultry easily, first place the meat in the freezer for about twenty minutes or until it is firm to the touch. Then cut it, against the grain, into slices and shred.

Cooked foods such as the Steeped Chicken with Spicy Sauce (page 105) are also shredded. Here, the textural quality of the chicken is enhanced by being hand-shredded, rather than with a cleaver or knife. Although it is coarser, hand-shredded food holds the sauce better.

SLICING

This is the conventional method of slicing food. Hold the food firmly on the chopping board with one hand and slice straight down into very thin slices. If you use a cleaver rather than a knife for this, hold the cleaver with your index finger over the far side of the top of the cleaver and your thumb on the side nearest you to guide the cutting edge firmly. Hold the food with your other hand, turning your fingers under for safety. Your knuckles should act as a guide for the blade.

There is a technique for splitting food into two thinner pieces while retaining its overall shape. It is can be used for cutting chicken breasts in half, for example. The cleaver with its wide blade is particularly suitable for this. Hold the blade of the cleaver or knife parallel to the chopping board. Place your free hand on top of the piece of food to keep it steady. Using a gentle cutting motion slice horizontally through the food.

OTHER PREPARATION TECHNIQUES

BUTTERFLYING POULTRY

This technique is used for preparing duck or chicken. You begin by splitting the fowl open from the back and removing the backbone. Then flatten the carcass with the palm of your hand. A bamboo stick or chopstick is usually inserted to hold the bird flat. I have used the French method, which is to make two small holes on either side below the breastbone, and I tuck the legs through these holes. I find it holds the carcass quite firmly.

THICKENING

Cornstarch blended with an equal quantity of water is frequently used in Chinese cookery to thicken sauces and glaze dishes. Always make sure the mixture is smooth and well-blended before adding it.

VELVETING

Food such as poultry, pork, beef, fish, or seafood is often coated with egg white and cornstarch to seal in the moisture and flavor while the food is cooking. This technique is mainly used for chicken breasts, shrimp, scallops, or delicately flavored fish. The coated food is refrigerated for twenty minutes to allow the egg white to set. Then it is added to just-warmed oil to partially cook. The dish is quickly finished by stir-frying. This method of cooking produces particularly tender and moist textures.

COOKING TECHNIQUES

BLANCHING

This involves putting food into hot water or into moderately hot oil for a few minutes to cook it briefly but not entirely, a kind of softening-up process that prepares the food for final cooking. Blanching in water is a common technique used not only with harder vegetables, such as broccoli, but also to help remove surface fatty particles from meat, resulting in a cleaner and clearer sauce and taste. Vegetables are plunged into boiling, salted water for several minutes, drained, and then plunged into cold water to arrest the cooking process. In such cases, blanching usually precedes stir-frying which completes the cooking. Salt added to the blanching water enhances the flavors of the vegetables. All food blanched before stir-frying should be well drained.

BRAISING AND RED-BRAISING

Braising foods in a clay pot is one of the popular techniques of Hong Kong chefs. The foods are often first quickly browned by stir-frying which seals in the juices. Then they are turned into a clay pot and braised over high heat. The resulting dishes are rich in flavor; meat cooked in this way is also very tender.

Red-braising, which is also known as red-cooking, is simply the technique by which food is braised in a dark liquid such as soy sauce. This gives food a reddish-brown color, hence the name. The sauce that results can be saved and frozen for reuse, becoming richer in flavor each time. This method of reusing braising liquid applies to meats and poultry, never fish or shellfish.

DEEP-FRYING

There are many Hong Kong recipes that call for the meat first to be plunged into either hot or moderately hot oil, drained, and then stir-fried. This partial cooking keeps the meat moist and tender because it is not subjected to intense heat. This cooking method creates juicy morsels of food that are then returned to the wok with sauce.

Then there is one of the most important techniques in Chinese cookery—deep-frying. The trick is to regulate the heat so that the surface of the food is sealed but does not brown so fast that the food is uncooked inside. The process does require a lot of oil. But deep-fried food is not greasy when properly done. The Chinese use a wok for deep-frying. Because of the wok's shape, frying in a wok requires less oil than a deep-fat fryer. Practice with a wok until you are sure of it. Before adding the oil to the hot wok, be certain that it is secure on its stand or, if it is flat-bottomed, that it sits firmly on the burner. A wok filled with hot oil should never be left unsupervised, and it should never be filled to more than half its capacity. To get a fresh tasting and very crisp surface, some recipes call for food to be deep-fried twice.

Some points to bear in mind when deep-frying:

Wait for the oil to get hot enough before adding the food to be fried. The oil should give off a haze and produce little wisps of smoke when it is the right temperature. Test the temperature by dropping in a small piece of food. If it bubbles all over, the oil is sufficiently hot. Thereafter, adjust the heat as necessary to prevent the oil from smoking or overheating.

Thoroughly dry food that is to be deep-fried with paper towels to prevent splattering. If the food is in a marinade, remove it with a slotted spoon and let it drain before putting it into the oil. If you are using batter, make sure all the excess drips off before adding the food to the hot oil.

In most cases, oil used for deep-frying can be reused. If you wish to reuse oil, cool it, and then strain it through several layers of cheesecloth or through a fine mesh strainer into a jar; this will remove any particles of food that will otherwise burn when reheated and give the oil a bitter taste. Label the jar according to what food you have cooked in the oil and only reuse it for the same thing. Oil for deep-frying can be used three times.

DRY-FRYING

This technique uses a small amount of oil and liquids to cook meat or vegetables for a long period of time to change their texture and to concentrate the flavors. In a wok over very low heat, continually stir the food to prevent burning.

～～～～～～～～～～～～～～～～～～～～～～～～～～～～～～～～～

POACHING

This is a method of simmering food until it is completely or partially cooked. It may then be put into soup or combined with a sauce and the cooking process continued.

REHEATING FOODS

Steaming is one of the best methods to reheat food because it warms the food without cooking it further or drying it out. To reheat soups and braised dishes, bring the liquid slowly to a simmer but do not boil. Remove food from the heat as soon as it is hot to prevent overcooking.

SHALLOW-FRYING OR PAN-FRYING

This technique is similar to sautéeing. It involves more oil than stir-frying but less than deep-frying. Food is fried first on one side and then on the other. Sometimes the excess oil is then drained off and a sauce added to complete the dish. A frying pan or a flat-bottom wok is ideal for shallow-frying.

SLOW SIMMERING AND STEEPING

These processes are very similar. In slow-simmering, food is immersed in liquid that is brought almost to a boil; the temperature is reduced so that it simmers, cooking the food to the desired degree. This is the technique used for making stock. In steeping, food is similarly immersed in liquid (usually stock) and simmered. The heat is then turned off and the residual heat of the liquid finishes off the cooking process.

STEAMING

Steaming has been used by the Chinese for thousands of years. Along with stir-frying and deep-frying it is the most widely used technique. In steaming, a gentle moist heat circulates freely to cook the food. This is an excellent method for bringing out subtle flavors and is particularly suitable for fish.

Here are the utensils you will need for steaming. A large bamboo steamer about ten inches wide: To use, put about two inches of water in a wok, bring it to a simmer, and place the bamboo steamer containing the food into the wok where it should rest safely perched above water level on the sloping sides. Cover the steamer with its lid. Replenish the water as required. Food is usually done when it is slightly firm to touch. Use a chopstick to test. Rack and plate: First choose a heat-proof plate that fits easily inside a wok or large roasting pan or pot. Then rub the plate with a small amount of cooking oil to keep it from sticking. Put the rack inside the wok or pan, add about two inches of water, and bring it to a simmer. Now put the food to be steamed on the oiled plate and lower the plate onto the rack. Cover the wok tightly and lower the heat to simmer and steam. Check the water level from time to time and replenish with hot water when necessary. Be careful when uncovering as there will be a rush of hot steam.

If you do not have a metal or wooden rack you might use a small empty can to support the plate of food. Remember that the food needs to remain above the water level and must not get wet. The water level should always be at least one inch below the edge of the plate.

STIR-FRYING

This is the most famous of all Chinese cooking techniques and the most widely used in Hong Kong. It is possibly the trickiest technique because success with it depends on having all the required ingredients prepared, measured out, and immediately at hand. It is also critical to have a good source of fierce heat. Quickly cooked in only minutes, stir-fried foods have the advantage of cooking in very little oil so they retain their natural flavors and textures. The process also preserves the foods' nutrients, which is a benefit for a healthy diet. It is very important that stir-fried foods not be overcooked or greasy. Using a wok is definitely an advantage when stir-frying as its shape not only conducts the heat well but its high sides enable the cook to toss and stir ingredients rapidly, keeping them constantly moving while cooking.

Having prepared all the ingredients for stir-frying, the steps are:

Heat the wok or skillet until it is very hot before adding the oil. This prevents food from sticking and ensures an even heat. Add the oil, and using a metal spatula or long-handled spoon, distribute it evenly over the surface. The oil should be very hot — indeed, almost smoking — before you add the next ingredient, unless you are going to flavor the oil. It is often better to have the wok too hot than not hot enough. This is also why a wok should be thick and heavy; it is better able to retain the heat.

If you are flavoring the oil with garlic, scallions, ginger, dried red chili or other seasoning, do not wait for the oil to get so hot that it is almost smoking. If you do, these ingredients will burn and become bitter. When the oil is moderately hot, toss the flavoring ingredients quickly in it for a few seconds. In some recipes these flavorings are then removed and discarded before cooking proceeds.

Now add the ingredients as described in the recipe and proceed to stir-fry by tossing them over the surface of the wok or pan with the metal spatula or long-handled spoon. Keep moving the food from the center of the wok to the sides. Stir-frying is a noisy business and is usually accompanied by quite a lot of splattering because of the high temperature at which the food must be cooked.

Some stir-fried dishes are thickened with a mixture of cornstarch and cold water. To avoid a lumpy sauce, be sure to remove the wok or pan from the heat before you add the cornstarch mixture, which must be thoroughly blended before it is added. The sauce can then be returned to the heat and thickened. You will know the sauce is ready when it thickens and turns clear.

VELVETING

Unique to Chinese cuisine, this technique gives a particularly delicious texture to meat and seafood. Heat the oil to moderately hot or just until bubbles gently form over the surface of a test piece of meat. Add the meat and stir carefully just to separate the pieces. Turn the heat off and allow the meat to sit in the oil as long as the recipe specifies. Turn the meat into a colander set inside a stainless steel bowl and drain well.

WINE IN THE CUISINE OF THE FRAGRANT HARBOR

BY DARRELL CORTI

It is difficult to try and blend what are two different aspects of culture — eating and drinking — particularly if one is Eastern and the other Western. In fact, it is probably appropriate that Hong Kong be the location for this effort since it is a city with essentially a Chinese milieu but a unique Western patina. It is difficult to imagine the effort made to superimpose British culture on an essentially Cantonese way of life. Yet it is this Anglicization of Cantonese culture that accounts for Hong Kong as we know it. It is this unique Hong Kong blending that proves two cultures can be combined.

This meshing reaches a high point with wine and food — wine from grapes as we in the West know it, and food as the Cantonese know it. Traditionally, grape wine is little used in Chinese cuisine. The very word Westerners translate as wine, "chiu," is practically a generic term for "(alcoholic) drink." This is not to say that grape wine is unknown. Even in the earliest days of China's history it was welcomed as an imported gift coming from vineyards in the remote corners of central Asia and, therefore, exotic and curious. Nothing much has changed!

Current Western taste in wine strives for a peculiar relationship of acidity, body, and fruitiness. At times this is discordant with the delicate taste of Hong Kong cuisine. This particular characteristic of wine called "balance" is sometimes uniquely disturbing with Hong Kong style dishes. Several factors enter into play. There can be the sharp contrasts between an appropriately balanced wine and the salt condiment that accompanies a simple white-cooked chicken dish. Most fermented ingredients in a dish require a red wine to stand up to their flavor and aroma, even if in Western eyes the dish would be served with a white wine. Ultimately, it is a matter of taste experience, but isn't this the most fascinating aspect of eating and drinking?

The cuisine of Hong Kong, open and receptive to almost any culinary idea, is a wonderful tapestry in which wine plays a minor role. In Hong Kong, wine acts as a social lubricant, promoting conviviality and enjoyment. There is no implication that certain wines go with certain dishes as we like to maintain in the West. Food and drink are meant to be enjoyed, not as a rigid system, slavishly followed as perhaps is often done in Western gastronomy. Just as one mixes his own condiments and seasonings for a dish, so, I feel, can the use of wine and other drinks be mixed in Hong Kong cuisine.

It is accepted wisdom in the West that Chinese cooking calls for white wine, more or less aromatic and sweet, as an accompaniment. Nothing could be further from the fact, but Westerners do like to pigeonhole ideas and remain convinced of their validity. Just as Hong Kong cooking has adapted to Western foodstuffs, cooking them to Chinese taste, perhaps we should not worry how they adapt to wine or not. It is foolish, in my view, to say that only one kind of wine will fit into a particular meal context. The Chinese notion of opposites — yin/yang —

operates in cuisine and it is logical that we should allow wine to fit the same pattern. In good menu construction, various dishes are put together to form a pleasing whole. They should not all be of the same kind, have the same ingredients, or tastes. Otherwise, it is much like a symphony programmer organizing a concert with all the pieces in the same key. Variety is the pleasure of a menu, and Hong Kong cooking exemplifies this.

To my mind, the aroma and taste of a dish is more important than the beverage that will wash it down. Unless a meal is served Western style, in courses, rather than having sections of it put on the table at the same time, as is appreciated by the Chinese, we are probably never going to be able to appreciate the peculiar subtlety and nuance of the perfect wine with the perfect dish in Hong Kong cuisine. To return to the symphony metaphor, it seems that the Chinese look at food and drink as instruments of an orchestra. The effect is an overall pleasant sound rather than a string of solos. Westerners would rather view the meal as the same orchestra yet allow each instrument its solo — which often seems more analytical than pleasurable. The experience is meant to be more than the sum of its parts.

The delicacy and lightness of Hong Kong cuisine has often made it difficult for me to put wine with it. Not only do the basic ingredients of a dish influence the wine selection, but sometimes its saucing or its condiments. I can state adamantly that no *one* wine goes well with a Hong Kong meal of several courses. If lucky, perhaps one wine will go well with a section of a meal, given, of course, that the meal has several courses to it or is a banquet.

Simple meals can and do go well with only one wine. The Hong Kong specialty of dim sum is a good case in point. For Western tastes, here is a meal perfect for champagne. The acid and bubbles make the delicacy of most dim sum sparkle. I can't imagine a better combination.

With a complex dish like Peking Duck as done in Hong Kong, the question is what to put with it. Look at the flavors, rich duck skin, plum sauce, spring onions. Which flavor takes precedence? Some would say duck. To me, the sauce is the dominant flavor and this is softened by the duck meat flavor and the freshness of spring onion. The wine needs to be slightly tannic to offset the meat's fatness and therefore red, fruity like the sauce, and fresh-tasting like the onions. Possibilities are young red wines such as Beaujolais from France, Zinfandel from California, or Chianti from Italy.

Dishes of seafood with powerful sauces made from fermented black beans need the accompaniment of powerful wines to stand up to the sauce. That these same fish sauced in Western fashion would be accompanied by white wine is of no interest in Hong Kong. What counts is the predominating flavor, and that requires a red wine, a full-bodied one at that.

Another context which must be considered is the climate and how this works on drinking habits. Hong Kong is humid and hot for part of the year, and wine can be a fatiguing beverage if not served at an appropriate temperature. Sometimes the niceties of table do not extend to refrigeration in Hong Kong. But then there is also the endemic terror of drinking anything cold, a fear Americans, in particular, know only in the reverse.

Once at the elegant home of young Hong Kong friends, I enjoyed a superb meal with banquet dishes served one at a time. There were six of us with as many dishes served. We began with a tiny silver pot full of Shoaxing wine warmed and served in tiny cups. Remarkably like warm oloroso sherry, it set up the appetite. A superb dish of golden threaded shark's fin with a huge piece of Yunnan ham in the center opened the meal. Accompanied by a remarkable old Madeira, served in Ming porcelain wine cups, the musky aroma of the ham and the unctuous flavor of the reduced stock used for the shark's fin were perfect with the pungent sharpness of the wine. Even the emperors could not have commanded a better dish or accompaniment. The next course of tiny rice birds (it was early fall and they were in season) stuffed with duck liver sausage and braised was accompanied by a Chambertin of sufficient age to be interesting yet not overly aged. Poured into Baccarat tasters, wide-bowled enough to allow the heady bouquet to come out, but not so tall as to be dangerous to those using the ivory chop sticks, the wine was as perfect as if it had been served in France with a dish of ortolans.

The Madeira and the Chambertin were two outstanding examples of the perfect blending of completely Hong Kong dishes with Western wines. Although I must admit that the aesthetic part did help somewhat, the idea is valid. Western wines and certain Cantonese dishes can go well together.

What happens in a normal banquet situation? It is a bit more complicated and not so easy to combine wine and food. At such a time you just sit back and take advantage of the chaos on your palate and savor the dishes, drinking after and not trying to combine tastes and balance flavors. The more complex the dishes and the more of them served, the less interesting wine becomes. At this point, it is only a beverage, one of many possibilities. Perhaps it is prudent to do as the natives do and have recourse to a good scotch and soda, or cognac and water, either of which is remarkably satisfying. In fact, only a real wine "connoisseur" would probably object, but then for him, whose only concern is the pedantic chase after wine, the food doesn't matter.

In a more ordinary situation, only a cold glass of hoppy beer is needed to complement the simple pleasure of going to a dumpling shop and experiencing the delight of a cabbage leaf-lined tray of steaming shark's fin soup dumplings with their satiny outside and full flavored hot soup contained inside. No wine for these delicacies; their simplicity is enhanced by the malty character of full-bodied Asian beer.

Home style cooking, salt fish fried rice as an example, is probably best served with simple, straightforward wines, preferably aromatic, light red wines that scour the palate and harmonize with the "baccala"-like character of the dried fish. Personally, I am quite fond of this dish, and find it deeply satisfying so accompanied.

At yet another extreme, desserts in Hong Kong cuisine are pretty much straightforward and simple. The standard custard tarts or fruit and almond *dou fu* can be made more satisfying if served with light, fruity, frothy wines like Asti Spumante from Italy or other light, muscat variety styles. They point up the insipid sweetness of some Asian fruit and temper the exotic ripeness of the others.

Given that most Hong Kong dishes are Cantonese in origin — where the flavors are quite delicate and basically simple — they taste of what they are made from. Wine can sometimes be an intrusion. Then I would not worry about what to serve, and would not serve anything. If it doesn't fit, don't force it. As T. C. Lai, the noted Hong Kong writer, says in his book *At the Chinese Table*, one should aim for balance of tastes (in a menu) and I think that this balance should not be undone by the forceful use of wine. It really is a matter of experiment.

DINING OUT
IN
HONG KONG:
A SHORT LIST

~~~~~~

Restaurant listings are notorious anywhere for being outdated the minute they are published. Hong Kong restaurants are no exception. Those listed here are mentioned in the book; they have a record of being in business for a long time as well as having consistently high-quality food that is typical of the *new* Chinese cooking of Hong Kong. However, one caveat: chefs do change as do restaurants. I hope you will have the same delicious experience I have had.

Yung Kee Restaurant
32-40 Wellington St., Central,
Hong Kong
Tel: 5-221624, 5-232343

Lai Ching Heen
The Regent Hotel
Salisbury Road, Kowloon
Tel: 3-7211211

Sun Tung Lok
Phase 3, Harbour City
25-27 Canton Road, G/F, Kowloon
Tel: 3-7220288

Lung Wah Restaurant/Hotel
22 Ha Wo Che, Shatin, N.T.
Tel: 0-611594

King Heung Restaurant
59-65 Paterson St. Causeway Bay,
Hong Kong
Tel: 5-771035, 5-767899

City Chiu Chow
1st/Fl., East Ocean Centre
98 Granville Road
Tsim Sha Tsui East, Kowloon
Tel: 3-7245383, 3-7236226

Eagle's Nest
Hong Kong Hilton
2 Queen's Road, Central, Hong Kong
Tel: 5-233111 Ext. 2501

Prince Court
Sutton Court, Harbour City
21 Canton Road, Kowloon
Tel: 3-668939

Chiuchow Garden
Tsimshatsui Centre, 2/F, Tsimshatsui East,
Kowloon
Tel: 3-687266

Guangzhou Garden
4/F, Tower 2, Exchange Square
8 Connaught Place, Central,
Hong Kong
Tel: 5-251163

Lee Gardens Hotel/Rainbow Room
22/F, Causeway Bay, Hong Kong
Tel: 5-777181

Oi Man Seafood Restaurant
No. 4, Ching Street
Lau Fau Shan, N.T.
Tel: 0-721504, 0-724330

Sichuan Garden
Gloucester Tower, 3/F
Central, Hong Kong
Tel: 5-214433, 5-263777

Spring Moon
The Peninsula Hotel
Salisbury Road, Kowloon
Tel: 3-666251

Wu Kong Shanghai Restaurant
27 Nathan Road, Alpha House Basement,
(Peking Road entrance), Kowloon
Tel: 3-667244

Flourishing Court
Prudential Centre, 216 Nathan Rd.
Tsim Sha Tsui, Kowloon
Tel: 3-7392308

KEN HOM is the author of a number of cookbooks including: *Ken Hom's East Meets West Cuisine* (Simon and Schuster) and *Asian Vegetarian Feast*. He also is the author of *Ken Hom's Chinese Cookery*, the companion book to the BBC television series that was shown throughout the world.

Besides writing, Ken Hom travels extensively to conduct cooking demonstrations and is a frequent guest on radio and television shows. For almost a decade, he has taught food and culture classes in Hong Kong. He now divides his time among his native United States, Europe and Asia.

DARRELL F. CORTI is a second generation Californian who has been directing the wine department of his family grocery business, Corti Brothers, since 1964. He is an associate member of The American Society of Enologists, and has participated in many wine and food organizations as well as consulted in Japan. He has written wine chapters for *The Book of California Wine* and *Ken Hom's East Meets West Cuisine*. Darrell F. Corti lives in Sacramento.

INDEX